The Aesthetic in Kant
A Critique

The Aesthetic in Kant

A Critique

JAMES KIRWAN

continuum
LONDON • NEW YORK

Continuum
The Tower Building
11 York Road
London SE1 7NX

80 Maiden Lane
Suite 704
New York
NY 10038

First published 2004

This paperback edition published 2006

© James Kirwan 2004

British Library Cataloguing-in-Publication Data
A catalogue record for this book is available from the British Library.

ISBN: 0-8264-7198-6 (hardback)
   0-8264-8778-5 (paperback)

Typeset by Servis Filmsetting Ltd, Manchester
Printed and bound in Great Britain by Biddles Ltd, www.biddles.co.uk

Contents

Acknowledgements

I would like to thank the two anonymous referees at Continuum for their many helpful suggestions.

Introduction

The significance of Kant's *Critique of the Power of Judgement* for contemporary aesthetics can best be brought out by considering the reaction to the text within German philosophy within a decade or so of its publication. On the one hand Kant was credited with having put an end to the domination of aesthetics by what Schelling described as the shallow and popular 'psychological principles of the English and French'; meaning the predominantly British tradition of the philosophy of taste, as exemplified by Shaftesbury, Hutcheson, Hume, Burke, Gerard, and Kames.[1] Aesthetics within this tradition had fallen quite naturally within the domain of 'moral philosophy', into enquiries and treatises on the passions and sentiments: that area which does indeed seem most nearly related to the modern discipline of psychology. Thus Burke, for example, had written that the object of his *Philosophical Enquiry into the Origin of our Ideas of the Sublime and Beautiful,* was 'a diligent examination of our passions in our own breasts . . . a careful survey of the properties of things which we find by experience to influence those passions . . . a sober and attentive investigation of the laws of nature, by which these properties are capable of exciting our passions'.[2] Usher, embarking on an analysis of the sublime, averred that what was required was 'a cause that accounts sufficiently for all the symptoms' manifested by the beholder.[3] So far, indeed, is aesthetics incorporated into 'moral philosophy' in the eighteenth century that it is easy now to overlook even highly developed treatments of aesthetics simply because they do not announce themselves as such.[4]

Hegel, reviewing Kant's predecessors, is dismissive of this whole tradition of analysing the aesthetic through the feelings of the subject: it is 'wearisome on account of its indefiniteness and emptiness, and disagreeable by its concentration on tiny subjective peculiarities'.[5] Such investigations, he felt, could never get far, since feeling is 'the indefinite dull region of the spirit; what is felt remains enveloped in the form of the most abstract individual subjectivity'.[6] According to Hegel, in order to truly plumb the depths of aesthetics – the subject matter of which is now to be confined to art – all consideration of 'mere subjectivity and its states' must definitely be relinquished.[7] Aesthetics did, of course, take his advice. It is because most subsequent aesthetics belong in the Hegelian rather than Kantian tradition that Kant's third *Critique* was, until quite recently, consistently interpreted, or misinterpreted, as a book about art.[8]

Kant's merit, then, for Schelling and for Hegel, would appear to be that, though he starts from the same antinomy of taste as the writers in the British tradition, and, indeed, covers very similar ground, he is content at last *not* to offer an explanation of the grounds of the aesthetic in terms of the psychology of the individual subject. As we shall see, in Chapter 3, Kant concludes that, while the determining ground of taste must lie in the supersensible substrate of humanity in general, nevertheless this substrate must remain indeterminate, for it necessarily transcends our faculty of cognition: 'The subjective principle, namely the indeterminate idea of the supersensible in us, can only be indicated as the sole key to demystifying this faculty which is hidden to us even in its sources, but there is nothing by which it can be made more comprehensible.' Yet, if this appeared to do away with the despised psychology, it is also precisely where Kant is inadequate in Schelling's and Hegel's estimation. He had remained, like his British predecessors, a philosopher of taste: he had approached the aesthetic as a matter of pleasant feeling rather than, as German idealism in general would have it, a matter of knowledge of the Idea or Absolute. (I refrain from enlarging on this notion of the aesthetic as transcendental revelation for two reasons: first, I have dealt with it at length elsewhere, and second, it is, frankly, not a notion that improves in intelligibility with exposition.[9]) Kant 'failed', according to Hegel, because he supposed that the reconciliation of the sensuous and the spiritual, the particular and universal, in the aesthetic to be 'only subjective in respect of the judgement . . . and not itself to be absolutely true and actual'.[10]

There were, then, two fundamental and interconnected effects of the *Critique of the Power of Judgement* on aesthetic speculation within German philosophy. The first was the provision of a philosophically respectable warrant to dismiss the kind of psychological speculation that had constituted aesthetics prior to Kant. Kant had declared, if not exactly proved, that such speculation was futile. This apparent deference to the power of Kant's thought was not, however, adventitious. It cleared the way for the emergence of a strain in aesthetics that was itself part and parcel of a reaction against Kant's own philosophy, insofar as that philosophy, in strictly separating the phenomenal from the noumenal, was exemplary of the anti-metaphysical standpoint of the Enlightenment. (Though Kant was in no way a religious sceptic, it would be fair to say that the censor who banned his *Religion within the Limits of Reason Alone* (1793), had a much firmer grasp of the natural direction of Kant's system than did Kant himself.) Eighteenth-century aesthetics, complained Schelling, had tried 'to explain beauty using empirical psychology, and in general treated the miracles of art the same way one treated ghost stories and other superstitions: by enlightening us and explaining them away'.[11] With the reaction at the turn of the century against the perceived ideals of the Enlightenment, miracles were back, and with them was to come that idealist notion of the aesthetic as a form of knowledge transcending knowledge, a 'nonsensuous knowledge', exemplified by the aesthetics of Schelling and Hegel.

This, then, is the second fundamental effect of the *Critique of the Power of Judgement*, or rather of the philosophical system of which it was a part, on the history of aesthetics: that it had set limits on the knowable that were bound to produce an *emotional* reaction. The aesthetics of German idealism partakes of the general nineteenth-century flight away from the 'coldness' of the preceding century, and back towards a sense of the holy. This reaction within aesthetics was indeed already underway before Kant wrote – Reid, recoiling from Hume, had attributed aesthetic merit to 'intrinsic excellence' – but it is doubtful that without the example of those eloquent and compendious spirits, such as Hegel, who were directly responding to Kant, this reaction would have so massively carried the day.[12] For carry the day it did. It is no accident that even at the beginning of the twenty-first century historical accounts of aesthetics still proceed from Kant to Hegel, and that the history of nineteenth-century aesthetics is constituted by a procession of German names, who, like Kant, are principally famous as great philosophers, succeeded by a mix of eminent Hegelians, and theologically committed prose-poets; Ruskin, Jouffroy, Cousin, Croce, Collingwood.[13] Moreover, it is noteworthy that, even as the secularization of thought once more appeared to gather momentum in the later nineteenth century, this form of aesthetics, which it would seem could hardly sustain itself without a commitment to something beyond the secular, nevertheless lost none of its hold.[14] In the twentieth century it was kept alive in the continental tradition by such figures as Heidegger, Gadamer and Lyotard.[15] In the ostensibly very different Anglo-Saxon tradition certain of its founding suppositions have prevailed simply by default: no credible alternative for a fundamental grounding of the aesthetic was put forward.[16] The vacuum left by Kant at the core of the aesthetic has remained a vacuum. Thus, little as the Anglo-Saxon tradition may otherwise owe to Hegel in terms of metaphysics, it does nevertheless follow him in the notion that aesthetics itself can be satisfactorily prosecuted even in the absence of an aesthetic theory; that, indeed, the proper study of aesthetics is not, or not principally, the aesthetic.[17] Moreover, while the Anglo-Saxon tradition rarely retains anything overtly transcendental, certain fundamental assumptions that have their basis in idealist/Romantic metaphysics – such as the notion of art as a means to wisdom – nevertheless, even in the absence of comparable metaphysical underpinning, tend to endure.

It is ironic, then, that Kant should so often be held up as the founding figure of modern aesthetics. (A judgement, however, often based on no more than the misapprehension that Kant was responsible for first identifying the realm of the aesthetic as the realm of disinterested pleasure.) For Kant is, historically, rather than philosophically, the culminating point of an eighteenth-century tradition that was deliberately rejected by the most influential figures in the subsequent history of aesthetics. Kant's text inaugurates nothing. More importantly, his most enduring legacy in aesthetics is a notion that would surely hardly have survived had it been attached to a less prestigious name: the notion that the grounds of aesthetic judgement are, by their very nature, unamenable to analysis, that the aesthetic cannot be rendered philosophically intelligible. As I have suggested above, the metaphysical aspirations of the aestheticians immediately succeeding Kant gave them a vested interest in embracing the proposition that, from a non-metaphysical point of view, the aesthetic was inscrutable. The persistence of this belief, albeit only implicit, in contemporary aesthetics is, however, given the extraordinary twentieth-century upheavals in other areas of philosophy, much more difficult to account for. The reasons for this persistence are, I believe, not merely historical, but rather lie, as the present work will attempt to demonstrate, in the nature of the aesthetic itself.

Why, then, at this point, offer yet another new reading of Kant? Not, or not principally, in order to clarify what happened in the past of aesthetics. Nor is the present work primarily concerned with attempting to demonstrate, or create, consistency in Kant's theory, or with pointing out such inconsistencies, or underdeveloped theses, as may be found in his exposition. (The existing commentaries of Guyer, and more recently Allison, both exemplary in their thoroughness, excellently fulfil such purposes.[18]) Where the present work differs from previous readings of Kant's text, aside from in the details of its interpretation, is in its fundamental purpose. For, the present work will attempt to show how Kant's *Critique* implies, through the very inconsistencies and obscurities for which it is notorious, a consistent theory of taste; though a theory which, in undermining the 'disinterested' aspect of such judgements, renders the phenomenon of aesthetic judgement quite unsuitable for the epistemological/ethical ends which aesthetics since Kant has either explicitly, or implicitly, wished it serve.[19]

In order to support this reading it will be necessary to set out what Kant does and does not establish in the *Critique*, and more importantly what lessons about the aesthetic and its role in the general economy of thought can be drawn from what Kant seeks and fails to establish. It is not only the eminence of Kant's work in the history of aesthetics that makes his text a suitable site for the examination of this theme of the untenability of disinterestedness. The very fact that, historically, it is Kant who brought to an end the psychological approach of the eighteenth century, and is thus responsible for bequeathing us the straight, and impossible, choice between the devil of idealist transcendentalism, and the deep blue sea of inscrutability, makes it appropriate that he should be my object here. Given this emphasis, then, it is a happy accident that a plethora of recent books on the third *Critique* (Cohen and Guyer *Essays on Kant's Aesthetics*, Schaper *Studies in Kant's Aesthetics*, Savile *Kantian Aesthetics Pursued*, McCloskey *Kant's Aesthetic*, Crawford *Kant's Aesthetic Theory*, Kemal *Kant's Aesthetic Theory: An Introduction*) appears to justify as necessary the choice of a title for the present work that, while perhaps awkward, is also apt. For Kant's text is here considered principally as an occasion for enquiry into the nature of the aesthetic.

It is, however, important to make a clear distinction here between the phenomenology that Kant presents and the inferences he draws from that phenomenology, often with the larger context of the 'critical project' in mind. I have no wish to play fast and loose with what the *Critique of the Power of Judgement* actually says. If a theory is to present itself as an advance on Kant, rather than simply a departure from him, its case will be stronger if it does not demand either a new phenomenology, that is, a basic definition of what aesthetic judgement seems to be, or, indeed, even the employment of different concrete examples to those Kant gives. At the same time I have no intention of deferring to what Kant establishes merely by fiat, or leaving unquestioned what is merely assumed for the sake of argument. Since I am anxious to forestall, as far as possible, potential misunderstanding (particularly among Kantians) of the intentions of this work, I will enlarge on this point here, even at the risk of running ahead of myself.

The most likely foreseeable objection to this work as an interpretation of Kant's text concerns its treatment of the ideality of the judgement of taste in that text.[20] It might well be objected that the present work misrepresents Kant insofar as it treats his account of judgements of taste as if that account were based solely on the properties of such judgements. On the contrary, it could be argued, Kant's account is based on the derivation of what would have to be the basis of a judgement of taste *if* that judgement was to have any legitimate claim to universal validity.[21] (For it is the possibility of such a claim, to a 'subjective universality', that Kant is interested in at this point in the critical project as a whole.) Therefore, to be truly a judgement of taste, in Kant's account, a judgement must be grounded in a certain relation between the imagination and the understanding: in the *a priori* structures that make cognition possible, and which can be presumed to be uniform. For only on such a basis could aesthetic judgement legitimately claim universal validity. Thus Kant is not saying, as perhaps my account would seem to suggest, that any particular judgement that believes itself to be a judgement of taste can be said to be the direct expression of a common sense (though it implies that some must be) but only that *if* taste's claim to universal validity and necessity is to be legitimate then we must assume a common sense as the only possible basis of such subjective universal validity. Kant, in this reading, is simply not faced with a straight choice between the judgement of taste being contingent and its being necessary, since, on the presumption that if a judgement is truly one of taste then by definition it has universal validity, he can assert that if a judgement is a true judgement then it is, by nature, necessary.

On this reading it could be said that I am seriously misrepresenting Kant when, for example, I present conflicts between the contingency and the necessity of judgements of taste as present or implicit in his text, or when I emphasize the role of the consciousness of the subject in determining whether a judgement is or is not one of taste. Such questions, it could be said, simply do not arise for Kant, since it is the different groundings of the feelings involved that constitute the distinctions I posit as problematic. While the feelings themselves may be indistinguishable, and the proposed groundings empirically indemonstrable, nevertheless, *if* there is to be the possibility of any legitimately claiming universal validity, it must be because they are at least potentially grounded in that play of the faculties that would render them universally valid.

The problem with this thesis is, of course, that not only are these different groundings not themselves possible objects of experience, but also it is only the presupposition of a valid claim to universal validity that justifies the appeal to them. They receive some support from the intuition of apparently 'disinterested' pleasure that the subject experiences in the moment of judgement, though, of course, Kant's own account, at least according to the above reading, does not even accept this feeling as evidence that a judgement of taste has been made. (That is, the subject can be wrong about whether or not they have made such a judgement, since the phenomenology of that feeling does not guarantee its grounds.) If this is all Kant has to offer us with regard to aesthetic judgement – what it *must be if* it is to have a legitimate claim to universal validity – then, frankly, Kant has nothing to offer on the subject. For, on this reading, the *Critique of the Power of Judgement* is both viciously circular in its arguments, apropos the nature of the aesthetic, and, in laying down unverifiable *a priori* conditions for what will count as legitimate examples of the object of enquiry (taste), intellectually pernicious as well.

My reluctance to stay within the circularity in Kant's account that is created by the demand for a legitimate claim to universal validity will be perhaps especially evident in my treatment of the sublime, where I have collapsed some of Kant's distinctions (as between sublimity and dependent beauty), and introduced others (as between a 'true' and a 'false' sublime) in a way that runs counter to the requirements of this demand. In dealing with the sublime I have made much of the fact that there is no means, in practice, of distinguishing what Kant defines as the sublime, that is, a feeling arising from imagination's failure to meet reason's demands, and other feelings which are felt as sublime but which arise from the sacrifice of one interest of sensibility to another stronger interest of sensibility. To this it might be objected that since, for Kant, the sublime *is* a feeling arising from imagination's failure to meet reason's demands, then any feeling that is grounded in some other way, even if phenomenologically indistinguishable, is simply not Kant's sublime and not germane to an analysis of Kant. Again to defer to such an objection leads to a kind of apriorism that would render the *Critique* hermetic, and hence useless for aesthetics. The conditions Kant lays down for a judgement to be sublime are those conditions the judgement must fulfil if it is to legitimately claim universal validity. Yet the existence of such a legitimate claim is not, after all, a given: Kant must establish its existence from the facts of the aesthetic, not derive the facts of the aesthetic from its presupposition. Surely a theory that can cover every instance of sublimity, without having to make indemonstrable distinctions, is the better theory. Moreover, in the course of his analysis, Kant gives ample material for the construction of such an alternative account. It is, indeed, a measure of the philosophical integrity of Kant's phenomenology of taste that the claim to subjective universal validity cannot be introduced except as a presupposition.

I have preferred, then, in the present work, to concentrate on developing a theory of the grounds of the aesthetic on the basis of what Kant establishes, that is, the properties of judgements of taste as they are given to the subject and the empirical facts concerning the operation of taste, rather than what he presupposes. Such a principle of commentary is not so peculiar as it might first appear, since all interpretations aim at the best *possible* reading. However, insofar as I am concerned here with what the aesthetic itself may be as I am with what Kant's account can be made to mean, I have perhaps pushed this hermeneutic principle further than I would if the integrity of Kant's text in relation to the rest of his philosophy were my only object.[22] It is not, however, necessary to step right outside Kant's philosophical world in order to discover an alternate grounding to the phenomenon he describes. One does not, for example, need to deny either that the judgement of taste is cognized as necessary, or that there is fundamental uniformity to human nature, in order to arrive at a different account of how these two postulates might be related. What is necessary, however, is that the legitimacy of the judgement of taste's claim to subjective universal validity should be left in question.

The closing decades of the twentieth century saw the publication of several excellent full-length commentaries and a wealth of articles on 'Kantian aesthetics'. Even now, it is a rare event for an issue of any of the major journals of aesthetics to appear without an article that concerns itself with one of the topics to be touched on hereafter. At the time of writing there is (for better or worse) no more scrutinized or controversial text in aesthetics than the *Critique of the Power of Judgement*. Despite this attention, however, there still remain a great many open questions, not merely regarding the interpretation of specific points in that text but also regarding its overall consistency, and ultimate significance for modern aesthetics. Such is the complexity (or, as some commentators would have it, confusion) of Kant's text, that any assertion about it – even one that pretends to be no more than descriptive – can only be made in the face of a contrary preexisting interpretation. Ideally this work would have begun with the present Chapter 5, or even 6, that is, with some agreed interpretation of what Kant was attempting, and what he had achieved, and confined itself exclusively to the necessary critical reconstruction that would highlight those fruitful discords which are my main subject. However, as the intense scholarly interest which Kant's text has aroused in the last few decades amply attests, an uncontroversial thumbnail sketch of Kant's aesthetics is, at present, quite simply impossible.[23]

Therefore, although my main interest in Kant's text does not often overlap with the central concerns of the existing secondary literature – epistemology, ethics, the nature of art, the consistency of Kant's critical project as a whole, the rise of the bourgeoisie, a potential political role for 'judgement' – it is, nevertheless, necessary that the present work acknowledge the diversity of interpretation to be found in this literature by making explicit the understanding of Kant's text upon which it is based. (For reasons of space and clarity, however, direct engagement with this secondary literature is confined to notes to the text.[24]) Though my own purpose here is to make sense of taste, to find an alternative solution to Kant's antinomies, I hope that the solutions to several currently contentious questions in the interpretation of Kant's text which are here advanced may prove useful to those whose attention to the text is motivated by other interests.

From the point of view of the existing literature, however, there is one large omission from the present work that must be noted. That epistemological and ethical concerns have dominated the recent resurgence of interest in Kant's third *Critique* would seem to follow naturally from the fact that Kant himself proposes that the 'key' to the problem of taste lies in the realm of the epistemological, in the 'harmony of the faculties'. It was, indeed, Kant's avowed intention that the *Critique of the Power of Judgement* should be a completion of his critical project as a whole. It is not, of course, the case that all recent commentators on Kant have accepted that the third *Critique* does represent the 'bridge' between reason and understanding that Kant intended it to be, nor is there general agreement that the 'riddle of taste', as Kant presents it to us, must ineluctably lead to a conclusion in these terms. Yet all recent commentators have largely given over their commentaries to an elucidation of what sense Kant's solution to the riddle of taste can be made to bear in Kant's own terms. Insofar as I do not believe that Kant's exposition does lead ineluctably to the kind of solution he provides, nor, indeed, to the necessity for the introduction of any kind of epistemological account, a rehearsal of the relationship of the third *Critique* to the critical project as a whole would have been strictly redundant.[25]

The present work will, then, in contrast to a great deal of the existing secondary literature, concentrate exclusively on the problem of taste. (Here again the outsider might find it puzzling that the same discipline could take Kant's work itself as seminal while yet considering the principal subject of that work theoretically all but negligible.) To this end, then, I shall be steering as straight a course as possible through Kant's exposition to what I take to be his final thesis, in order to proceed from there (albeit by regression) to my own critique. The scope of the present work, then, is much narrower that that of the *Critique of the Power of Judgement* itself; I will, for example, be largely ignoring what Kant says about the social role of judgements of taste, and the genesis of art. This work will be concerned almost exclusively with the phenomenology of taste that Kant presents, and, more specifically, with drawing out the implications of that phenomenology in order to show why I believe Kant was premature in his verdict on the inscrutability of taste.

Chapters 1 and 2 set out the nature of the judgement of taste as it is described in the *Critique of the Power of Judgement*, and seek to establish that the indispensable condition of a judgement of taste is that it represents the subject's feeling of immediate delight in the object so designated. Because of this apparent autonomy, the object of taste appears to the subject to be an object of necessary delight, though reflection on the differences that do, as a matter of fact, exist in taste, should inform that subject that the object, paradoxically enough, is only an object of 'necessary' delight for them. Kant's analysis, I argue, does not lead to a definition of 'judgement of taste' as a judgement on an object of necessary delight, but rather as a judgement on what is cognized by the subject as an object of necessary delight.

Chapter 2 deals particularly with Kant's contentious distinction between free and dependent, or adherent, beauty, and argues that the distinction can be shown to turn on the extent to which we are conscious that a concept has been active in the process of cognizing the object which is the object of our judgement of taste; so that the ultimate touchstone of whether a judgement of taste is a judgement on a free or a dependent beauty is the subject's feeling of whether it is the one or the other. Dependent beauty (*pulchritude adhaerens*), it is suggested, is best identified with judgements on aesthetic merits (in the modern rather than Kantian sense) other than beauty itself. Chapter 2 also proposes that the kind of concept we discern in dependent beauty takes the form of what Kant calls an aesthetic idea: 'that representation of the imagination that occasions much thinking though without it being possible for any determinate thought, i.e., *concept*, to be adequate to it, which, consequently, no language fully attains or can make intelligible'.

Having dealt in Chapters 1 and 2 with the question of what judgements of taste are, Chapter 3 turns to Kant's explanation of their grounds. This chapter deals with Kant's notoriously unsatisfactory proposition that the determining ground of taste lies in the supersensible substrate of humanity in general, in the subjective finality of nature for the power of judgement. It argues that it is possible to provide an alternative grounding for the phenomenon that is Kant's starting point, and, moreover, that this grounding is immanent in Kant's own account. We gain some hint of its possibility from the specific examples of taste in operation that Kant gives, though it is only in the ostensibly 'supplementary' critique of the sublime that these hints are more fully developed. For it is specifically in dealing with the sublime that Kant's account shows how the conceptual may be introduced into taste without compromising its apparent autonomy. Though Kant denies that judgements on the sublime are judgements of taste at all, it will be my contention in Chapter 4 that Kant's own account shows otherwise and that, consequently, Kant's analysis of the grounds of the sublime is, in effect, the analysis of a particular form of dependent beauty. An examination of the structure of the aesthetic idea involved in this form of judgement of taste will, therefore, carry us beyond that, in effect, ineffable grounding of taste which Kant provides.

Chapters 5 and 6 propose that the form of the idea discerned in the sublime does, indeed, conform to Kant's description of the aesthetic idea: it is not identifiable with an idea which can be cognized by the subject as grounded in either logic, or desire, it accounts for the subject's discernment of the object as an object of 'disinterested' pleasure, and it is ultimately unintelligible to that subject: the subject may feel that the idea somehow justifies the judgement but is unable to show how it does so. Most importantly, the form which the idea takes will also account for how the aesthetic idea can be entertained as inextricable from the pleasure, while yet that pleasure also appears to be a pleasure 'in' the object, rather than in the idea itself.

Chapters 7 and 8 offer two further examples of judgements of taste, on dependent and free beauty respectively, taken from the text, showing the constitutive role of the aesthetic idea in each case, and accounting for the original distinction between these forms of judgement in terms of their different grounding. The first example is one that Kant himself brings forward to illustrate the notion of the aesthetic idea; the second is an instance of free beauty that Kant renders problematic in his exposition of the 'pure' form of taste. I conclude from these examples that Kant has shown, albeit inadvertently, the operation of an interest in the judgement of taste; despite the fact that it is a defining characteristic of the experience of such judgements that they should be cognized, by the subject, as disinterested. I also propose how this cognizance of disinterest might be rendered necessary by the form of interest involved.

Chapter 9 summarizes the conclusions of the book, and explicitly links the judgement of taste to Kant's own description of vain wishing, that is, to 'the presence of desires in man by which he is in contradiction with himself'.

In his preface to the *Critique of the Power of Judgement* Kant, in explaining his reasons for turning to aesthetic judgement, writes that if there is to be a metaphysics, 'the critique must previously have probed the ground for this structure down to the depth of the first foundations of the faculty of principles independent of experience, so that it should not sink in any part, which would inevitably lead to the collapse of the whole'. It is a central thesis of this present work that, in fact, the aesthetic is to be identified with that 'vain-wishing', those 'fantastic desires', that Kant describes, in the *Critique of the Power of Judgement* itself, as the chief psychological obstacle to the process of Enlightenment. Although there is no space in the present work to address the broader historical and philosophical issues that might arise from setting these two facts beside one another, I must record here my conviction that such a juxtaposition does *not* have profound implications for what has come to be known as 'the Enlightenment project'. In order to show how it might one would first need to prove, what seems highly improbable, that a rational basis for taste is necessary to this project. The only lesson of more general application to be derived from Kant's unsuccessful attempt to push the aesthetic, in the form of the sublime, in the direction of the rational is that taste (as I have attempted to show in my *Beauty*) cannot be co-opted to serve the interests either of the cognitive or the ethical. Indeed, it is to Kant's credit that, in keeping with most British eighteenth-century thinking on the subject, he does not believe that the aesthetic in general can be so co-opted to either the true or the good. That particular fallacy had to wait until the following century, which then bequeathed it to the twentieth. Perhaps the century now beginning will finally see its demise.

Except where otherwise specified I have used Guyer and Matthews' translation of the *Kritik der Urtheilskraft* throughout, only departing from it in my preference for 'dependent beauty' over 'adherent beauty' as a translation of Kant's *anhängende Schönheit*, and, for aesthetic reasons, in rendering the translators' boldface (to signal Kant's *Fettdruck*) as italic.

1

The Description of Taste I:
Immediacy and Necessity

It is no longer necessary, as it would have been twenty years ago, to begin with the declaration that in dealing with Kant's aesthetics we are not going to be dealing with what is now the central concern of aesthetics: art. While Kant has many interesting things to say about art, the construction of a philosophy of art is manifestly not the object of the *Critique of the Aesthetic Power of Judgement*. It is now generally acknowledged that to read Kant's work translating each proposition concerning 'beauty' or 'taste' into one about the grounds of our enjoyment or evaluation of art can only lead to the conclusion that Kant has, at the very least, started from the wrong place. That Kant's work was so read for so long is a tribute to the power of the Romantic thesis discussed in the Introduction.

Nevertheless, another assumption, deriving perhaps more remotely from Romanticism, is still liable to come between Kant's text and us, specifically, his use of the word 'judgement'. For Kant's 'judgement' is, as we shall see, something that *happens to us* rather than something we do, in the sense that arriving at a judgement by conscious deliberation is something we do. ('The very *feeling*', as Hume had put it, 'constitutes our praise or admiration.'[1]) For this reason Kant should not be interpreted as saying 'When you want to make a judgement of taste you should do this', but rather 'There are judgements called "judgements of taste", and this is how to recognize when you are making such a judgement'. A great deal of confusion may be saved by bearing this in mind.

There is a sense, however, in which Kant's definition of the judgement of taste might be taken as prescriptive (though in a different sense from the one intended above). Kant, as was noted in the Introduction, is concerned to show how the judgement of taste must be grounded if it is to have a legitimate claim to subjective universal validity. This introduces a requirement that the judgement of taste to be truly such should be able to make this claim, even though the legitimacy of the claim in any particular judgement is indemonstrable. At the same time, Kant must concede as a fact that one subject feels *x* is beautiful and *y* is not, while another feels just the opposite. Since both subjects experience their feeling as a judgement of taste, if anybody is ever to be right that they have made a 'true' judgement of taste (though it is not a given that anybody ever should be), then, somebody must be wrong. Therefore the *verifiable* fulfilment of the conditions laid down for a feeling to qualify as a judgement of taste is not sufficient to prove that the feeling is such a judgement: it is possible to believe, even on the soundest possible grounds, that one is making such a judgement, and yet be failing to do so. It is, of course, difficult to conceive of the ideal form of judgement that this state of affairs implies otherwise than as a model, that is, as something that may be prescribed. Self-evidently, however, given that fulfilment of the sufficient conditions of making a judgement of taste is indemonstrable, whatever prescriptive force the definition may have can concern only a ban on misnaming what one is *aware* could not possibly be a judgement of taste.

If, then, Kant's *a priori* requirement that the judgement possess universal validity is set aside, what remains in his account may be taken as principally descriptive: an exposition of the verifiable necessary (if not, according to Kant's stipulative definition, sufficient) conditions of a judgement of taste. The following is, then, concerned with the phenomenological question of the conditions Kant lays down for a feeling at least to lay claim (legitimately or otherwise) to being a judgement of taste.

THE SUBJECTIVITY OF THE JUDGEMENT OF TASTE

An indispensable condition of the attribution of beauty to an object, according to Kant, is that the subject should take an (apparently) immediate pleasure in that object.[2] (We shall postpone until the next chapter, consideration of the use of 'beauty' here. The modern reader would no doubt be more comfortable with 'aesthetic value/merit', but it is, nevertheless, worth persisting, for the moment, as far as possible with Kant's terms.) Insofar as we 'discern' beauty not by any process of cognition but by the feeling of pleasure it arouses, which feeling denotes nothing in the object, its ground 'cannot be *other than subjective*':[3]

> If pleasure is connected with the mere apprehension (*apprehensio*) of the form of an object of intuition without a relation of this to a concept for a determinate cognition, then the representation is thereby related not to the object, but solely to the subject . . .[4]

This is not, however, a peculiarity of judgements of taste. The perception of a thing as agreeable or good shares, according to Kant, the same characteristic of appearing to be a determination of the object while, in fact, being 'the determination . . . of the subject and its feeling'.[5] Thus, under the rubric 'aesthetic' Kant actually includes four different categories of judgement: on beauty, on goodness, on agreeableness, and on sublimity. What these judgements have in common is that in them we discover what is purely subjective in the representation of an object, that is, what constitutes its reference to the beholder, independent of any determination of the object for the purpose of knowledge.[6] Where the discernment of beauty differs from these other 'aesthetic judgements' (feelings of pleasure or displeasure in an object or representation) is that in the case of beauty we feel this pleasure *apart from any interest* in the object: 'One only wants to know whether the mere representation of the object is accompanied with satisfaction in me, however indifferent I might be with regard to the existence of the object of this representation.'[7] In contrast, any satisfaction that we associate with the idea of the object's real existence is interest and, as such, is always connected with desire.[8] In this way Kant sets beauty in contrast to both the agreeable, which gratifies, and the good, which is esteemed.[9]

In the case of the good, a thing may be, for example, *good for something* when it pleases as a means, or even *good in itself* when it pleases on its own account, but in both cases, since we can ask ourselves whether something is mediately or immediately good, it cannot be said to please immediately, rather it pleases by means of a concept and therefore implies an interest.[10] The agreeable, though it does please immediately, is like the good in that it too is determined by the represented bond of connection between the subject and the real existence of the object.[11] It is, therefore, only in the apparently *contemplative* satisfaction associated with the beautiful that no concept is involved, and only this satisfaction, in contrast to the pleasure we take in either the agreeable or the good, can be properly termed 'immediate', in the sense of disinterested and aconceptual.[12] Thus while there may be many kinds of judgement, the ground of determination of which lies in a sensation connected with the feeling of pleasure, it is, according to Kant, only when the pleasure is judged to be combined necessarily with the representation (that is, independent of any grounding in, or provision of, a concept of the object), so that the combination appears to hold not simply for the subject but for everyone who passes judgement, that the object of the representation can properly be called 'beautiful'.[13]

To say that the satisfaction is felt *apart from any interest* in the object is not, of course, to say that the object, or its real existence, must necessarily be a matter of indifference to the subject.[14] We may be interested in the existence of a beautiful object because it is beautiful but this does not make the pleasure we feel, that is, our ascription of beauty to the object itself, in any sense dependent on this interest. Hutcheson had put the matter succinctly when he wrote that, though we may 'pursue beautiful objects from self-love, with a view to obtain the pleasures of beauty, as in architecture, gardening and many other affairs, yet there must be a sense of beauty, antecedent to prospects of even this advantage, without which sense these objects would not be thus advantageous, nor excite in us this pleasure which constitutes them advantageous'.[15] Any particular object, then, may be at the same time both desired by, and beautiful to, a subject, providing there is a pleasure for that subject not merely in the anticipation of the satisfaction of the desire, but also, and apart from this anticipation, in the mere representation of the object.[16]

THE CLAIM TO UNIVERSALITY

It is, however, not enough, according to Kant, that beauty should please immediately; it must also please 'universally'.[17] He is not, however, despite a certain undertow in the vocabulary both here and elsewhere, making an appeal, as did some of his eighteenth-century predecessors in their more pragmatic moments, to consensus as a guarantee of what is, in some sense, *really* beautiful.[18] This may be taken rather as part of Kant's stipulative definition of the 'true' judgement of taste. As such, then, it can play no part in a phenomenology of taste. However, there is a sense in which the very making of this claim to universality (though not its legitimation) is implicit in the way in which we experience the beautiful as an object of *necessary* pleasure.[19] Since the satisfaction the subject feels in beholding beauty is 'not grounded in any inclination of the subject (nor in any other underlying interest), but rather the person making the judgement feels himself completely *free* with regard to the satisfaction that he devotes to the object, he cannot discover as grounds of the satisfaction any private conditions, pertaining to his subject alone'.[20] The subject speaks of beauty as if it were a quality of objects, and the judgement logical ('*It* is beautiful'), that is, applicable to everyone perceiving the same object.[21] Moreover, the judgement appears to presuppose a necessary connection between representation and satisfaction, which is neither objective nor cognitive, nor inferable from universality of experience. It is a subjective necessity that nevertheless takes the form of an insistence that everyone ought to agree because its very existence implies that we share a common ground – a universal validity of feeling that does not rest on concepts, that is, a subjective universal validity.

The discernment of the beautiful, therefore, appears to imply the existence of a universality with reference to pleasure and displeasure, a *common sense*, and only on this presupposition, that is, only insofar as I put my judgement forward as *exemplary*, am I able to call anything 'beautiful'.[22] Did we not impute the satisfaction we feel to everyone, writes Kant, beauty would not exist, and there would be merely the agreeable.[23] This imputation, however, is only something implicit in our finding the object to be beautiful, in our feeling that the beauty is actually a quality of the object. (There is, of course, no other way of finding a thing beautiful, though we may recognize that something is, of its kind, a thing that others might find beautiful.) The common sense remains, then, only an ideal of the subject at the moment of judgement; nothing is postulated in our judgement except the *possibility* of that judgement being valid for everyone, its universality 'is represented . . . only as subjective'.[24] For, in fact, 'the judgement of taste is always made as a singular judgement about the object'.[25]

Beauty, then, appears to us immediately, in the manner of a sensation: it is only because we do not ascribe our pleasure to any private interest that this pleasure does not appear as a 'private sensation', but rather as a quality of the object.[26] It is, therefore, only in this way, that is, in our inability to account for beauty as a matter of private sensation, and referable to our individual desire, that the implied 'universal voice' is present:

> The judgement of taste does not itself *postulate* the accord of everyone (only a logically universal judgement can do that, since it can adduce grounds); it only *ascribes* this agreement to everyone, as a case of the rule with regard to which it expects confirmation not from concepts but only from the consent of others. The universal voice is thus only an idea . . . Whether someone who believes himself to be making a judgement of taste is in fact judging in accordance with this idea [of the concurrence of others] can be uncertain; but that he relates it to that idea, thus that it is supposed to be a judgement of taste, he announces through the expression of beauty. Of that he can be certain for himself through the mere consciousness of separation of everything that belongs to the agreeable and the good from the satisfaction that remains to him . . .[27]

The claim to the agreement of others, 'as if' the judgement were objective, is present, then, only as implicit in the subject's *feeling* that the beauty belongs to the object: it is another way that this feeling of objectivity, definitive of the judgement of taste, could be formulated.[28] It may appear, says Kant, that describing a flower as beautiful is 'merely to repeat its own claim to everyone's satisfaction', that is, tantamount to asserting that beauty is to be taken for a property of the flower itself, a property which 'does not correspond [as does the agreeable] to the difference of heads and so many senses, but to which instead the latter must correspond if they would judge it'. This is not, however, the way the matter stands: 'For the judgement of taste consists precisely in the fact that it calls a thing beautiful only in accordance with that quality in it by means of which it corresponds with our way of receiving it.'[29] If, then, we abstract Kant's *a priori* demand that the judgement of taste, to be truly such, must possess an (indemonstrable) legitimate claim to universal validity, what we are left with from the descriptive part of his account is this; if it feels like beauty, then it is beauty.

This fundamental point is well brought out in Kant's example of the young poet who refuses to be dissuaded from the conviction that his own poem is beautiful even by the joint contrary verdict of everyone else acquainted with the poem. So long as the effect of the poem on him is one of immediate satisfaction, there is no way of establishing that his judgement on the poem is not a true judgement of taste.[30] It will certainly appear to others that his pleasure has some connection with either the agreeable or the good, that is, that it is attributable to some *interest* in the object. However, so long as he has no consciousness of the role these connections may be playing in his pleasure, that is, so long as his poem appears beautiful (immediately pleasing, *apart from any interest*) to him, then he is satisfying all the conditions that anyone *could* satisfy in order to legitimately claim that the judgement they are making is one of taste.[31] It may be, according to Kant, that later, when his power of judgement has been 'made more acute by practice', he will come to agree with his critics on the merits of his work, but only if he truly has ceased to find it beautiful will this new (negative) judgement be a judgement of taste.[32] While taste may be 'improved' or 'sharpened', in the sense of coming closer to some prevailing norm (if that is improvement), any particular judgement which takes this, or any other abstract principle, into consideration, is, by definition, not a judgement of taste.

A judgement of taste that demonstrates 'bad taste' (that is, runs counter to a prevailing consensus) is still, as far as it is possible to determine, a judgement of taste. This is a point Kant seems to concede in dealing with the partial young poet: despite gesturing towards the existence of a standard of good taste (it may be 'made more acute by practice'), he is not disqualifying any sense of immediate pleasure in an object from being called 'taste', since taste is an immediate sense of pleasure. It is for this reason that Kant says that the establishment of principles of taste is 'absolutely impossible':

> For I must be sensitive of the pleasure immediately in the representation of it, and I cannot be talked into it by means of any proofs. Thus although critics, as Hume says, can reason more plausibly than cooks, they still suffer the same fate as them. They cannot expect a determining ground for their judgement from proofs, but only from the reflection of the subject on his own state (of pleasure or displeasure), rejecting all precepts and rules.[33]

These, then, are the necessary conditions Kant lays down for us to justifiably claim that the judgement we have made is one of taste, and not some other kind of judgement. Kant does not, however, appeal to this 'justification' as a possible way to negatively establish a standard of taste in the manner that, for example, Hume does when he asserts that the collective verdict of those possessing a 'strong sense, united to delicate sentiment, improved by practice, perfected by comparison, and *cleared of all prejudice*' will provide a 'true standard of taste and beauty'.[34] Kant does, however, make what appears a rather similar claim elsewhere when he is excluding any possibility of charm or emotion contributing to taste. The presence of such elements as determining factors in the judgement, he asserts, disqualifies such judgements from a claim to 'universal satisfaction'.[35] This much follows from his stipulative definition of 'judgement of taste'. The conclusions he draws from this point are not, however, warranted even by that definition, if they are taken as reflections on what it is possible to positively, rather than negatively, establish about any particular judgement. For he here claims that while charm may sometimes be 'passed off for' the form, such a misunderstanding 'can be eliminated by careful determination of these concepts'.[36] The possibility of a verifiable standard of taste suggested, but not warranted, by the possibility of such elimination, appears to lead Kant's argument beyond itself; for he immediately afterwards invokes 'genuine taste' as if it were a given standard:

> As for the opinion that the beauty that is attributed to the object on account of its form may well be heightened by charm, this is a common error and one that is very detrimental to genuine, uncorrupted, well-grounded taste, although charms [such as colour in painting] may certainly be added beside beauty [which, in the case of painting, would reside in the composition] in order to interest the mind through the representation of the object beyond dry satisfaction, and thus to serve to recommend taste and its cultivation, especially when it is still crude and unpractised. But they actually do damage to the judgement of taste if they attract attention to themselves as grounds for the judging of beauty. For it is so far from being true that they contribute to taste that, if taste is still weak and unpractised, they must rather be accepted cautiously, as foreigners, only to the extent that they do not disturb the beautiful form.[37]

Though, as we saw in the Introduction, to satisfy the demand for subjective universal validity, Kant must ultimately claim that differences in taste are somehow attributable to some subjects' failure to recognize that their pleasure is based on an interest, he does not believe that there is any way of showing which subjects these are, or, conversely, which apparent judgements of taste are satisfying the sufficient conditions of 'true' judgements of taste. It would not, then, be legitimate to fasten on Kant's drawing of limits to what may at least properly *claim* to be a judgement of taste, in order to attribute to Kant the kind of untenable normative thesis that Hume advances, or, indeed, that the above passage from Kant suggests: the argument that, since interest or ignorance may be supposed to sometimes distort taste, any taste that is demonstrably disinterested and informed must be 'correct'. For it is impossible to demonstrate genuine disinterest, and thus to separate 'genuine, uncorrupted, well-grounded' taste from any other sort that merely believes it is such and cannot be shown to be otherwise. Only, then, where the judgement does not even lay claim to subjective universal validity, that is, where the subject is merely making an error in vocabulary (the rectification of which implies no change in feeling) when they claim the judgement is one of taste, can this criterion of disinterestedness serve a discriminating function.

There are, then, two points fundamental to Kant's discussion, two matters of fact that we must accept if we are to understand it at all. Firstly, that sometimes objects appear to please us immediately. Secondly, that an object which pleases in this way may legitimately be called 'beautiful' by the one who is pleased. These two propositions were commonplaces of Kant's time and still are commonplaces outside the academic study of aesthetics. The necessity of emphasizing them here will become clear if we digress for a moment to consider the afterlife of the *Critique of the Power of Judgement*.

BEAUTY AS AESTHETIC MERIT

Kant, as we have seen, is quite specific, about what he means by 'beauty': it is that thing which we see, or do not see, with our own eyes – apparently regardless of understanding, preparation, comparison, the opinion of others, and so on.[38] For Mothershill such a characterization makes beauty a 'mindless pleasure', trivializing it into relativism or subjectivism, and, since her 'beauty' is actually aesthetic merit, that is, a class containing any quality we may admire in art, she has no difficulty in proving the inadequacy of Kant's definition.[39]

'Mindless pleasure' is, however, rather a good summary of Kant's characterization of beauty: if we ignored the negative connotations of the phrase, it would do quite well as shorthand for his 'pleasure attendant on a mere reflection upon a given intuition'. Indeed it is precisely insofar as it is a mindless pleasure that taste is interesting to Kant. Moreover Kant himself, as we shall see in the next chapter, does use the word 'beauty', albeit in the apparently oxymoronic form of 'dependent beauty', to refer to what we would now call 'aesthetic merit'. (The term 'aesthetic merit' itself would be, by his own definition, so general – including both the desirable and, if this is a separate category, the good – as to be useless.) This, then, would seem to justify Mothershill's charge that Kant reduces the experience of art to a 'mindless pleasure'. On the other hand, Kant does deal with the ideas involved in the experience of art at some length, and does allow a role for concepts in that experience; hence, as we shall see, the qualification 'dependent' in 'dependent beauty'. However, he is principally interested in what we now call 'aesthetic merit' at the level at which it shares common fundamental characteristics with that mindless pleasure which is the experience of what he terms 'free beauty', that is, the bare reflection upon a given intuition. The fundamental characteristic that art has in common with this form of beauty, a characteristic which Kant believes justifies using 'beauty' for both, is that, despite the fact that the cognition of art obviously involves concepts, the pleasure we *ultimately* derive from it is still a matter of taste, that is, it is a pleasure that is apparently undetermined by either desire or rational concepts.

To understand a play by Shakespeare we need, at least, to understand the language, to understand, if only at the crudest level, its symbolic relationship to reality (that it is a play), to understand the sequence of actions as a plot, and so on. Some would say, and the existence of the subject 'Literature' implies, that in order to 'fully appreciate' it we must understand a great deal more. However, having said all this, whether the play is moving or not is still a matter of whether we *feel* it is moving or not, and it is this feeling, rather than any deference to whatever concepts may be involved in the experience, that is the arbiter, for any particular subject, of whether the play does or does not possess the aesthetic merit of being moving. Critics, as Kant says, may be able to argue more plausibly than cooks, but they must still share the same fate.

We shall return to this matter of the concepts involved in what Kant calls 'dependent' or 'adherent' beauty later, but for the moment it is sufficient to note that modern commentators are usually approaching the question from a quite different angle.[40] In resurrecting the word 'beauty' as a blanket term for aesthetic merit, and yet wishing to discuss that aesthetic merit in terms of the concepts upon which the cognition, though not, ultimately, the evaluation of the work depends, it is inevitable that much of what Kant writes about beauty will appear strikingly, almost wilfully, counter-intuitive. For such comment-ators are usually approaching the experience in terms of precisely what separates aesthetic merit from what Kant calls 'pure' or 'free' beauty, that is, the obvious involvement of concepts in the cognition of the object.[41]

There is, then, a fundamental conflict between the Kantian notion of beauty and the recent use of 'beauty' to mean aesthetic merit. For, while Kant is con-cerned with the definition and explanation of a specific immediate effect, aes-thetics is concerned with the process of cognizing and evaluating a quite different range of effects. Mothershill, for example, questions the *usefulness* of such concepts as 'intrinsic value' and 'pleasing in itself', as if they were intended not as description but as explanation, and thinks it is a shortcoming in Kant that he 'neglects' the contribution of critical study to the formation of judge-ments.[42] It is, indeed, the immediacy of taste that is the first casualty of this misappropriation. Mothershill, for example, writes that the perception of 'great and serious beauty' may require prolonged study and critical analysis; a correct 'assessment' only being possible where the subject allows for and removes whatever may be 'prejudiced', that is, subjective in 'his' response.[43] Likewise Savile (who specifically says that his analysis is intended to cover 'natural' cases of beauty) writes that, since beauty is a satisfactory answer to a problem in style, only a response to an object that derives from a proper under-standing of this problem is fit to enter into a judgement of the object's 'beauty'; so that appreciation cannot be divorced from clarity of vision and accuracy of understanding, both of which may be corrected by the intellect.[44] Hence we find this trend in aesthetics constantly counselling the subject to follow just that course, in pursuit of 'true judgement', which Kant holds up as the anti-thesis of the process, that is, deference to principles, or to the opinions of others, either individually or as embodied in a canon.

> [It] is required of every judgement that is supposed to prove the taste of the subject that the subject judge for himself, without having to grope about by means of experience among the judgements of others and first inform himself about their satisfaction or dissatisfaction in the same object, and thus that he should pronounce his judgement not as imitation, because a thing really does please universally, but *a priori*. . . . Taste makes claim merely to autonomy. To make the judgements of others into the determin-ing ground of one's own would be heteronomy.[45]

Ultimately, making 'beauty' the subject of what are perhaps quite defensible characterizations of the experience of art (depending, that is, on how we define 'aesthetic' in the non-Kantian sense) requires that even the most fundamental defining characteristics of taste, as the perception of beauty, be denied. Thus Mothershill writes that

> although I know what I *intend* to do in uttering the words 'This rose is beautiful', the question whether my intention has been executed, that is, whether I have actually *made* a judgement of taste, must remain open.[46]

Not, however, 'open' in the sense that, in deference to the demand for universal validity, this same question is left incorrigibly open by Kant. For, Mothershill can hold that when she perceives beauty she is actually perceiving a property of the object as objectively present as colour or size; so that, consequently, another may 'confirm' our opinion of an object, and there are objects of 'beauty' (that is, canonical works of art) 'whose claim to our admiration and reverence are beyond dispute'.[47] Likewise Savile finds that he can easily solve the difficulty of accounting for those 'beauties [canonical works] that do not attach but leave us indifferent or even repel', by denying that pleasure is an intrinsic quality of our experience of 'beauty' (meaning art), and, therefore, irrelevant to the analysis of beauty: 'Non-normal beauty can be set aside as of little theoretical interest or importance.'[48] Normal beauty, in this scheme, is as near to objective as makes no matter. This objectivist line of thought reaches its apotheosis in Mothershill's statement: 'Not everything that people take to be beautiful *is* beautiful.'[49] 'Beautiful' here has completely lost its meaning.[50]

Not surprisingly, then, Mothershill specifically takes Kant to task for holding that the young poet's perception of the beauty of his own poems, made in defiance of public opinion, could yet be a genuine judgement of taste.[51] For, she argues, does not Kant say elsewhere that the least hint of 'interest' disqualifies the perceiver? The point is, however, that the poet genuinely does see beauty when he reads his poems, that is, no *conscious* interest is involved, no admixture (from the poet's point of view) of the agreeable or good. (And even his rational recognition that such an adulteration might be the case is, precisely in being rational, irrelevant.) For Kant any judgement that is really, *for the subject*, a judgement of taste, and not any other sort of judgement, can lay claim to being a judgement of taste; for Mothershill a 'genuine judgement' is one that is 'right' about the aesthetic value of a given object: they are simply talking about different things – though, unfortunately, using the same words to do so.[52]

The purpose of this digression, then, has been to defend the existence of Kant's object in the *Critique of the Power of Judgement*, that is, the judgement of taste, in its full antinomical splendour. Such a defence is rendered necessary by the fate that the concept of beauty, and consequently Kant's work, has suffered at the hands of the philosophy of art. (This is by no means a merely contemporary phenomenon: although I have concentrated only on recent manifestations of the misappropriation of beauty these are, in point of vocabulary at least, no more than the resurrection of themes that are to be found in aesthetics throughout the whole of the nineteenth and the early part of the twentieth centuries.[53]) Critics and aestheticians have gone on reasoning with considerably more plausibility than cooks, but taste remains taste.

Kant's use of 'taste' and 'beauty' is worth defending for two reasons. First, despite the fact that the desire to make the value of art autonomous, and consequently intrinsic, has often brought the definition of 'aesthetic' close to that of 'beauty', it is obvious that if 'aesthetic merit' is to mean 'what art is valued for', and 'aesthetic' to mean 'the cause of this value', it is not possible to identify beauty with the aesthetic. (Still less so if 'aesthetic' is understood to be substantive rather than verdictive.) The latter term has, at present, no settled definition, but whatever common denominators, arising from its association with 'art', we can find among its various uses, these are obviously not identifiable with the properties of beauty *per se*. Second, it is, at best, confusing to use 'beauty' for two disparate areas of experience. While it may be possible to find other terms for the kind of 'judgements' or reactions that are the subject of aesthetics, if we renounce the use of 'beauty' for that form of perception of which simply feeling is the necessary (and perhaps sufficient) condition, we will be hard put to replace it.[54]

THE APPEARANCE OF UNIVERSALITY

As we have seen, it is fundamental to Kant's account that a judgement of taste should be 'the reflection of the subject on his own state (of pleasure or displeasure), rejecting all precepts and rules'.[55] The subject knows 'he' is making a judgement of taste 'through the mere consciousness of separation of everything that belongs to the agreeable and the good from the satisfaction that remains to him': if it feels like beauty then it is beauty.[56] Moreover, since we experience the beautiful object as an object of necessary satisfaction, that is, we can discover no *personal* reasons to account for the pleasure, either in terms of the agreeable or the good, we speak of beauty as if it were a quality of the object itself – thereby implying that we are speaking with a 'universal voice'.

However, Kant goes on to insist that because of this implied, if only ideal, universality it would be ridiculous for someone to say 'This is beautiful *for me*', that is, to hold that everyone has their own taste in the beautiful in the same manner as they have a taste in the agreeable.[57] After all, he continues, do we not blame someone for judging differently from ourselves, and deny that they have taste? To say that everyone has their own taste when it comes to beauty, he concludes, would be equivalent to saying that there was no such thing as beauty, or 'aesthetic judgement' at all.[58] Indeed, immediately after claiming that it is the subject's own consciousness of the absence of anything belonging to the agreeable or the good from the satisfaction that is felt that makes that satisfaction a judgement of taste, Kant goes on to qualify the remark by saying that although such a consciousness should guarantee that the judgement is one of taste, nevertheless the subject cannot be sure that it is such a judgement since they must be aware that their judgements have not always met with universal agreement, that is, that they have previously made 'erroneous judgements'.[59]

It is such remarks as these that I had in mind when speaking of a certain undertow in Kant's work towards the notion of consensus as a guarantee of what is really beautiful. The question must, however, arise at this point whether it is here necessary to invoke the notion that judgements of taste can be divided (in accordance with Kant's stipulative definition) into those which erroneously lay claim to speak with a 'universal voice', that is, those feelings that are only apparently judgements of taste, and those feelings which legitimately make this same claim, and are, by virtue of this, really judgements of taste. Such an appeal would obviously resolve the conflict. Equally obviously, however, given the effective short-circuiting of any analysis this would involve, it would be better, if at all possible, to avoid such a removal of the argument to the realm of the empirically indemonstrable. Let us see, then, what Kant can actually establish with regard to the significance of 'erroneous' judgements without appeal to a stipulative definition of the judgement of taste.

Even granting that the subject has not always met with universal agreement, it does not follow that the subject must conclude that when this happened it was because the original judgement was 'erroneous', that is, in some way, not a judgement of taste. For if a judgement of taste is necessarily 'the reflection of the subject on his own state (of pleasure or displeasure), rejecting all precepts and rules', who is to judge when another has made an erroneous judgement? And how can one rely on the judgements of others? The subject may be well aware that universal agreement to their judgement is not forthcoming but it does not follow from this that they have grounds for assuming the original judgement was not one of taste. Indeed, contrary to what Kant here asserts, it is the proposition that everyone *cannot* have their own taste when it comes to beauty that would be equivalent to saying there was no such thing as judgements of taste.

This last position, as we saw above, is the line that Kant elsewhere takes. It is perhaps best, then, to interpret Kant in these passages on 'erroneous judgement' as insisting on the separation of the beautiful from the agreeable and the good, rather than asserting the universal validity of some judgements. In finding an object beautiful, it must appear to the subject 'as if' the beauty were a property of the thing. For this reason the admission that the object is beautiful merely for oneself appears to constitute a denial of one of the fundamental conditions of the judgement's being one of taste. In any particular instance in which I am ostensibly making a judgement of taste, says Kant, I cannot justify calling the thing 'beautiful' simply by saying that it is beautiful *for me*.[60] This is not to say that the subject counts on others agreeing or has found that they do agree, but rather that the very act of finding the object 'beautiful' must, in some sense, take the form of a demand for the agreement of others.[61]

The subject's demand for this agreement is made on the basis of that 'common sense' which is apparently implied by the immediacy of the judgement itself. The beautiful 'claims' to deal in universal rules.[62] It follows from this, according to Kant, that in describing something as beautiful we are also insisting that 'everyone *should* approve of the object in question and similarly declare it to be beautiful'.[63] However, though this is what is implied in calling a thing beautiful (as opposed to good or agreeable), whether this demand also takes place as a separate claim aside from the calling of a thing beautiful is debatable. As Kant himself says, the 'ought' in judgements of taste is only pronounced conditionally. Indeed he implicitly concedes that we cannot claim unconditioned necessity for judgements of taste when he contrasts such judgements both with taste in the agreeable, which, being devoid of any principle, does not give rise to the idea of necessity, *and* cognitive judgements, that is, those instances where we can point to a definite objective principle and, thereby, claim 'unconditioned necessity' for the judgement.[64]

The judgement of taste can lay claim to necessity only insofar as it appears, by default, exemplary of some form of common sense. The immediacy of beauty – that is, its lack of any apparent reference to the agreeable or the good – leads us to infer a sense that we 'assume' to be universal.[65] Yet this is only an assumption, and, even in Kant's account, the subject is not only completely justified in calling the object beautiful on the basis of their own feelings but is in fact prohibited from making such a judgement on any other basis. Thus the definition of the beautiful drawn from this section states not that the beautiful is an object of necessary satisfaction but that it is an object which 'is cognized without a concept as' an object of necessary satisfaction.[66]

Kant, as we shall see in the next chapter, does in fact make the dubious transition from the *felt* necessity of judgements of taste to the *real* necessity of such judgements, though his argument for doing so can be seen to comprise (once the presupposition of the existence of a subjective universal validity is removed) of no more than an appeal to the properties of judgements of taste hitherto considered. However, Kant posits this necessity in a form that precludes our being able to appeal to it in any given case, so that, in fact, this 'solution' in no way solves the problem of how we are to account for, and, more importantly, justify accounting for, differences in taste in practice.

The question for the present, however, is whether Kant is justified, purely on the basis of his phenomenology of judgements of taste, in asserting that the immediacy of beauty, its appearance as an object of necessary satisfaction, actually does entail or justify our 'blaming' others for judging differently in the way he describes:

> In all judgements by which we declare something to be beautiful, we allow no one to be of a different opinion, without, however, grounding our judge-

ment on concepts, but only on our feeling, which we therefore make our ground not as a private feeling, but as a common one.[67]

In reality, of course, this is simply not always the case: it is remarkably easy to agree to differ about matters of taste.[68] That is, it is possible to find a thing beautiful and at the same time realize that it exists as such for me, and would not be beautiful for someone else. (Given that beauty appears to be a quality of this object, this should not be – but here we are concerned with what is rather than what should be.) We do not, after all, consider anyone who does not find the same thing beautiful either incapable, or somehow beyond the pale of what we take to be our common humanity: we are not astounded, or, at least, not so often as we should be. *De gustibus non est disputandum*, after all. Moreover, experience readily shows us that our tastes change over time; a fact which, more than any other, should make us aware of the provisional, in the sense of personal, nature of judgements of taste. Thus, while almost everyone will on occasion blame someone's taste in the case of 'bad taste', few would feel blame was appropriate in those cases where someone simply did not see (feel) the beauty they themselves saw (felt).

This certainly throws some confusion into the account, since it seems impossible for beauty to appear 'objective' and yet be intuited as subjective: how can I ascribe beauty to the object without ascribing the feeling to everyone who might look at it? Perhaps the answer is simply historical (as the parentheses in the last sentence of the previous paragraph suggest), that is, perhaps I am incapable of taking beauty as a quality. If the expression 'It is beautiful for me' seems equally unusable today it is surely not because most people feel that it is a contradiction in terms but rather because it appears tautological: the personal qualification is redundant. (Moreover the expression implies that there might be some other way in which a thing could be beautiful!) This position, however, does not necessarily compromise the perception of the judgement of taste as disinterested, or aconceptual; not, at least, *at the moment of judging*.

Assuming that it is not mere solipsism or indifference on my part that leads me to relinquish the universal claim for beauty it must follow that the beautiful is 'cognized . . . as the object of a *necessary* satisfaction' in some peculiar fashion.[69] This leads to another possible objection to Kant's insistence on our making a universal claim: that if beauty really was felt, unequivocally, to be an object of (universally) necessary pleasure, and appeared so even to reflection, there would be no 'problem of taste' such as the one Kant has posited. Instead there would simply be the problem of why some people are insensible to beauty, or perceive it where it is not present. For many writers on the subject, of course, this has been the problem of beauty. Kant's characterization of aesthetic intolerance, if taken simply as a comment on the critical manners of his time, could be illustrated with myriad instances. ('One can see', writes Diderot apropos his own worship of Richardson, 'that there is in matters of taste, as in matters of religion, a kind of intolerance of which I disapprove, but which I can only avoid in myself by an effort of reason.'[70]) But, as we have seen, Kant's own argument so far does not justify any 'standard of taste' aside from a personal one, nor, as we shall see, does it prove that taste itself necessarily entails belief in such a standard. According to his own lights, then, it is going too far to claim that the very existence of the judgements of taste either necessarily entails aesthetic intolerance, or necessarily excludes justifying a particular judgement by an appeal to one's own feelings. The partial young poet, after all, must be aware, as a matter of empirical fact, that he is alone in his judgement of the beauty of his poems, and yet Kant is in no position, as it were, to deny that the poet's judgement is one of taste.

To some extent the problem here lies in Kant's moving away from the mere description of taste and towards a proposed grounding; everything he has said so far could imply this aesthetic intolerance, but it is by no means a necessary conclusion. Consider the case of an optical illusion; knowing that the pencil half-immersed in water is straight both will and will not make it look straight. Likewise it is possible to entertain the notion of an object that is a necessary source of satisfaction only to oneself. This may be what Kant means when he describes the universality in question as represented only subjectively: there is some admixture of that reference to the self, implicit but not reflected upon, which we realize more fully in the agreeable.

In the case of the agreeable, according to Kant, it is quite permissible to correct one who declares that Canary-wine, the colour violet, or the sound of wind instruments, 'is agreeable' by reminding them that they should add a personal qualification.[71] It would be foolish, he says, to argue over such preferences as if they were matters of logic. Yet we have all, though hopefully only at some early stage in our lives, entered into just such futile controversy. (Indeed it would seem rather childish now even to insist on the personal qualification, since we understand it to be necessarily implied by the initial statement.) It is Kant's contention in this same passage, as we have seen above, that since this particular kind of aesthetic satisfaction is immediate, disinterested, and, therefore, apparently necessary, it must stand on a different footing. This may be so, yet it does not follow that we can therefore feel justified in placing our judgements of taste on the same plane as logical judgements or even that we always do. (Moreover, we must keep this 'apparently' constantly in mind.) As Kant himself says, since feeling pleasure immediately in the representation of the object is the touchstone of beauty, while critics may be able to reason 'more plausibly' than cooks, especially, we might add, in connection with the beautiful in art, where we can point to definite properties to which we believe the beauty can be attributed, nevertheless, the critic and the cook must still share the same fate: that is, they can logically demand no agreement from another apropos the beauty of the object except on the basis of that other's reflection upon their own state of pleasure or displeasure.[72]

Six years after the publication of the *Critique of the Aesthetic Power of*

Judgement, in a polemic against what Kant sarcastically designated the 'superior' tone of certain contemporary philosophical writings, there is an interesting verbal echo of his assertion that our judgements of taste 'demand' the agreement of everyone:

> The principle of wanting to philosophize under the influence of higher *feeling* is, among all principles, the one best suited to produce a superior tone. For who will contest my own feelings? If I can make it credible that this feeling is not merely subjective *in me* but can be demanded of everyone and is therefore held to be objectively valid and rationalized as a piece of knowledge, therefore not as a mere concept but an intuition (apprehension of the object itself) – if I can make this credible, I have a great advantage over those who must first justify themselves before they are allowed to celebrate the truth of their assertions.[73]

To posit a truth on the basis of feeling – and Kant has allowed no other measure than feeling in connection with taste – is, then, for Kant, by no means a legitimate philosophical move.

Moreover, as Kant's very method of enquiry presumes, reflection itself should make us aware that even if our judgement does appear necessary to us this does not, either in practice or theory, imply that it is a universally necessary judgement. Admittedly, this would appear to import some degree of inconsistency into the subject's state of mind at the moment of judgement, but since we have started from a set of antinomies, this inconsistency is not, in itself, an argument against either of the two conflicting propositions – that beauty, unlike the agreeable, is cognized as an object of necessary satisfaction, and that we are reflectively aware that beauty, like the agreeable, is such only for ourselves. After all we can say, with regard to the immersed pencil, both that it 'looks bent', since we undeniably perceive an angle, and that it 'looks straight', since we also perceive that we are viewing it in water, and can, therefore, take into account the refractive properties we know are attributable to this medium. With respect to beauty of course we are ignorant of the medium; indeed, no medium appears. Kant has not, at this stage, addressed this question, though, as we shall see, it is a question that becomes more urgent as his account of judgements of taste becomes more detailed.

To conclude this chapter I wish to anticipate, to some extent, this question of the nature of the 'medium' that gives rise to an object appearing as a beautiful object. In order to do so it is necessary to rehearse what Kant has said so far, and to draw out some of what his account might imply. Principally there is the idea that the immediacy, or felt necessity, of the judgement of taste leads us to presume, if only by default, the possibility of a common ground for that judgement. Such a presumption seems justified, if not by a universal uniformity of taste, then at least by the fact that the *experience* of finding things beautiful is sufficiently uniform to justify us calling it the same experience even when its objects differ. Does this also allow us to presume that this common ground is, or should be, expressed in a common way? In theory it should. The justification for this being the same as for the original supposition of a common ground, that is, that if taste is immediate, if, as Hume says, there is no space available between the perception and the judgement in which the understanding might refract perception, then individual differences, aside from organic ones, should not affect its operations.[74] However, as a matter of fact, there are differences in taste. We might get around this difficulty if we could point to the objective principle at work in judgements of taste but, as Kant says, this is not possible.

Another way would be if we could *demonstrate* when the subject is either not really making a judgement of taste, or has not really apprehended the same object. But even were such a demonstration possible in the first case, or successful in the second, this would still only leave us with a broadened consensus rather than an objective principle. Apropos the possibility of proving that someone has believed themselves to be making a judgement of taste when really they were making another kind of judgement, the point made in the early part of this chapter must be borne in mind: it is the pleasure in, not the awareness of, the object that is cognized as disinterested, so that merely to discover a potential or even real interest the object might have for the subject is not to prove anything about the quality of the pleasure they are deriving from it when they claim it is beautiful.

Differences in taste would seem to indicate that the operation of taste is itself in some way effected by individual differences, and, therefore, that it is either not immediate, or rather only immediate given the particular subject, that is, that it is something potentially peculiar to the *individual* subject which is the medium we are seeking. (By this I do not mean to imply that the individual distorts the operation of some ideal capacity for making true judgements of taste, but rather that – leaving entirely to one side all questions of 'true' and 'false' – all particular judgements of taste *depend upon* factors that are only contingently present in the individual subject.) The judgement of taste is, as Kant says, cognized as immediate (necessary), for it is by this immediacy that we recognize the judgement as one of taste. It would seem, then, that whatever it is in the subject that leads to the attribution of beauty, that is, that creates the refraction of perception into judgement, its operations must be hidden from the subject at the moment of judgement.

The question of whether the above is, in fact, the case, and what such refraction might imply about the grounds of taste, is, however, a matter that we must postpone. For we have still to complete the examination of Kant's own exposition.

2

The Description of Taste II: The Role of Concepts

The disinterested, aconceptual nature of beauty, the universality apparently implicit in its lack of grounding either in a subjective end (as a *source* of satisfaction) or an objective end (as a *source* of the good), leads Kant to assert that the sole foundation of the judgement of taste must be the 'form of purposiveness' of an object or its mental representation.[1] The judgement of taste, in other words, does not deal with any concept of the nature or of the possibilities of the object, but simply with the relative bearing of the representative powers so far as determined by representation itself: '*Beauty* is the form of the *purposiveness* of an object, insofar as it is perceived in it *without representation of an end*'.[2]

This form of purposiveness that the object has for us in a judgement of taste can be contrasted, says Kant, both with *external objective purposiveness*, that is, usefulness, and *internal objective purposiveness*, that is, the perfection of the object.[3] He rejects both on the grounds that they would involve making the judgement of taste reliant on concepts. This is obviously so in the case of the useful, but Kant holds that it is equally so in the case of perfection. For in estimating any objective purposiveness we require both a concept of what sort of thing the object is, and an estimate of how closely the particular example comes to what we conceive of as the perfection of such things: as he says, 'the mere form of a *perfection*', divorced from a concept of type and, therefore, function, is a contradiction in terms.[4]

In deriving that aspect of the definition of the beautiful that is contained in this section ('*Beauty* is the form of the *purposiveness* of an object, insofar as it is perceived in it *without representation of an end*') Kant adds a footnote to counter the possible objection that we are capable of cognizing a form as useful without also cognizing a particular end for that form. He puts forward the example of a Stone Age implement:

[Although] they clearly betray by their shape a purposiveness the end of which one does not know, [they] are nevertheless not declared to be beautiful on that account. Yet the fact that they are regarded as a work of art is already enough to require one to admit that one relates their shape to some sort of intention and to a determinate purpose. Hence there is also no immediate satisfaction at all in their intuition. A flower, by contrast, e.g. a tulip, is held to be beautiful because a certain purposiveness is encountered in our perception of it which, as we judge it, is not related to any end at all.[5]

It has appeared to some commentators that Kant is here asserting that the very quality of being artificial precludes the possibility of being beautiful. Kant's main emphasis in the note, however, is on the idea that being unable to determine the objective purposiveness of the object is not the same as considering the object independently of the concept of an objective purposiveness. He is not, then, saying that we do not perceive the implement as beautiful because it is artificial, but rather that simply being unable to cognize the function of the implement is not sufficient grounds for the object appearing as beautiful.

The form of the note does, nevertheless, invite some confusion by the contrast it draws between the implement and the flower. In the case of the flower, Kant writes, we meet with a certain purposiveness merely in its perception. This would appear to imply that the flower, being without a purpose, is necessarily beautiful, or, at least, potentially beautiful in a way that the implement cannot be. This is not, as we shall see, what Kant wishes to assert; neither, indeed, is it something that can be deduced from what he has said so far. For if uselessness is not a sufficient condition for a thing's being beautiful then neither is it, in Kant's account, a necessary condition either. It is the bare form of purposiveness in the representation whereby any object is *given* to us, so far as we are conscious of it, that inspires the satisfaction of beauty. If we did not refer, or were not conscious of referring, the form of the implement to a hypothetical use then we might also meet with a certain purposiveness in its perception, that is, find it beautiful. A pure judgement of taste, says Kant, is possible even in respect of an object with a definite internal end, providing 'the person making the judgement either had no concept of this end or abstracted from it in his judgement'.[6] On the other hand there are various ways the representation of the flower might be given to us (as herbalists, botanists, or gardeners) that would imply either an estimate of usefulness or perfection.[7] It is not, then, that the flower is intrinsically beautiful or potentially beautiful while the implement is not. Hence Kant's definition of 'beauty' not simply as the form of purposiveness in an object, but rather as that purposiveness 'so far as perceived' in the object apart from the 'representation' of some end.

FREE AND DEPENDENT BEAUTY

However, having defined the judgement of taste by the exclusion of any role for concepts, either of use or perfection, Kant then appears to retract this very definition. There are, he says, two forms of beauty: 'free beauty', or beauty which presupposes no concept of what the object should be, and 'dependent beauty', which does presuppose such a concept, and consequently an answering perfection in the object.[8] 'Dependent beauties' are, therefore, appendant, for a concept of the good enters in, and, according to Kant, mars the purity of the judgement of taste in just the same way as would an admixture of the agreeable.[9] This would seem to indicate that 'dependent beauty' is not beauty at all, though Kant persists in using the word 'beauty' to refer to this species of apparently normative judgement, which, while it may involve satisfaction, would not appear to be aconceptual after the fashion of the beauty he has hitherto described.

It would be convenient to be able to say that Kant, in distinguishing between 'free beauty' and 'dependent beauty', is merely qualifying his earlier definition: '*Beauty* is the form of the *purposiveness* of an object, insofar as it is perceived in it *without representation of an end*'.[10] But it is difficult to see how such a definition can be reconciled with the assertion that there is a 'dependent' form of beauty. Indeed, this distinction, between free and dependent beauty, is generally taken as one of the more arcane moments in the *Critique*.[11] It is worth noting, however, that some distinction of this kind was no novelty at the time Kant was writing. The author of the article 'Beauty' in Chambers' *Cyclopaedia* had distinguished between a beauty that is ascribed according to the approbation of the mind, and a beauty that is ascribed according to the excitation of 'agreeable Sensations'; concluding, rather unhelpfully, that 'There is therefore *Beauty* and *Beauty*'.[12] Kames had made a similar distinction, likewise without feeling the need to reconcile what the distinction implied, between relative beauty, which is perceived where a notion of adaption to purpose enters into the subject's reaction, and intrinsic beauty, for which 'no more is required but singly an act of vision'.[13] If we also bear in mind how theoreticians and critics at this time used the word 'beauty' both to denote an immediate and ineffable effect, and (usually in combination with an article) to denote effects, most commonly in art, the production and enjoyment of which were presumed to be largely, if perhaps not wholly, intelligible, we can see that this distinction, or lack of distinction, may have arisen from the unavailability of the word 'aesthetic' as it is now used.

According to Kant, while free beauty is self-subsisting, dependent beauty is conditioned by the concept of a particular end for the class of objects to which the object belongs. The parrot, the humming-bird, the bird of paradise, a number of Crustacea, designs *à la grecque*, ornamental foliage, all music without words, and so on, have, says Kant, no intrinsic meaning, represent nothing, and are thus free beauties.[14] In contrast, the beauty of human beings, horses, buildings, and so on, presupposes a concept of the end that defines what the thing has to be, and consequently a concept of its perfection.[15]

This is not, of course, to say that flowers are free beauties of nature *in themselves*. For, as we saw above, while a botanist may know the true nature of the flower, and be able to judge its internal and external purposes, nevertheless, in finding the flower beautiful (freely beautiful), the botanist, as Kant says, 'pays no attention to this natural end', hence no 'perfection' of any kind underlies the judgement.[16] This is purely, then, a matter of the way in which, at any particular time, the representation of the object is given to the subject. The flower tends towards free beauty because, as Kant comments, 'hardly anyone other than the botanist knows what sort of thing a flower is supposed to be'.[17] By contrast, the inclusion of horses in the list of dependent beauties may seem a little odd until we consider that in 1790 a horse was most likely to strike the average subject principally as a functional object. (Thus Reynolds, in 1759, though he rejects the idea that 'fitness to the end proposed' for an object can be a criterion of beauty, since 'we always determine concerning its beauty, before we exert our understanding to judge of its fitness', nevertheless in the same place writes that 'had a horse as few good qualities as a tortoise, I do not imagine that he would be esteemed beautiful'.[18]) Indeed, though Kant gives buildings in his list of dependent beauties, and in particular churches, palaces, arsenals and summer houses, it is the very example of a palace which he uses at the beginning of the *Critique* to outline the conditions of a pure judgement of taste. There he writes that in making a judgement of taste on a palace nothing is relevant except 'whether the mere representation of the object is accompanied with satisfaction, however indifferent I might be with regard to the existence of the object of this representation'.[19] Now he asserts that there may be a form of judgement of taste in which some concept of the function of the class of palaces plays a role in this representation:

> A judgement of taste in regard to an object with a determinate internal end would thus be pure only if the person making the judgement either had no concept of this end or abstracted from it in his judgement. But in that case, although this person would have made a correct judgement of taste, in that he would have judged the object as a free beauty, he would nevertheless be criticized and accused of a false taste by someone else, who considered beauty in the object only as an adherent property (who looked to the end of the object), even though both judge correctly in their way: the one on the basis of what he has before his sense [a pure judgement of taste on a free beauty], the other on the basis of what he has in his thoughts [a judgement of taste applied intentionally on a dependent beauty].[20]

It would appear, then, despite Kant's provision of a list of free and dependent beauties, that the distinction he is drawing is not one between different kinds of objects, rather the distinction depends on whether or not the subject refers, or is conscious of referring, the beauty to a concept of the object.

The text will not, then, support an interpretation of 'dependent beauty' as either beauty in art or artistic merit. Though art is a useful resource for examples of dependent beauty, if we are to interpret this form of beauty as aesthetic merit (in this restricted sense) there is no reason why it should be confined to art.[21] Moreover, as we have seen, Kant does not intend such a restriction.

Neither, of course, can this distinction between 'free' and 'dependent' be made into a hierarchy with the 'purer' as a 'higher' form. Although Kant ultimately does place natural beauty above art from a moral point of view, it should be noted that this ranking will not reflect back on the distinction between free and dependent beauty: his list of objects appropriate to the former kind of judgement includes only ornament and music from the arts, yet in his evaluative ranking of the arts music comes lowest, while his most emphatic example of dependent beauty – poetry – comes highest.[22]

Although the distinction is not, then, between the intrinsic natures of different kinds of objects, it is easy to imagine how the kind of object or its properties might act (though never absolutely) as limiting conditions on the kind of beauty that the subject discerns in them. The flower, to most of us, is unlikely to present itself as a dependent beauty; the horse to most of Kant's contemporaries was unlikely to present itself as a free beauty. Things which do not obtrude their 'intrinsic meaning', their internal or external purposiveness, on us are more likely to be judged (that is, to strike us) as free beauties.[23] On the other hand, to claim that no form of concept entered into the judgement that a line of poetry was beautiful, that is, to claim that the meaning of the words had nothing to do with the beauty, would be a very difficult position to maintain.[24] However, whether this obtrusion of internal or external purposiveness takes place, or is cognized as taking place, is necessarily a matter for the subject at the moment of making the judgement: whether the subject can be said to be making a judgement of free or dependent beauty depends upon whether they *feel* they are making the one or the other.[25]

THE AESTHETIC IDEA

A judgement is called 'aesthetic' according to Kant 'precisely because its determining ground is not a concept but the feeling (of inner sense) of that unison in the play of the powers of the mind, insofar as they can only be sensed'.[26] How, then, can we justify proposing a form of beauty into which the conceptual enters, or, rather, which appears to depend in some way upon concepts? It might be that Kant wishes us to understand the word 'beauty' in the expression 'dependent beauty' figuratively. (We now use the word 'beauty' as a synonym for 'fine' in just this way – 'a beautiful meal', 'a beautiful solution'.) Kant, after all, asserts that the presence of a concept in dependent beauty mars its 'purity' as an aesthetic judgement.[27] Yet he does not seem to wish to debar such judgements from being judgements of taste, that is, in some way distinct from judgements which are based exclusively either on the agreeable or the good: in discussing 'dependent beauty' he speaks of the *combination* of aesthetic and intellectual pleasure, not the substitution of the former with the latter.[28] There is, however, another way in which we can interpret 'dependent beauty'; in accordance with the way that Kant himself distinguishes it from 'free beauty', combined with the concept of the 'aesthetic idea' he advances in a later part of the *Critique*. This interpretation yields a scheme that Kant does not, in fact, advance, though it can serve to resolve several problems in his text.

As we saw above, the freedom or adherence of a beauty depends upon whether of not some form of purposiveness, aside from the mere purposiveness of the representation of the object, obtrudes itself on the consciousness of the subject in the act of making a judgement of taste upon that object. Hence Kant, it seems, was conscious of referring the beauty of horses to the presence of those properties of the horse that make it a useful animal, though to us, now, a horse is more likely to appear as a free beauty. This is not to say that a horse *qua* beautiful object is any different for you than it was for Kant, but only that you are less likely to feel that a concept is in play in your judgement.[29] (Reynolds was surely too confident in assuming that the subject can know whether the understanding has exerted itself in a given judgement.) In those cases (such as the line of poetry) where the obtrusion of internal or external purposiveness appears ineluctable we are obliged to refer the beauty to the concepts we associate with the class to which the object belongs. (In the case of the poetry, for example, this would be, among other things, the meanings of the words as they exist independently of the particular poem.) Where the nature of these associated concepts can be, to some extent, determined, it appears possible for the subject to distinguish in the object the properties or effects to which that subject believes their own judgement of taste can be referred (the line is beautiful 'because it is profound').

There are a host of properties or effects, running the spectrum of dependence upon the conceptual, from 'profound' (or even 'thought-provoking') to the likes of 'graceful' and 'melodious', which denote an approbation in terms of taste, and the presence of which, like beauty, is, for the subject, ultimately a matter of taste, which are yet obviously not identifiable with beauty, either in effect or in perceived immediacy. These properties or effects, I would argue, are what are now more likely to be called 'aesthetic properties' or 'aesthetic merits' rather than 'beauties'.[30] (The term is not, of course, available to Kant: his 'aesthetic judgement' also denotes judgements on the good and the agreeable, so that the term 'aesthetic merit', if he had used it, would have been fairly useless, being equally applicable to what is contemplated, what is edifying, and what is edible.[31]) That such effects refer to concepts is clear from the fact that we are capable of distinguishing them into kinds, and even degrees within any particular kind. That such effects are, nevertheless, not absolutely determined by concepts is likewise clear from the fact that the presence or absence of some (for example, profundity), or even the merit of others (for example, cuteness), are still matters of taste in precisely the same way as is the presence or absence of free beauty. It is this last point which justifies Kant's use of the term 'beauty' in the expression 'dependent beauty', though, as was said earlier, given that the experience of free beauty (modern 'beauty'), and dependent beauty (modern 'aesthetic merit'), is qualitatively different, it would have saved a great deal of confusion if Kant and his contemporaries had opted for a different term – Addison's 'pleasures of the imagination' for instance – to denote the latter.[32] However, merely rechristening 'dependent beauty' as 'aesthetic merit', even if the strategy were not attended with so great a potential for misunderstanding, would not, in itself, given that the substitute is also ambiguous, explain Kant's intention in making the distinction under discussion. Let us, therefore, return to his explanation.

Kant describes the way in which 'beauty' may be referable to, or dependent on, concepts without actually being determined by a definite concept in his discussion of what he calls 'aesthetic ideas'. An aesthetic idea, he writes, is

> that representation of the imagination that occasions much thinking though without it being possible for any determinate thought, i.e. *concept*, to be adequate to it, which, consequently, no language fully attains or can make intelligible.[33]

The representations of the imagination, according to Kant may be termed *ideas* insofar as they have some semblance to objective reality, that is, they 'at least strive [strain] toward something lying beyond the bounds of experience, and thus seek to approximate a presentation of concepts of reason (of intellectual ideas)'.[34] The ideas of the imagination become aesthetic ideas when they prompt so great a wealth of associations as to defy comprehension in a definite concept:

> [In] this case the imagination is creative, and sets the faculty of intellectual ideas (reason) into motion, that is, at the instigation of a representation it gives more to think about than can be grasped and made distinct in it (although it does, to be sure, belong to the concept of the object). . . . [The] aesthetic idea is a representation of the imagination, associated with a given concept, which is combined with such a manifold of partial representations in the free use of the imagination that no expression designating a determinate concept can be found for it, which therefore allows the addition to a concept of much that is unnameable, the feeling of which animates the cognitive faculties and combines spirit [*Geist*] with the mere letter of language.[35]

Kant gives the particular example of language as a form which can be infused with 'spirit' at the end of the above quotation because the passage occurs in the course of a consideration of a poem by Frederick the Great, but any object which is capable of sustaining a symbolic interpretation, that is, any object, might be the object of an aesthetic idea.[36]

Kant does not, however, intend to say that aesthetic ideas belong exclusively to art. Indeed at one point he asserts that all beauty, whether in nature or art 'can in general be called the *expression* of aesthetic ideas'.[37] This raises some problems for the thesis that free beauty can be distinguished from dependent beauty by the dependence of the latter on aesthetic ideas. Kant, however, qualifies his statement about the ubiquity of aesthetic ideas in beauty by asserting that in the case of the beauty of art the idea is excited through the medium of a concept of the object, whereas in the beauty of nature a bare reflection upon a given intuition, 'without a concept of what the object ought to be, is sufficient for arousing and communicating the idea of which that object is considered as the *expression*'.[38] As we have seen in connection with the implement and the flower, the distinction between art and nature that is made here is not tenable in this form within Kant's general scheme. It is perhaps best, then, to understand Kant as here invoking his original distinction between dependent and free beauty – the former being in some way tied up with, though not determined by, a concept, the latter being, or appearing to be, a bare reflection upon a given intuition.

That Kant's account is confused at this point by the introduction of the discussion of art becomes clear if we juxtapose two general statements that he makes about the relationship between art and nature with respect to beauty. In the *Critique of the Aesthetic Power of Judgement* he writes that 'the purposiveness in the product of beautiful art, although it is certainly intentional, must nevertheless not seem intentional; i.e. beautiful art must be *regarded* as nature, although of course one is aware of it as art'.[39] Yet in the *Critique of the Teleological Power of Judgement* he appears to say just the opposite:

> Beauty in nature, since it is ascribed to objects only in relation to reflection on their *outer* intuition, thus only to the form of their surfaces, can rightly be called an analogue of art.[40]

According to Kant, then, art can only be beautiful if it appears, in some sense, as nature, and nature can only be beautiful if it appears, in some sense, as art. That is to say, art must appear like nature in order to be beautiful insofar as, though concepts are obviously involved in art, in order for the concept to take the form of an aesthetic idea it cannot be a definite concept; if all that we discern in a work of art is the intention to produce a definite concept then that work, while perhaps it may appeal to our reason (we may judge the success or otherwise of the work in fulfilling its manifest intention), cannot be said to be making an appeal to our taste.[41] To appeal to our taste (to be *schöne Künste*) it must appear to us that the pleasure we feel is attributable to that object as an object devoid of any specific end. Our estimate of the object, even if we are aware that it is not made independently of any concept, must nevertheless appear to be a response to something in excess of that conceptual element – the effect must be greater than the sum of the parts. This excess will appear to the subject, paradoxically, as something less than a concept, that is, as the 'superficial form' of the object, the object in itself. Hence, though we remain intellectually aware that the object (as a product of art) and its properties were intended to appeal to our taste, if the object actually succeeds in doing so it does so only insofar as this intellectual awareness comes to appear irrelevant, that is, insofar as the object appears, like nature, to be devoid of a definite end with respect to our judgement. (Kant's point here finds obvious confirmation in the way in which such epithets as 'contrived', 'manipulative', 'obvious', and others cognate, are so readily reached for as terms of aesthetic condemnation, and also in the perennial struggle of aesthetics to prove that art and propaganda are somehow mutually exclusive. In Chapter 7 we will see how Kant's own treatment of the distinction between poetry and rhetoric turns on this question of perceived intention.)

In the passage from the *Critique of the Teleological Power of Judgement*, on the other hand, Kant looks at the same relationship between art and nature as it appears to the intellect rather than to taste: we know that fine art is intended to create beauty, and that beauty is 'ascribed to objects only in relation to reflection on their *outer* intuition, thus only to the form of their surfaces'; if, therefore, we find the same phenomenon in nature it appears, by analogy, to be similarly intended. (Kant, of course, definitely rejects the possibility of saying that nature is actually so intended.[42]) In both art and nature, then, beauty is a matter of the 'superficial form' of the object. In the case of a 'beautiful' art object (that is, an art object with aesthetic merit) we are more likely to be conscious of the role of a concept in our judgement, though if this judgement is one of taste, the concept involved must take the form of an aesthetic idea, as Kant defines it, which form of idea, as we shall see, can equally well belong to nature. Likewise art, in those of its manifestations that do not obtrude a conceptual element (designs *à la grecque*, ornamental foliage, music *without words*), can appear, according to Kant, to be an object of free beauty. Kant's distinction between the beauty of art and nature on the grounds that the former is the result of a bare reflection upon a given intuition, while the latter is excited through the medium of a concept, is not, then, warranted by his own presentation.[43]

But if this distinction between two kinds of beauty cannot be made to apply to the intrinsic properties of different kinds of objects (natural or artificial) it does nevertheless correspond to, and help to clarify, his earlier distinction between free and dependent beauty. The freedom or dependence of a particular beauty depends upon whether or not we are conscious of an aesthetic idea at work in our response. An object is judged a free beauty if the judgement feels like a bare reflection upon a given intuition; an object appears as an dependent beauty if we feel that our judgement is somehow attributable to a concept, though since this concept takes the form of an aesthetic idea, the judgement nevertheless remains one of taste, since our approval is not ultimately explicable in terms of a definite concept. This, it seems, is what is at the root of Kant's apparently obscure distinction.

In examining Kant's distinction between free and dependent beauty I have mostly concentrated on the problem of accounting for 'dependent beauty', since the definition that he gives of it appears, at first sight, self-contradictory. In order to clarify Kant's contentious distinction, however, it was necessary to

treat the notion of 'free beauty' – a bare reflection upon a given intuition – as
though it were, in itself, unproblematic. This is justified insofar as, up to this
point, we have only been concerned with describing how taste strikes one
rather than with what taste is. At some stage, however, we must get to the
point of accounting for this strange, antinomy-ridden form of judgement. But
before returning to free beauty there is one final point to be made in connection with 'dependent beauty'.

THE STANDARD OF TASTE

Kant, as we saw in Chapter 1, appears to absolutely reject the notion of a standard of taste. (While he appears to invoke such a standard in §§13–14 in his
rejection of a role for charm or emotion, in fact, since it is neither warranted
by his phenomenology, nor indeed possible according to his stipulative
definition of judgement, its emergence at this point can best be viewed as itself
the result of an emotional requirement arising from the felt universal validity
that characterizes every judgement of taste.) There can be, he says, no 'objective rule of taste that would determine what is beautiful through concepts', no
rule by which one is compelled to find something beautiful: in order to decide
if a thing is beautiful we must look with our own eyes, just as if our satisfaction depended on sensation, reasons or principles being foreign to the sphere
of the beautiful.[44] For this reason, he holds, it is useless to look for a principle
of taste, a universal criterion of the beautiful involving definite concepts; such
a thing would be inherently contradictory. Even though it may appear that
the accord of all ages and all nations as to the beauty of certain objects gives
us an empirical criterion of beauty, this criterion is 'weak and hardly sufficient
for conjecture' on universal grounds.[45] Moreover we cannot appeal to such a
criterion in any particular instance without renouncing that autonomy of
judgement that constitutes 'taste':

> [It] is required of every judgement that is supposed to prove the taste of the
> subject that the subject judge for himself, without having to grope about
> by means of experience among the judgements of others and first inform
> himself about their satisfaction or dissatisfaction in the same object, and
> thus that he should pronounce his judgement not as imitation, because a
> thing really does please universally, but *a priori*.[46]

The archetype of taste, according to Kant, is a mere ideal which each person
'must produce in himself', though it is, ultimately, incapable of being represented by means of a concept.[47] Such an ideal, he continues, if we do believe
ourselves to possess it, cannot be an ideal of free beauty but must be fixed by
a concept of objective purposiveness, for otherwise we would not have to seek
for it. It cannot, then, belong to a pure judgement of taste but must be partly
intellectual.[48]

This ideal of the beautiful, he asserts, should not be confused with the *normal idea* for the genus – which is merely a floating image of the archetype underlying all particular examples.[49] Though such a *normal idea* might be fixed by a concept, it is not the archetype of beauty but rather the archetype of correctness (which he suggests may be a necessary, though it is certainly not a sufficient, condition of beauty).[50] A representation that comes close to this archetype may please, but only because it is correct, not because it is beautiful. Even the human figure, Kant argues, though it may imply an ideal, only sustains such an ideal as the expression of the *moral*, as the outward manifestation of benevolence, purity, strength, equanimity, and so on, and therefore an interest is involved: 'judging in accordance with such a standard can never be purely aesthetic [since it involves reason], and judging in accordance with an ideal of beauty is no mere judgement of taste'.[51]

There can be no rules of taste, according to Kant, because a judgement of taste is, by definition, determined by the feeling of the subject, not by any concept of an object.[52] What then of 'dependent beauty' (or 'aesthetic merit', in the modern sense), in which Kant appears to allow a role for the conceptual in judgements of taste? In dependent beauty, however, though reason is, as Kant says, put into 'motion', in the form of imagining, this motion does not culminate in a definite concept.[53] We may be able to point to the general ideas that are at play in the object insofar as we believe these ideas have a constitutive role in our judgement of taste on the object, but we are still not able to *reasonably* deduce the judgement from those ideas in such a way that we might compel another, through their reason, to concur in our judgement. I may say I like this line because it is profound, and even that the profundity lies in its expressing this or that proposition, in this or that way, about the world, but I cannot prove that an object is profound, or graceful, or exciting, or whatever, *in itself*. (Indeed, the further we go in this direction, that is, the more precisely we define the propositional value of the object, as any piece of criticism which takes this course will show, the weaker the claim that the judgement can be logically deduced appears.) Thus it is quite possible for two people to be able to agree on every proposition concerning an object except those that are evaluative.

This matter is especially relevant to art for two reasons. Firstly because what Kant calls 'dependent beauty' is most likely to be discerned in connection with art. Secondly, art objects are enduring appeals to taste: Shakespeare exists in the world in a quite different way to the cloud formation I saw, alone, one afternoon five years ago.[54] Whole libraries have been written (and are everyday being enlarged) on the conceptual aspects of objects that are thought worthy of such attention only because they have appealed to taste. At this very moment, in innumerable institutions, subjects are being obliged to write essays on the properties of objects in which they may see no aesthetic merit whatsoever, in order to pass examinations set by teachers who, implicitly at least, are subscribing to the belief that if their students only do concentrate on the conceptual properties of these objects they will come to *feel* the aesthetic merit which has been attributed to them. This state of affairs has produced a curious parallel between the eighteenth century and the present day. For whatever reason, whether, as some believe, because of the rediscovery of the classical, or, perhaps more plausibly, because the eighteenth century was enamoured of consensus in everything, writers on taste in that century were eager, if unable, to establish a standard of judgement, a 'good taste'. The twentieth century, though apparently indifferent to the notion of taste itself, has enshrined just such an idea in the process of humanistic education.[55] I am not here referring to the existence of any particular canon of works, but merely to the assumption that art objects are legitimate objects of a study that has their 'intrinsic' (as opposed to, for example, historical) value as its end.[56] This fact has tended to render obscure the distinction between the discernment of the concepts that an object gives rise to and a judgement of taste upon that object, that is, the very distinction that Kant is here making.[57]

While understanding may appear to have a role in the judgement of taste, this role is an auxiliary one. The role of the understanding is not to cognize the beautiful object ('Am I experiencing beauty?'); this is done by the sense, but rather to determine the judgement of the sense and its representation ('Is it this object or that, this property or that which I find beautiful?') according to its relation to the subject and the subject's internal feeling. Though the understanding may discern what is the true object of the judgement, nevertheless, it cannot ultimately determine what judgement of taste is joined to the object. As Kant says, in the experience of dependent beauty the train of thought of which we are conscious, while no doubt germane, to the concept of the object, nevertheless 'gives more to think about than can be grasped and made distinct'.[58] The analysis of such a train of thought may issue in rules of taste in the sense that it may provide *a posteriori* rules for the production of an object that is likely to appeal to taste (as Reynolds can say that if you paint thus or thus you *should* produce such and such an effect which has hitherto generally pleased), but such rules are only rules either for the production of an object or for better enabling the subject to determine the source of an effect, they are not rules for determining the judgement of taste itself.

> To be sure, taste gains by this combination of aesthetic satisfaction with the intellectual in that it becomes fixed and, though not universal, can have rules prescribed to it in regard to certain purposively determined objects. But in this case these are also not rules of taste, but merely rules for the unification of taste with reason . . .[59]

These rules, or deductions, are the grounds of that plausibility which the arguments of critics enjoy, according to Kant, over the arguments of cooks, though ultimately the arguments of both critics and cooks must defer to the same arbitration: the subject's reflection upon their own state of pleasure or displeasure.[60]

THE FREEDOM OF FREE BEAUTY

Despite the amount of attention given here to dependent beauty, this form of beauty, as its name implies, is described within the *Critique* as a variation on, or as Kant at one point calls it, an 'adulteration of', the fundamental form of beauty, that is, free beauty. Dependent beauty is, for Kant, still a form of beauty – by virtue of the fact that the ascription of it to an object is finally a matter of the subject's taste – yet it is an adulteration insofar as free beauty, which is cognized as a bare reflection upon a given intuition, without the mediation of concepts, appears the more immediate, the 'purer' form. We have seen above that Kant's dependent beauty is best understood as a description of what is now known as 'aesthetic merit' (if we exclude, for the moment, beauty itself from the list of possible aesthetic merits), since with aesthetic merit we are conscious of an ability to refer our judgement to some concept of the object, even to the extent of being able to classify the kind of concept involved, and to argue plausibly, if not decisively, about the merit of the object in relation to others in which we discern a similar conceptual element. The experience of aesthetic merit is, then, qualitatively different from the experience of beauty (Kant's 'free beauty'), though, as Kant's use of the word 'beauty' to characterize the former implies, the subject's consciousness of the mere presence of a concept in dependent beauty does not in itself exempt this form of judgement from the fundamental antinomy of taste with which we began.

Today a great deal of attention is given to the kind of concepts which are at play in Kant's dependent beauty, a good deal less to the way in which this form of 'beauty' might depend upon such concepts, and almost none to the question of why there should be such a thing as beauty, or judgements of taste, at all. This last question arises most urgently in connection with free beauty, for with free beauty, that is, with what is now simply, and commonly, called 'beauty', it is of the essence of the judgement to appear unmediated by a concept: no obtrusion by a concept of internal or external purposiveness is cognized as taking place within the judgement. This intractability on (free) beauty's part has led to beauty's neglect as an object of study. (The 'return to beauty' within the world of letters at the end of the twentieth century will not qualify as 'study'.) Consequently we are now in the rather odd situation of approaching a subject central to a work by an academically revered philosopher, yet one that is hardly any longer an academic subject: the nature of (free) beauty.

A true child of his age, Kant found nature, unconstrained by artificial rules and lavish, to be the most unfailing source of beauty. We find beauty, he writes, not in that order which imposes an irksome restraint upon the imagination, but rather most often and most consistently in what gives the imagination scope for play.[61] It is only what is natural, or 'taken to be nature', he says, that can arouse an immediate interest in its beauty.[62] This, as we have seen, is not consistent with the way in which he elsewhere distinguishes free from dependent beauty on the grounds of the subject's consciousness. (While it is easy to see how certain natural objects can become dependent beauties, it is much more difficult, though not impossible, to conceive of an intended object appearing to possess free beauty.) However, what is principally interesting at this point is Kant's use of the phrase 'taken to be nature', for it is this 'taken to be' which points to the possibility of the conceptual, in some form, being able to enter into 'free' beauty without compromising its immediate character as such.

Kant himself provides an instance of the kind of mistake he means in the case of the bird's song which he cognizes as a free beauty and yet realizes would strike him as 'utterly tasteless' were he to discover it was artificially produced:

> Even the song of the bird, which we cannot bring under any musical rules, seems to contain more freedom and thus more that is entertaining for taste than even a human song that is performed in accordance with all the rules of the art of music: for one grows tired of the latter far more quickly if it is repeated often and for a long time. But here we may well confuse our sympathy with the merriment of a beloved little creature with the beauty of his song, which, when it is exactly imitated by a human being (as is sometimes done with the notes of the nightingale) strikes our ear as utterly tasteless.[63]

This would suggest, as Kant himself comments, that he has perhaps confused what he *thought* was a judgement on the immediate, free beauty of the song with what was in fact a judgement on a dependent beauty in which a feeling of 'sympathy with the merriment of a beloved little creature' played some role. If this was the case, if his perception of his own judgement was mistaken and the bird's song was not in itself, that is, as mere sound, beautiful for him, then some concept must have been involved in that apparently bare reflection on a given intuition. For, if no concept of the object was originally involved, then no change in the concept of the object ('It is natural' to 'It is artificial') should affect the judgement. The difficulty cannot be resolved simply by saying that it is the bird's song coupled with the bird's singing that is the beautiful object, for, as Kant says, for him the song is 'merriment', and the bird is a 'dear little creature'. Even if it were merely that the object is the bird's singing of the song this itself makes provenance part of the 'form' of the song.

On reflection the 'beautiful song' begins to look less like an object of immediate, necessary satisfaction, and more like the accidental occasion of some other feeling, the beginning of a chain of association. For at least some concept is involved (that of the bird), and quite possibly an interest (sympathy, and the concept of nature as a suitable object of sympathy). Still we might say that the concept, or even the concept of the interest, is a beautiful object, that is, an object of an aconceptual, disinterested, necessary satisfaction. And if we were to discover that these apparently beautiful concepts did, in fact, rest on others, or on some interest, then we could simply again postpone what we designated as the beauty of the 'bird's song'. Such a potentially infinite regress would render our initial definition of beauty, as 'disinterested satisfaction', irrefutable – though it would also rule out the possibility of using the word 'beautiful' to describe what we *merely perceived* as beautiful, that is, would leave us without a judgement that was distinguishably a judgement of taste. This result does not, of course, raise any problem for Kant insofar as he posits the judgement of taste as ideal. But, if we suspend the requirement of subjective universal validity upon which this ideality rests, such empirical complications become of more moment.

In the same section Kant goes on to give another example of the kind of 'mistake' that it is possible to make in judgements of taste. Beautiful objects, he writes

> are to be distinguished from beautiful views of objects (which on account of the distance can often no longer be distinctly cognized). In the latter, taste seems to fasten not so much on what the imagination *apprehends* in this field as on what gives it occasion to *invent*, i.e. on what are strictly speaking the fantasies with which the mind entertains itself while it is being continuously aroused by the manifold which strikes the eye, as for instance in looking at the changing shapes of a fire in a hearth or of a rippling brook, neither of which are beauties, but both of which carry with them a charm for the imagination, because they sustain its free play. [64]

As in the example of the bird song, Kant here posits that the subject may cognize as a free beauty (the sound, the view, the flames, the movement of the water) an object that is actually constituted by a concept. The example of the flames and the rippling brook is problematic, since it would be difficult to establish whether the reverie is the cause or the effect of the attribution of beauty. The example of the subject's confusing a beautiful view of an object with a view of a beautiful object seems, however, more germane to the present question.

Of course if the subject asserts that the view is beautiful then, at least according to the criteria for a judgement to legitimately lay claim to being a judgement of taste, it must be allowed that the view is beautiful for the subject. But it is conceivable that someone might attribute the beauty to the object itself when, in fact, the beauty really depended, for them, on the view. (As, for example some mountains may appear beautiful at a great distance but not so at closer range; not because the whole may now be less visible, but because details which appear as blemishes, are now *more* visible. One thinks of Gulliver's experience among the Brobdingnagian Maids of Honour; which suggests that nothing, indeed, is beautiful independently of point of view.) In this case, as in the case of the bird song, there is a mistake not in the feeling that something is apparently beautiful for one – an impossibility – but rather in the attribution of the beauty. In both cases the misattribution arises from a lack of awareness of the role of the context (distance in the case of the view, the concept of naturalness in the case of the bird song) in determining the judgement. That this context or provenance does *determine* the judgement is implicit in Kant's dismissal of artificial bird song, even if sensuously indistinguishable from the real thing, as 'utterly tasteless'.[65] What is significant here is that such a mistake is possible: the context or provenance can be, for the subject, part of the form of their beautiful object without that subject being aware that this is the case.

Such misattributions are not, of course, peculiar to free beauty. The young poet who is partial to his own poems genuinely does, as Kant allows, perceive a kind of beauty (aesthetic merit) in the poems themselves: there is no *perceivable* admixture of interest in his judgement. Later, Kant surmises, he may come to see them as others do, but the crucial point is that when he makes his initial judgement he really does see them as having an intrinsic value, he sees them in a different way to others. For the poet there is a penumbra around the words, that is, the aesthetic idea, which he intended the lines to convey, but which, unfortunately, the lines in themselves invoke in no one but himself. He has, in short, confused a beautiful view of an object with a beautiful object; a beauty in which certain concepts are at play, with a beauty that he believes requires no additional concept. (It is not, of course, necessary that the subject be the author in such a case – many changes in taste obviously involve the decay of such a penumbra.) Kant's definition of the aesthetic idea as 'a representation of the imagination, associated with a given concept, which is combined with such a manifold of partial representations in the free use of the imagination that no expression designating a determinate concept can be found for it' would indeed lead us to expect that the actual definition of what is the dependently beautiful object (or what precisely are the aesthetic merits of an object) would be a far from simple issue.[66] The history of criticism, and even the fact that criticism has a history, bears out that such is the case. But free beauty, as immediate, that is, in apparently relying on no concept of the object at all, should not find itself, as it does in the case of the bird song and the beautiful view, encountering the same possibility of misattribution that dependent beauty's dependence implies.

Some commentators on Kant, as we saw in Chapter 1, take the line that Kant's free beauty does not, in effect, exist. For having made the distinction between dependent (conceptual) beauty, and free (immediate) beauty, Kant then seems to concede that the latter, too, is potentially dependent. He notes that nature does indeed at times appear to 'display herself as art', in the sense that a natural object, as is apparently the case with the bird's song, 'interests through its beauty only insofar as a moral idea is associated with it', that is, insofar as it appears to embody a language in which nature speaks to us with the semblance of a 'higher meaning'.[67] Indeed, even in the exemplary case of the flower, it could plausibly be argued that its beauty is dependent on the very *concept* of its being *gratia sui*.[68]

Kant nevertheless feels that we may distinguish between those expressions that give rise to dependent beauty, and the 'semblance' of expression in nature, which perhaps gives rise to free beauty. In the case of the latter, he asserts, it is 'not this [association with a moral idea], but rather the quality inherent in it by means of which it qualifies for such an association, which thus pertains to it internally, that interests immediately'.[69] In other words, while the beauty of dependent beauty is attributable to that dependence, in the case of the 'free' beauty of nature, even where dependence emerges as a condition of the effect (to discover the object was artificial would destroy the effect), we should not attribute that effect to the dependence, to the expressive force which the object acquires through our cognizance of its provenance. There is, it would seem, a contradiction here; for Kant appears to make provenance at once a condition of, and yet accidental to, the beauty of the object. Moreover, he appears to be able to make the provenance accidental only by an appeal to that subjective universal validity, and its correlative of inherently beautiful objects, that is itself a mere presupposition.

Yet what the instance of the bird song demonstrated is that, despite Kant's perception of his judgement as one of free beauty, there was, for him, no 'inherent character' of the beauty of the song *in itself*. It was not the beauty of the song that qualified it for partnership with moral ideas, but rather an apparently unconscious partnering, by Kant, of the song with moral ideas that qualified it to be beautiful.

Kant cannot, then, justify a distinction between free and dependent beauty by appealing to the notion of inherent beauty, for, even if the idea of inherent beauty were not a highly dubious deduction to make from the nature of judgements of taste as he himself has described them, the instance of the bird song demonstrates how even when we are apparently responding immediately to the 'beauty of an object' it is possible that this immediate response depends upon a conceptual reconstruction of that 'object'. The 'inherent' properties of our object, then, may not immediately strike the eye or ear but may rather be, as it were, made inherent by the mind. Reflection reveals to Kant that the 'inherent' character of the form of the bird's song included, for him, the concept that a bird was producing it. Even if he cannot clearly define the concept (of nature as an object of sympathy) which he feels might be at play in the judgement, there is at least one concept that Kant allows must be present – that of the song being a product of nature: that whatever is being expressed by the song, this expression is coming directly from nature at the moment we hear it. It was upon the concept that this was so, that his original judgement depended. Thus there are at least two concepts to which the judgement must defer – the joy-ousness (for thus he characterizes the expression) of the song, and the idea that nature is 'expressing herself'.

Indeed Kant himself, as we saw above, at one point states that all beauty (free or dependent, natural or artificial) is the '*expression* of aesthetic ideas'.[70] He nevertheless still distinguishes between free and dependent beauty on the grounds that in the former the idea 'must be occasioned by a concept of the object', while in the latter 'the mere reflection on a given intuition, without a concept of what the object ought to be, is sufficient for arousing and communicating the idea of which that object is considered as the *expression*'.[71] Yet, not only is it difficult to imagine how an idea might arise from, or be perceived as being expressed by, an object to which we attach no concept whatsoever, but this is also a state of affairs which Kant nowhere in the *Critique* describes. Even the 'free beauties of nature', as we have seen, appear to depend upon at least one concept: naturalness. It could be argued, then, that there can be no such thing as a bare reflection upon a given intuition simply because there is no such thing as a bare form (a form which we cognize without the intervention of some kind of concept) for such a reflection to be a reflection on.[72] Certainly Kant in his single analysis of an instance of free beauty (the bird's song) does not describe such a bare judgement.

To argue against the very existence of (free) beauty in this way, however, would be to argue beside the point. For the fact remains that Kant initially perceived his judgement on the bird's song as a judgement upon a free rather than an dependent beauty: it felt to him, despite what introspection later revealed, that he was making a bare reflection upon a given intuition. The experience, then, was qualitatively different from an experience of dependent beauty, insofar as the role of the concept (of birds, nature, and whatever these might imply for Kant) involved was not apparent to him at the moment of making the judgement: the form *appeared* bare to reflection.

The freedom of free beauty, then, depends, I would suggest, not on that beauty's being undetermined by a concept, but rather upon that beauty's being cognized, at the moment of judgement, as undetermined by a concept.

CONCLUSION

As a description of the way we perceive judgements of taste Kant's account is complete, though in reproducing that account it has been necessary to make connections and draw conclusions – particularly in connection with dependent beauty – that Kant himself neither makes nor draws, and which, indeed, often run counter to Kant's intentions. Some of this reconstruction may be justified as the working out of what is implicit in Kant's text, but much of it, as I have indicated along the way, is a matter of limiting the pretensions of taste to subjective universal validity solely to what the Kantian phenomenology of taste will bear. If, however, we take Kant's primary concern to be the establishment of what the judgement of taste *must be if* it is to legitimately claim universal validity, then, where my engagement with Kant's text has deferred to the principle of giving priority to his phenomenology, the interpretations made can be said to run directly counter to Kant's intentions.

However, whether we view the ground so far covered either as a description of what necessary conditions a judgement must fulfil to legitimately lay claim to being a judgement of taste, or as a description of what necessary conditions a judgement must fulfil in order to legitimately lay claim to subjective universal validity, the fact remains that this exposition is obviously not intended by Kant to be, in itself, a theory of taste. Indeed the more he enlarges upon the phenomenology of this form of judgement the more antinomical it seems to become. What we have hitherto been considering is merely the prelude to a theory of taste: the delineation of what facts such a theory must account for. Before, then, turning to Kant's explanation of the grounds of the judgement of taste, that is, the cause of beauty, it is worth reviewing what these facts are.

The indispensable condition of a judgement of taste, according to Kant, is that it represents the subject's perception of their own immediate satisfaction in the object designated. (This holds irrespective of whether or not we accept the further conditions imposed by Kant's stipulative definition of 'judgement of taste'.) This satisfaction is immediate in the sense that, even when, as in dependent beauty, we are conscious that a concept is at play in our cognizance of the object as the object of our judgement, nevertheless the feeling of pleasure we experience is not explicable in terms of that concept: the judgement is not *arrived at* by any process of cognition (in the manner of a judgement on truth). Neither is the judgement explicable in terms of a discernible interest (in the manner of a judgement on the good or the agreeable). Any judgement that appears autonomous in this manner can at least lay claim to being a 'judgement of taste'. Moreover this claim is, in practice, irrefutable: neither the discovery of an interest in connection with the object, nor even a new contrary judgement on the object, can retrospectively refute it. This follows from the indemonstrability of the grounds of the judgement, which precludes both the possibility of verifying that a discoverable interest is actually a determining condition of the judgement, or, in the case of a new contrary judgement, the possibility of giving precedence to one judgement over another (notwithstanding the general prejudice that all our changes in taste represent improvements.)

Because of this apparent autonomy of the judgement, the beautiful object appears to the subject to be an object of *necessary* satisfaction, though reflection on the differences that do, as a matter of fact, exist in taste, should inform that subject that the object is only apparently an object of *necessary* satisfaction for themselves. Since the subject is the sole possible arbiter of what is beautiful (for that subject) – whatever feels like beauty is beauty – it follows that we cannot define beauty as an object of necessary satisfaction, but only as an object that is *cognized* as an object of necessary satisfaction.

The sole foundation of a judgement of taste, according to Kant, is the 'form of purposiveness' of an object or its representation, so far as this representation does not involve a representation of an end. However, judgements of taste can be distinguished into two fundamental forms: judgements of free beauty and judgements of dependent beauty. Dependent beauty (or 'aesthetic merit' in a non-Kantian sense) is discerned where we are conscious that a concept has been active in the process of cognizing the object which is the object of our judgement of taste. That we perceive there is some concept involved in the judgement does not, however, mean that the judgement is the outcome of a logical deduction: we still feel that the end point of that process is an object of disinterested, that is, apparently necessary satisfaction. Dependent beauty, then, appears to involve concepts but not to be absolutely determined by concepts. The involvement of concepts in the cognition of the object does, however, make the experience of this kind of beauty qualitatively different from the experience of free beauty (or 'beauty' in the modern sense). The ultimate touchstone of whether a judgement of taste is a judgement on a free or a dependent beauty is the subject's *feeling* of whether it is the one or the other.

The kind of concept that we discern in dependent beauty takes the form of an aesthetic idea: 'that representation of the imagination that occasions much thinking though without it being possible for any determinate thought, i.e. *concept*, to be adequate to it, which, consequently, no language fully attains or can make intelligible'. It is for this reason that we cannot show how any judgement is absolutely determined by the concept or concepts involved, or, consequently, use such concepts to establish rules of taste.

Free beauty, in contrast, does not appear *to the subject* to be mediated by any concept of the object, though the possibility of the subject's mistakenly attributing beauty to an object that is not the actual object of judgement shows that this appearance of immediacy does not necessarily rule out the possibility that a concept of the object is a determining condition of that object as an object of free beauty for the subject.

This last point is a peculiarity of taste that Kant demonstrates but does not dwell upon: that beauty can depend upon a concept, not only without the subject being aware that this is so, but also only on condition that the subject remains unaware that they are entertaining that concept. Kant, as noted above, explicitly claims that all beauty is the expression of aesthetic ideas, but this does not prevent him from drawing a distinction between 'dependent beauty' (in which the dependence on an aesthetic idea is cognized by the subject as a condition of the object's beauty for that subject) and 'free beauty' (in which such a dependence is not cognized by the subject). Aside from the isolated assertion that all beauty depends on aesthetic ideas, and the instance of the bird song, which demonstrates how this might be so, Kant does not directly address this peculiarity of free beauty, though it is a peculiarity which any theory of taste must account for.[73]

The aesthetic idea, then, which may perhaps be entertained either consciously or unconsciously by the subject, while it does not determine the judgement in the sense that the judgement cannot be logically deduced from that idea, nevertheless does play some kind of determining role in the cognizance of the object as a beautiful object, and, therefore, we may presume, in the experience of beauty itself. The aesthetic idea, then, however it arises, seems likely to be the 'medium' mentioned at the end of Chapter 1: that medium which refracts the object to make it appear either possessed of aesthetic merit (if we are in some way conscious of the *idea*) or beautiful (if we are not conscious of the *idea*).

Kant, then, would probably not endorse Hume's observation that, in matters of sentiment, there is no space between perception and judgement in which the understanding may operate to influence that perception.[74] The contrast is, however, only a matter of appearance. Hume appeals to the immediacy of the sentiment specifically to emphasize that in judgements arising from sentiment the subject is necessarily the sole judge of whether that sentiment is or is not present, and, since the presence of a sentiment is registered in terms of feeling, the subject, as a judge of their own sentiments, is infallible.[75] Kant's supposition of the aesthetic idea is not incompatible with such a position. For though in the case of dependent beauty the aesthetic idea must, in one sense, 'come between' an object and the subject's cognizance of that object as a beautiful object, yet, in another sense, that *idea* is itself the object of the subject's judgement: whatever the sensuous object involved, for the subject who finds it beautiful the aesthetic idea which it expresses is constitutive of that object *qua* beautiful object. The hypothesis of the aesthetic idea does not, then, in itself solve the problem of taste: there is still a gap between the consciousness of the *idea* and the positing of value – a gap that cannot be filled with a connection that would depend upon the aesthetic idea's lending the object either agreeableness or goodness, since this would render the judgement on the object into something other than a judgement of taste. This state of affairs is precisely what we find in practice: someone may be able to show me, even to the extent of their own satisfaction, the meaning which they believe gives their object its aesthetic value (dependent beauty), yet my understanding of what they communicate does not entail my sharing their feeling about the object.[76]

The case of the bird song shows how an aesthetic idea may 'come between' an object and the subject's cognizance of that object as a beautiful object. The very fact that the role of the concept in the judgement was hidden from the subject (the judgement was apparently made upon a 'free beauty'), and yet turned out to be decisive for that judgement (Kant found the sound 'utterly tasteless' when divorced from the concept), might lead us to believe that merely by discovering the presence of the concept we have accounted for the beauty. Reflection, and a consideration of the structure of dependent beauty, reveals, however, that this is not the case. For the aesthetic idea, even when it is consciously entertained does not account for the feeling of pleasure which the object inspires. We cannot, in the absence of a demonstrable appeal by the object to our sense of the agreeable or the good, make the transition from the properties of the object (including the *idea* it inspires) to a judgement of taste, that is, what is ostensibly a value judgement, upon that object. Indeed, in the case of the bird song (as free beauty) the problem of explaining this gap is compounded, for, even though the beauty seems, retrospectively, dependent on the concept, it would be problematic to say that it was attributable to the concept, since the *idea* itself was not cognized at all in the original judgement: the object that was cognized as the object of necessary satisfaction was not the *idea* but rather the 'bare form' of the sound itself. This same state of affairs should also warn us against the temptation to reduce free beauty (beauty) to the status of a form of unacknowledged dependent beauty (aesthetic merit).

So far, then, Kant has shown that taste is a very perplexing phenomenon indeed. The question now, however, is no longer 'What is a judgement of taste?' – this he has established in its full antinomical splendour – but rather 'Why is there taste?' At this point we must turn to Kant's proposal for the final cause of 'beauty', the *a priori* principle in which he believes taste is grounded.[77]

3

The Grounds of Taste

Kant summarizes the problem to be addressed in the *Critique of the Power of Judgement* thus:

> How is a judgement possible which, merely from *one's own* feeling of pleasure in an object, independent of its concept, judges this pleasure, as attached to the representation of the same object *in every other subject, a priori*, i.e. without having to wait for the assent of others? [1]

With regard to the notion that the subject attributes the pleasure to every other individual, this, as we have seen, means in practice no more than that, as Kant says, since the subject can find no personal reason for the satisfaction that is felt, 'he must . . . regard it as grounded in those [conditions] that he can also presuppose in everyone else; consequently he must believe himself to have grounds for expecting a similar pleasure of everyone'.[2]

There are two alternatives, according to Kant, to the idea of an *a priori* principle of judgements of taste. One is the idea that the judgement of taste is a disguised judgement of reason on the perfection discovered in a thing, only called 'aesthetic' due to some confusion in reflection. If this were so the solution to the antinomy of taste would be simply that the objects of such judgements are not mere phenomena, but rather things-in-themselves.[3] This alternative is, he believes, sufficiently refuted, by his analysis of the nature of such judgements.

The second alternative given by Kant to the idea of an *a priori* principle in judgements of taste is that such judgements, like judgements of the palate, depend upon the contingent 'organization of the subject'.[4] If such were the case, he continues, a judgement would only deserve to be considered 'correct' insofar as '*it happens* that many people agree . . . because the subjects are contingently organized in the same way'.[5] What Kant means here by 'organization', leaving aside for the moment the true dead-end of physiology, is perhaps best brought out by his discussion of psychological interpretations in the first introduction to the *Critique of the Power of Judgement*.[6] Such explanations, he writes, must be forever hypothetical, and for every three plausible psychological theories we may have of any mental event it is an easy matter to think of an equally plausible fourth.[7] (That Kant does not, however, entirely reject the employment of psychological concepts, in a modern sense, can be seen from the crucial role he makes subreption play in the sublime. This is, of course, a psychological explanation, and it is a relatively easy matter to think of several less plausible ones.) With regard to the explanation of the judgement of taste, that is, a judgement which 'gives itself out to be universally valid', it would be, according to Kant, 'absurd' to attempt to explain the origin psychologically, since, if such an explanation were successful, it would prove that such a judgement 'could make absolutely no claim to necessity, precisely because its empirical [psychological] origin can be demonstrated'.[8]

At this point we run head-on into the parameters of Kant's project in the *Critique of the Power of Judgement*: the establishment of what the judgement of taste would have to be in order to legitimately claim at least the potential for subjective universal validity. For nothing that Kant actually establishes about taste within the *Critique* supports the objection he here makes to such a limited idea of 'correctness' as approximation to a consensus, or leads ineluctably to the rejection of any thesis that would require such a conclusion. Rather the argument here presupposes that the judgement of taste be at least capable of being 'correct' in the wider sense of possessing universal validity. At this point, then, we must absolutely distinguish between the phenomenological observation that the judgement appears (universally) necessary, and Kant's *a priori* demand that the judgement actually be (universally) necessary. Indeed, the urgency of that demand may be gauged from the fact that it leads to the supposition of the necessity of particular judgements on particular objects: a supposition that does not even logically follow from supposing the necessity of the judgement of taste *per se*. The whole notion of 'correctness', as it appears here, is strictly superfluous.

The hypothesis that Kant here rejects, on the grounds that some judgements *must* be able to claim necessity, that is, the hypothesis that the judgement might be necessary only for the individual, and as a result of the contingent organization of that individual, is very similar to that which Hume puts into the mouth of his sceptic in the 'Essay on the Standard of Taste':

> All sentiment is right; because sentiment has a reference to nothing beyond itself, and is always real, wherever a man is conscious of it. . . . [A] thousand different sentiments, excited by the same object, are all right: Because no sentiment represents what is really in the object. It only marks a certain conformity or relation between the object and the organs or faculties of the mind; and if that conformity did not really exist, the sentiment could never possibly have being. Beauty is no quality in things themselves: It exists merely in the mind which contemplates them; and each mind perceives a different beauty. One person may even perceive deformity, where another is sensible of beauty; and every individual ought to acquiesce in his own sentiment, without pretending to regulate those of others.[9]

Kant's rejection of such scepticism here, like Hume's own rejection of it (and the overwhelming rejection by the nineteenth century of Alison and Jeffrey's system-atized form), appears to rely more on the unpalatability of the idea that there is no such thing as a 'correct' judgement of taste (or, in Kant's terms, one that can 'legitimately claim universal assent') than on any counter arguments that might either be grounded in his phenomenology or even arise from the presupposition that aesthetic judgement should possess subjective universal validity.[10] Before pursuing this question, however, we must turn to the *a priori* principle of taste that Kant favours over the two alternatives (that taste is disguised reason, or that it is contingent) which we have seen him reject above. This grounding, as we have now seen, must not only account for the phenomenology of taste as it has been outlined in the preceding two chapters but also accommodate the presup-position of a legitimate claim to subjective universal validity.

According to Kant, since the judgement of taste is not determinable by con-cepts, and yet appears to presuppose a principle (insofar as the satisfaction is immediately connected with the representation), its ground must be in the subjective formal conditions of judgement in general, and can only be deduced from those formal conditions.[11] All judgement, he continues, requires a representation by the imagination (for the intuition and arrange-ment of the components of intuition) and by the understanding (the concept of the unity of this arrangement). If, as in the case of taste, the determining ground of the 'objectivity' of the representation is to be conceived of as inde-pendent of any concept of the object, 'it can be nothing other than the state of mind that is encountered in the relation of the powers of representation to each other insofar as they relate a given representation to *cognition in general*'.[12] Moreover the cognitive powers brought into play by this represen-tation must, since no definite concept restricts them to a particular rule of cog-nition, be engaged in a 'free play'. The mental state of the judgement of taste is, then, according to Kant, 'a feeling of the free play of the powers of repre-sentation in a given representation for a cognition in general'.[13]

The ground of the pleasure of beauty is, therefore, to be found in the uni-versal condition of reflective judgement, that is, in the 'purposive correspon-dence of an object (be it a product of nature or of art) with the relationship of the cognitive faculties among themselves (of the imagination and the under-standing) that is required for every empirical cognition'.[14] Every given object, according to Kant, 'brings the imagination into activity for the synthesis of the manifold, while the imagination brings the understanding into activity for the unification of the manifold into concepts'.[15] The disposition of the cog-nitive powers in relation to one another will however differ from object to object. What distinguishes the beautiful object is that it (somehow) calls forth that disposition of cognitive powers in which 'this inner relationship is optimal for the animation of both powers of the mind (the one through the other) with respect to cognition (of given objects) in general'.[16] The proper-ties such an object must possess are not specified in the *Critique of the Aesthetic*

Power of Judgement, but at the beginning of the *Critique of the Teleological Power of Judgement* he writes that there are forms 'so specifically suited to [our power of judgement] that by means of their variety and unity they serve as it were to strengthen and entertain the mental powers (which are in play in the use of these faculties), and to which one has therefore ascribed the name of *beautiful* forms'.[17]

Kant is, then, ultimately a formalist after the manner of Hutcheson, whose *Inquiry into the Original of our Ideas of Beauty and Virtue* had appeared in 1725; though he does not, of course, follow his predecessor in positing a separate 'internal sense' responsible for taste.[18] (Hutcheson believed that the judgement of taste was a discernment, by an autonomous 'sense' of taste, of manifestations of 'uniformity amidst variety' in the external world. He accounts for the pleasure accompanying the judgement by appealing to the fact that the ability to discern such ordering is advantageous to us in organizing our knowledge and, hence, in prosecuting those actions upon which our happiness depends.[19]) Moreover Kant believes, as did Hutcheson to a more limited extent, that there are such things as universally beautiful forms, since, he says, we may presume, on the basis of our more general assumption of that *common sense* which is the 'necessary condition of the universal communicability of our cognition', that this optimal ratio must be the same for everyone.[20] However, he also writes that, since no one else can judge for us, insofar as there is 'no empirical *ground of proof* for forcing the judgement on anyone', the universality of the grounds of taste is ultimately indemonstrable.[21] At an earlier stage, as we have seen, Kant avers that this common sense is an 'ideal norm', and that the mere presumption of it in judgements of taste does not prove such a presumption is justified.[22] It is difficult to see, however, given the way in which Kant grounds taste, how he can allow that there might be legitimate differences between what are nevertheless true judgements of taste, though we might conjecture that the form of the aesthetic idea, that is, the constituents of the variety and the uniformity, may vary from subject to subject through individual configurations of the association of ideas; so that the optimal ratio would be universal, but the objects that inspired it would differ from person to person. (Such a relativistic solution is suggested by Hutcheson's analysis.) This is what was meant by the assertion that a notion of 'correctness' should be superfluous in Kant's account, and the suggestion that its presence indicates a non-philosophical, as it were, motive.

It is, according to Kant, the 'animation of both faculties (the imagination and the understanding) to an activity that is indeterminate but yet, through the stimulus of the given representation, in unison, namely that which belongs to a cognition in general' that constitutes 'the sensation whose universal communicability is postulated by the judgement of taste'.[23] This harmony of understanding and imagination is not, he insists, represented as a concept, for if it were we would have to allow that our consciousness of this relation would be intellectual, and so, not bearing on pleasure or displeasure, it would not manifest itself as taste. Indeed, the only way for the harmony to make itself known is by sensation:

> [Since] the beautiful must not be judged in accordance with concepts, but rather in accordance with the purposive disposition of the imagination for its correspondence with the faculty of concepts in general, it is not a rule or precept but only that which is merely nature in the subject, i.e. the super-sensible substratum of all our faculties (to which no concept of the under-standing attains), and so that in relation to which it is the ultimate end given by the intelligible in our natures to make all our cognitive faculties agree, which is to serve as the subjective standard of that aesthetic but unconditioned purposiveness in beautiful art, which is supposed to make a rightful claim to please everyone. Thus alone is it possible that the latter, to which one can prescribe no objective principle, can be grounded on a sub-jective yet universally valid principle *a priori*.[24]

These proposed grounds of beauty are, Kant says, inferred solely from a con-sideration of the 'formal peculiarities' of the judgement of taste (they are what the I-know-not-what, in being such, must be), though, of course, he begins §31, 'On the method of the deduction of judgements of taste', by character-izing a deduction as a 'guarantee of . . . legitimacy'.[25]

The above reference to the 'supersensible substratum' of the subject's facul-ties stands in need of explanation. For there is another way in which Kant for-mulates the resolution of the antinomy of taste which has led some commentators to interpret Kant's explanation of taste as an example of the kind of metaphysics he seems anxious to reject in the rest of his work.[26]

The problem of taste, according to Kant, is that its judgements appear to be both based on concepts (insofar as they appear to have *a priori* universal validity) and not based on concepts (we can point to no concept that will account for them).[27] To remove this conflict, he suggests, we must show that 'concept' here bears two different senses. That the judgement of taste must have some reference to a concept, he asserts, does not necessarily mean that this concept be demonstrable – a concept of the understanding, determinable by means of predicates borrowed from sensible intuition and capable of cor-responding to such an intuition. There are also, according to Kant, transcen-dental rational concepts of the supersensible, which lie at the base of all sensible intuition and which are, therefore, incapable of being further deter-mined theoretically, that is, of corresponding to a sensible intuition. These he believes are the two different senses of 'concept' that we meet with in formu-lating the antinomy of taste.

Kant's introduction of the supersensible into the grounds of beauty might be interpreted as anticipating that shift, already discussed in the Introduction, by the generation that followed him, to a quasi-Neoplatonic theory of beauty as a revelation of the Absolute. Later Croce went so far as to link Kant's analysis with Neoplatonic thought, identifying Kant's appeal to the supersensible with a tendency to mysticism: a 'mysticism without conviction or enthusiasm, almost in spite of himself, but very evident nevertheless'.[28] It is important to note, then, the limits which Kant himself draws, both in the *Critique of Pure Reason* and, indeed, in the writings that followed the *Critique of the Power of Judgement*, to what may be predicated of the supersensible. We cannot, he says, be conscious of our experience over time as *ours* unless we are also conscious of that experience as only one possible series of experience of a unified objective world that exists apart from our subjectivity. Moreover, this awareness must be implicit in the concepts employed within experience, as, for example, the concepts of persistence and causality. There cannot be experience without this fundamental distinction between a temporal order of subjective impressions and the existence of a unified and enduring world. (A 'unified' world in the sense of one which we must tacitly *assume* to be ultimately intelligible, or 'adapted', to our powers of cognition.) This opens the way for a distinction between the appearance of things, that is, our knowledge of things such as they affect us, and those things as they exist independently of our knowledge of them, that is, the supersensibly real, or noumenon.

The function of the concept of the noumenon in Kant's overall scheme should, then, be purely negative: we presuppose its existence to prevent us confusing what we know with what is, that is, with what we might *conceivably* know. 'Conceivably' is the important word here, for the transcendent, the non-sensible, cannot, by definition, belong to this category.

> If by 'noumenon' we mean a thing so far as it is not an object of our sensible intuition, and so abstract from our mode of intuiting it, this is a noumenon in the negative sense of the term. But if we understand by it an object of a non-sensible intuition, we thereby presuppose a special mode of intuition, namely, the intellectual, which is not that which we possess, and of which we cannot comprehend even the possibility. . . . The concept of a noumenon is thus merely a limiting concept, the function of which is to curb the pretensions of sensibility; and it is therefore only of negative employment. At the same time it is not arbitrary invention; it is bound up with the limitation of sensibility, though it cannot affirm anything positive beyond the field of sensibility.[29]

If we accept this distinction between rational concepts, as they may be presumed to belong to the noumenon, and concepts as they belong to sensible intuition, then it becomes possible to say that taste is founded on a (transcendental) concept, though one which is incapable of being represented by a concept (of the understanding) such as would make the judgements of taste determinable by proofs.[30] To remove the antinomy in 'aesthetic judgement' we are compelled to look beyond the horizon of the sensible to that point in the supersensible where all our faculties are united *a priori*.

An *aesthetic idea* cannot become a cognition, because it is an *intuition* (of the imagination) for which a concept can never be found adequate. An *idea of reason* can never become a cognition, because it contains a *concept* (of the supersensible) for which no suitable intuition can ever be given. Now I believe that one could call the aesthetic idea an *inexponible* representation of the imagination, the idea of reason, however, an *indemonstrable* concept of reason. Of both it is presupposed that they are not entirely groundless, but rather . . . are generated in accordance with certain principles of the cognitive faculty to which they belong . . .[31]

To say that taste depends upon a principle that, since it is constitutive of cognition, is not open to direct experience other than through its effects, does not, then, constitute an appeal to mysticism.[32] The effect of this appeal to the 'supersensible substratum' of the subject's faculties is, however, to make it apparently easier for Kant to imply the existence, though not the determinability in practice, of an absolute (if subjective) standard of taste, a notion which, as we saw in Chapter 1, does not properly belong to either his characterization of judgements of taste, or, indeed (except as a presupposition), to the deduction, discussed above, that he provides.[33]

This, then, is Kant's solution to the antinomy of taste: the determining ground of taste lies in the supersensible substrate of humanity in general, in the subjective purposiveness of nature for the power of judgement. We cognize nothing in respect of the object, and our judgement is singular, yet the sensation which accompanies our intuition is based on a universal, *a priori* ground – the *indeterminate* concept of the supersensible substrate of phenomena. Moreover, insofar as this concept is *a priori* it must remain indeterminate, for it necessarily transcends our faculty of cognition: it can only be experienced as a sensation, that is, a feeling of pleasure. This, Kant believes, is as far as it is possible to go in exploring the ground of taste:

> We cannot do any more than remove this conflict in the claims and counterclaims of taste. To provide a determinate objective principle of taste, by means of which its judgements could be guided, examined, and proved, is absolutely impossible; for then it would not be a judgement of taste. The subjective principle, namely the indeterminate idea of the supersensible in us, can only be indicated as the sole key to demystifying this faculty which is hidden to us even in its sources, but there is nothing by which it can be made more comprehensible.[34]

His solution to the antinomy of taste, the riddle of beauty, is, as he says almost apologetically, deduced solely from the logical form of judgements of taste, and 'the way in which the phenomenon is derived from the power of judgement does not have all the distinctness that one can rightly demand elsewhere'.[35]

A number of Kant's transitions are, indeed, palpably precipitous. His dismissal of the possibility that judgements of taste might depend upon the contingent 'organization of the subject' presupposes precisely what should be in question at this point in the argument, that is, the legitimacy of the claim to necessity, the real universal validity of judgements of taste. Moreover, irrespective of whether we are prepared to grant Kant his 'supersensible substrate of humanity in general', its introduction here does not in fact provide a solution to the antinomy of taste, quite simply because there is no reason to presume that the judgement of taste is a *direct*, unmediated, expression of the workings of the faculties. If we remove the supposition of subjective universal validity, and remain purely with the logical form of the judgement as it emerges from Kant's phenomenology, it can be seen that there must remain the possibility of a third term in the equation: some other principle, contingent or otherwise, that is responsible for particular judgements. While some form of common sense may be deduced from the existence of taste *per se* (from the fact that there is such a thing as aesthetic experience), it does not follow from this that the content of any judgement of taste is explicable simply by reference to this common sense. It does not follow merely from the existence of fear that we can claim universal validity for our claim that this particular object is fearful. Indeed, in the case of fear we might at least point to a principle of danger, implicit in all such judgements, in order to assert some degree of at least general validity for any particular one (it might bite, bites are painful, etc.); but where is the *demonstrable* principle in a perception of beauty?

Given the very opacity of the grounds of taste, and the observable variety in tastes, Kant's ruling out of further enquiry, merely because the contingency of judgements of taste would be counterintuitive, does not seem justified. Indeed, given how the basic antinomy in question arises from the subject's own sense of the objectivity of the judgement, it may be that a counterintuitive explanation is precisely what is required.

It is, I believe, possible to provide an alternative grounding for the phenomenon which is Kant's starting point, and to do so without taking the path we have already seen certain commentators taking, that is, without denying that taste is taste.[36] Moreover, as I have already suggested, this grounding is immanent in Kant's own account, once the *a priori* demand for universal validity is suspended. We have gained some hint of its possibility from the specific examples of taste in operation that Kant gives – the bird's song, the young poet on his own work – though it is only in the 'supplementary' critique of the sublime that these hints are more fully developed. For it is particularly in Kant's account of the sublime, and his grounds for separating the sublime from taste, that we can begin to see how the conceptual may be introduced into taste without compromising its apparent autonomy.

4

The Sublime

At the end of the last chapter Kant's treatment of the sublime was described as 'supplementary' to his critique of taste. Kant himself does not bracket judgements on the sublime together with judgements on the beautiful: rather he divides aesthetic judgement into four kinds – the agreeable, the good, the beautiful, *and* the sublime.[1] At the same time, it is perhaps misleading to describe it as 'supplementary', for though Kant separates the sublime from taste, not only does he continue, in his analysis of the sublime, to pursue the task of legitimizing a claim to subjective universal validity, but even achieves a more plausible result than he does in connection with taste.[2] Indeed, Kant's explanation of the cause of the sublime is generally far more detailed, and accessible, than his explanation of beauty.

It will be the contention of this chapter that, despite Kant's opinion to the contrary, judgements on the sublime are, in fact, judgements of taste, and that, consequently, Kant's analysis of the grounds of the sublime is the analysis of a particular form of dependent beauty. An examination of the structure of the aesthetic idea involved in this 'beauty' should, therefore, carry us beyond that, in effect, ineffable grounding of taste which Kant provides.

THE FORM AND FEELING OF THE SUBLIME

Kant's exposition of sublimity is very different in form to his exposition of beauty. With beauty he devotes a great deal of space to a description of the judgement, little to the kinds of objects that might inspire it, and a bare minimum to its grounds. With sublimity, by contrast, the kinds of objects that inspire the judgement are delimited at the outset, and the proposed grounding is expounded in tandem with the description of the judgement. It will be necessary later to separate the phenomenon from this proposed grounding, but for the moment we will proceed more or less in step with Kant.[3]

The sublime is like the beautiful, according to Kant, in that it pleases on its own account, is not a judgement of sense or logic, involves no knowledge of the object, and professes to be universally valid: like a judgement of taste it is a claim 'merely to the feeling of pleasure and not to any cognition of the object'.[4] Kant does not, however, propose categorizing the sublime as a taste, but rather as a *feeling*. One of the principle reasons for this distinction is the difference he posits between the beautiful and the sublime in their respective relationships to form: the beautiful in nature, according to Kant, is always a question of form, and hence of limitation, but the sublime 'is to be found in a formless object insofar as *limitlessness* is represented in it, or at its instance, and yet it is also thought as a totality'.[5] While with beauty the satisfaction is 'connected . . . with the representation of *quality*', with the sublime the pleasure is coupled with the representation of *'quantity'*.[6] The beautiful presupposes that the mind is in *'calm* contemplation', and preserves it in this state; the sublime is characterized by a *'movement* of the mind connected with the judging of the object'.[7]

It is this last, that is, the consciousness of 'mental movement', which is at the root of what Kant claims is the 'most important and intrinsic' distinction to be drawn between beauty and sublimity:

> [Natural] beauty (the self-sufficient kind) carries with it a purposiveness in its form, through which the object seems as it were to be predetermined for our power of judgement, and thus constitutes an object of satisfaction in itself, whereas that which, without any rationalizing, merely in apprehension, excites in us the feeling of the sublime, may to be sure appear in its form to be contrapurposive for our power of judgement, unsuitable for our faculty of presentation, and as it were doing violence to our imagination, but is nevertheless judged all the more sublime for that.[8]

Thus, while we may 'quite correctly' call objects 'beautiful', we cannot call objects 'sublime', since the sublime 'cannot be contained in any sensible form, but rather concerns only ideas of reason', of which no adequate presentation is possible: a stormy ocean is not in itself sublime, it only inspires sublimity in some subjects.[9] Self-subsisting natural beauty on the other hand suggests a purposiveness in the object itself relative to the employment of judgements of taste: it appears intended to please, it gives an 'indication' of something purposive for judgement in nature itself: 'For the beautiful in nature we must seek a ground outside ourselves, but for the sublime merely one in ourselves and in the way of thinking that introduces sublimity into the representation of [nature]'.[10] This attitude of mind, this 'movement', is experienced as a 'the feeling of the momentary inhibition of the vital powers and the immediately following and all the more powerful outpouring of them'; it appears to the subject as a 'something serious in the activity of the imagination', in which displeasure is a necessary condition of the pleasure involved.[11] It takes, according to Kant, two fundamental forms, depending on whether it arises in connection with cognition (the *mathematically* sublime) or desire (the *dynamically* sublime).[12]

The mathematically sublime is inspired by whatever appears to the subject to possess *absolute* greatness, that is, greatness not as it might be calculated mathematically, but rather 'a magnitude that is equal [comparable] only to itself'.[13] (This is Kant's justification for situating the sublime not in things themselves 'but only in our own ideas'.) The measure of the sublime is, then, subjective: it is the presentation of absolute magnitude 'so far as the mind can grasp it in one intuition'.[14]

> Nature is thus sublime in those of its appearances the intuition of which brings with them the idea of its infinity. Now the latter cannot happen except through the inadequacy of even the greatest effort of our imagination in the estimation of the magnitude of an object. [15]

This occurs when the size of the object is such that 'the imagination fruitlessly expends its entire capacity for comprehension' on it. [16]

Although Kant specifies nature as the source of such phenomena in the sentence quoted above, in fact he draws on examples both from nature and art in order to illustrate what kind of objects might encourage the imagination to make this vain effort. Moreover, since it is the 'cast of mind' inspired, rather than the object which occasions this inspiration, which, he claims, should, more properly, be called sublime (despite his own tendency to talk of sublime objects), there seems no obvious reason at this point for his distinguishing between the natural and the artificial. We shall return to this distinction at a later stage, but for the moment both sorts of example will do to demonstrate what Kant means by phenomena that convey the idea of infinity.

If we attempt to imagine the size of the universe, writes Kant, we will almost certainly encounter the sublime. For, in trying to form an estimate, starting from the height of a man, then a mountain, then the earth's diameter, then the extent of the solar system, and so on, 'we always arrive at ever greater units'.[17] The greatest effort of the imagination proves inadequate to the task, and thus, though the distances involved may be finite, our intuition of the phenomenon itself conveys the idea of infinity. The same holds true even with objects that might appear more easily intuitable as wholes. The interior of St Peter's at Rome, or the pyramids from a certain distance, will, according to Kant appear sublime, not because the objects in themselves could not be measured, but because they cannot be measured in a single intuition by the subject from that subject's vantage point. The subject's imagination can only take in part of the whole at a time, for, in the time it takes to complete an apprehension of this whole, what was first apprehended is no longer present to the imagination, 'and the comprehension is never complete'.[18] In this way, even what is demonstrably finite can convey to the subject that which gives rise to the 'mathematically sublime'.

The dynamically sublime, according to Kant, gives rise to the same feeling as the mathematically sublime, but it is occasioned by a different kind of intuition. It is aroused by our contemplating, from a position of safety, an object that expresses the potentially lethal power of what is outside us, an object, that is, which, in other circumstances, would naturally be a source of terror: overhanging rocks, thunderclouds, lightning, volcanoes, hurricanes, stormy oceans, high waterfalls, war, God, and so on.[19] Our estimate of the object takes the form of simply *thinking* of the case of our wishing to offer some resistance to the force displayed, and recognizing that all resistance would be 'completely futile'.[20] Yet the estimate is not felt simply as fear, but rather, as the same kind of mixed pleasure – 'delightful horror' – that attends, or constitutes, the mathematically sublime.[21]

THE GROUNDS OF THE SUBLIME

The point at which Kant's exposition of the sublime is here separated from his deduction of the sublime may appear largely arbitrary. Kant himself presents them simultaneously; almost as if, indeed, a consciousness of the cause of the sublime were given to the subject at the moment of experiencing the sublime. (Though, as we shall see later, Kant in no way wishes to assert that such is the case.) It might even be argued that in what Kant has said so far, he has already posited more than is given in the experience. Against this it must be said that a great many of his contemporaries would have agreed with the description of the feeling given above as in itself a definition of sublimity, though they might have differed as to the precise cause they proposed for that feeling.[22] I, too, believe that I know what he is talking about, despite only a few of his examples of sources of sublimity being, at present, to my taste.

The task of an analysis of the sublime is, of course, to account for the quality of feeling involved in terms of the qualities of its object and the propensities of the subject. Though the qualities of the objects that occasion sublimity fall, in Kant's scheme, into two fundamental forms, and it will be necessary to deduce grounds for each separately, ultimately they are reunited in a common feeling – the sublime – by their common grounding in the propensities of the subject.

The *mathematically* sublime, as we have seen, is occasioned by the attempt to comprehend phenomena that in their intuition convey the idea of their infinity.[23] Kant's task, then, is to explain why we feel satisfaction in our incapacity to comprehend the phenomena, that is, why we are pleasurably overwhelmed instead of merely overwhelmed. Indeed, being overwhelmed, in one sense, is part of the experience of the sublime: the 'excess' towards which the imagination is driven in its attempt to comprehend the intuition is, according to Kant, 'as it were an abyss in which it fears to lose itself'.[24] At the same time, the rational idea of such an extension is not excessive for the subject, for it is the subject's rational faculty itself that drives the imagination to attempt to comprehend the phenomenon.[25] In the experience of trying to imaginatively comprehend what exceeds the power of the imagination to comprehend, we experience a revelation of the fact that there exists in our own faculty of reason a 'nonsensible standard, which has that very infinity under itself as a unit against which everything in nature is small'.[26]

We can see how this works from the example of attempting to imagine the size of the universe. In trying to form our imaginative estimate, says Kant, we may begin with the dimensions of a man, then a tree, a mountain, the earth, the solar system, yet probably long before we have reached the dimensions of the solar system, we reach a point where the imagination feels it is almost impossible to keep up with that – the actual figures involved – which reason informs us is the case. The imagination, nevertheless, keeps striving to make the attempt, and, in doing so, represents 'all that is great in nature as in its turn small, but actually representing our imagination in all its boundlessness, and with it nature, as paling into insignificance beside the ideas of reason if it is supposed to provide a presentation adequate to them'.[27]

> [Just] because there is in our imagination a striving to advance to the infinite, while in our reason there lies a claim to absolute totality, as to a real idea, the very inadequacy of our faculty for estimating the magnitude of things of the sensible world awakens the feeling of a supersensible faculty in us; and the use that the power of judgement naturally makes in behalf of the latter (feeling), though not the object of the senses, is absolutely great, while in contrast to it any other use is small. [28]

The quality of the feeling arises from the fact that the subject's very incapacity to comprehend the phenomena imaginatively gives rise to the consciousness of an unlimited faculty of the same subject, one that gives our mind 'a superiority over nature itself even in its immeasurability'.[29] Moreover the mind can only *feel* the presence of this faculty, that is, from an aesthetic (in the Kantian sense) estimate of it, by means of a felt incapacity; hence the pleasure of the sublime is mediated by displeasure.[30] The 'abyss', which is repellent to 'mere sensibility', becomes a source of attraction through the consciousness it awakens of the omnipotence of a supersensible faculty.[31]

> The feeling of the inadequacy of our capacity for the attainment of an idea *that is a law for us* is *respect*. . . . Thus the feeling of the sublime in nature is respect for our own vocation, which we show to an object in nature through a certain subreption . . . which as it were makes intuitable the superiority of the rational vocation of our cognitive faculty over the greatest faculty of sensibility. The feeling of the sublime is thus a feeling of displeasure from the inadequacy of the imagination in the aesthetic estimation of magnitude for the estimation by means of reason, and a pleasure that is thereby aroused at the same time for the correspondence of this very judgement of the inadequacy of the greatest sensible faculty in comparison with ideas of reason, insofar as striving for them is nevertheless a law for us. That is, it is a law (of reason) for us and part of our vocation to estimate everything great that nature contains as an object of the senses for us as small in comparison with ideas of reason; and whatever arouses the feeling of this supersensible vocation in us

is in agreement with that law. . . . [The] inner perception of the inadequacy of any sensible standard for the estimation of magnitude by reason corresponds with reason's laws, and is a displeasure that arouses the feeling of our supersensible vocation in us, in accordance with which it is purposive and thus a pleasure to find every standard of sensibility inadequate for the ideas of the understanding. [32]

Precisely why the revelation of such a faculty, or even of the harmony between this revelation and what we are, should occasion pleasure – a pleasure, moreover, which appears to the subject not as the result of a 'revelation' at all, but, on the contrary, merely as a necessary concomitant to the contemplation of an object – is still, at this stage, an open question. In order to understand why Kant believes he has given an adequate grounding for this form of the sublime we will have to look beyond the *Critique of the Power of Judgement*. For the moment, however, it remains to situate the sublime in that work itself.

Just as the exposition of the dynamically sublime was more straightforward than the exposition of the mathematically sublime, so its grounding also turns out to be a much simpler matter. The dynamically sublime, as we have seen, takes the form of our picturing to ourselves the case of wishing to offer some resistance to a force against which we realize all resistance would be futile.[33] It is occasioned, then, by the contemplation of whatever expresses such a force to us, providing we contemplate that object from a position in which it is not actually necessary to offer resistance to the force expressed.[34] It is the act of imagining this futile resistance that renders the object sublime, or rather, as Kant has it, it is in this act of imagining that the sublime resides: in voluntarily imagining a resistance which we nevertheless know to be futile we discover a 'courage to measure ourselves against the apparent all-powerfulness of nature'.[35] Although the resistance, and therefore the courage, is entirely hypothetical, the propensity to entertain the notion of such a resistance does, according to Kant, 'elevate the strength of our soul above its usual level', insofar as it reveals the '*vocation* of our capacity' that might enable us demonstrate such courage.[36]

Just as in the mathematically sublime a consciousness of our own limitations revealed within us a non-sensuous standard, in the rational faculty, which demonstrated the pre-eminence of the mind over nature, even in its immeasurability, so in the dynamically sublime, a consciousness of our own sensuous limitation reveals a similar standard transcending the sensuous:

[The] irresistibility of [nature's] power certainly makes us, considered as natural beings, recognize our physical powerlessness, but at the same time it reveals a capacity for judging ourselves as independent of it and a superiority over nature on which is grounded a self-preservation of quite another kind than that which can be threatened and endangered by nature outside us, whereby the humanity in our person remains undemeaned even though the human being must submit to that dominion. In this way, in our aesthetic judgement nature is judged as sublime not insofar as it arouses fear, but rather because it calls forth our power (which is not part of nature) to regard those things about which we are concerned (goods, health and life) as trivial, and hence to regard its power (to which we are, to be sure, subjected in regard to these things) as not the sort of dominion over ourselves and our authority to which we would have to bow if it came down to our highest principles and their affirmation or abandonment. Thus nature is here called sublime merely because it raises the imagination to the point of presenting those cases in which the mind can make palpable to itself the sublimity of its own vocation even over nature.[37]

The moment of the dynamic sublime is then constituted by much the same 'check and discharge' of feeling as the mathematical sublime: we realize our weakness and at the same time discover, through regarding the object as a challenge rather than as simply overwhelming, a sense within us that estimates ourselves as independent of nature and superior to it. In both cases the mind abandons itself to the imagination and to reason without a definite end, and feels itself elevated in its own estimate of itself on finding 'the entire power of the imagination inadequate to its ideas'.[38]

It would appear, then, that the sublime arises whenever we thank God, or more properly ourselves, for our unconquerable souls. '*That is sublime*', asserts Kant, '*which even to be able to think of demonstrates a faculty of the mind that surpasses every measure of the senses*'.[39] Sublimity, in Kant's account, renders intuitable the supremacy of our cognitive faculties over our sensibility, and it is this intuition, coming hard on an intuition of the 'abyss' of our impotence, that is, in itself, sufficient as a cause for the feeling of pleasure we experience. The peculiar feeling of sublimity, then, is explicable in terms of this double movement of feeling, this vibration between repulsion and attraction, peril and rescue; an intuition of the inadequacy of the imagination combined with a rejoicing at what this inadequacy indicates. In the sublime the mind feels itself empowered to pass beyond the confines of sensibility, and does so at the very moment these confines are made most apparent. The satisfaction involved, according to Kant, is, in contrast to the *positive* pleasure of the beautiful, only *negative*, since it is 'a feeling of the deprivation of the freedom of the imagination by itself, insofar as it is purposively determined in accordance with a law other than that of empirical use'.[40] Yet we must not forget that this also involves redemption from the abyss into which sensibility would otherwise plunge: it is by means of the self-deprivation of the imagination that the mind 'acquires an enlargement and power which is greater than that which it sacrifices'.[41]

[The] imagination, although it certainly finds nothing beyond the sensible to which it can attach itself, nevertheless feels itself to be unbounded precisely because of this elimination of the limits of sensibility; and that separation is thus a presentation of the infinite, which for that very reason can never be anything other than a merely negative presentation, which nevertheless expands the soul. [42]

The 'infinite' that is discovered is an infinite within the mind. Sublimity is a revelation of our capacity to assert our independence in the face of the immeasurability or irresistibility of nature, 'to diminish the value of what is great according to these, and so to place what is absolutely great only in its (the subject's) own vocation'.[43]

The capacity that is revealed, or at least intimated, in the sublime, is one in the existence of which the subject may, in some sense, *take an interest*. In this respect we can see why Kant, though he places judgements on the sublime in the category of aesthetic judgements (alongside the agreeable, the good, and the beautiful), nevertheless does not place them in the category of judgements of taste, which he has defined as essentially 'disinterested'.[44] Why he does not place sublimity under the heading either of the agreeable or the good is a question we shall postpone until after we have dealt with what is, for the subject of taste, a far more pressing one: how Kant can justify making a distinction in kind between the judgement of taste on the beautiful, as he has described it, and that other form of judgement which is a judgement on the sublime.

THE DISTINCTION BETWEEN THE SUBLIME AND THE BEAUTIFUL

Kant, as we have seen, believes that a judgement on the sublime is like a judgement on beauty, that is, a judgement of taste, insofar as it appears to please on its own account, is not a judgement of sense or logic, involves no knowledge of the object, and professes universal validity in respect of every subject. However, he distinguishes it from judgements on the beautiful on the grounds of what he claims are three fundamental differences: the relationship of the judgement to *form*, the quality of *feeling* involved, and the difference in *grounding*.

Form: While the beautiful, according to Kant, is always a question of form ('quality'), and hence of limitation, the sublime, by contrast, 'is to be found in a formless object insofar as *limitlessness* is represented in it, or at its instance, and yet it is also thought as a totality'.[45] The sublime, then, is not

> a satisfaction in the object, as in the case of the beautiful (since it can be formless), where the reflecting power of judgement finds itself purposively disposed in relation to cognition in general; rather [it is a satisfaction] in the enlargement of the imagination itself. . . . Thus sublimity is not contained in anything in nature, but only in our mind . . . [It] must be sought only in the mind of the one who judges, not in the object in nature, the judging of which occasions this disposition in it.[46]

The sublime, then, is unlike beauty in that it is entirely separate from the idea of a purposiveness in nature: 'For the beautiful in nature we must seek a ground outside ourselves, but for the sublime merely one in ourselves and in the way of thinking that introduces sublimity into the representation of [nature]'.[47] A stormy ocean is not in itself sublime, it only inspires sublimity in some subjects.[48] Self-subsisting natural beauty on the other hand suggests a purposiveness in the object itself relative to the employment of judgements of taste: it appears intended to please, it gives an 'indication' of something final for judgement in nature itself.[49]

The quality of the *feeling*. While the beautiful, according to Kant, presupposes that the mind is in *calm* contemplation, and preserves it in this state, the sublime is characterized by a '*movement* of the mind' connected with the estimation of the object.[50] Moreover, this mental movement is one between repulsion and attraction, and the pleasure involved seems only to exist in contrast to the 'positive' pleasure we take in the beautiful, through the mediation of displeasure. While the beautiful is attended with a feeling of the furtherance of life, the sublime is more earnest ('something serious in the activity of the imagination'), and the pleasure associated with it arises only indirectly, that is, from the discharge of vital forces after a momentary check. Thus while 'natural beauty (the self-sufficient kind) carries with it a purposiveness in its form, through which the object seems as it were to be predetermined for our power of judgement, and thus constitutes an object of satisfaction in itself', in contrast that which, 'merely in apprehension, excites in us the feeling of the sublime, may to be sure appear in its form to be contrapurposive for our power of judgement, unsuitable for out faculty of presentation, and as it were doing violence to our imagination'.[51] Indeed, Kant's analysis of the sublime, which links the feeling to respect, leads him to characterize the pleasure involved in the sublime as 'only *negative*'.[52]

Grounding. It is a moot point whether Kant can actually be said to have provided a grounding of the beautiful. Nevertheless it is obvious that, whether we find the theory he advances adequate or not, it stands in sharp contrast to his treatment of the sublime. It should be borne in mind, in what follows, that in the *Critique* the sublime is treated after only part of the exposition of the beautiful, and before any attempt at its deduction. The fact that much of what Kant says about beauty at this stage does not quite square with what he later asserts may perhaps be attributable to this ordering.

Where the satisfaction appears to turn on the form of the object, as in beauty, the deduction of the judgement, according to Kant, has to be something 'added to' the exposition of the judgement.[53] With the sublime, by contrast, that is, with that which 'can be considered as entirely formless or shapeless, but nevertheless as the object of a pure satisfaction, and can demonstrate subjective purposiveness in the given representation', the satisfaction must properly be attributed not to the object but 'only to the manner of thinking, or rather its foundation in human nature'.[54] The beautiful object, then, is estimated as subjectively purposive '*for itself*', whereas the object involved in sublimity 'merely provides the occasion for becoming conscious of' the basis of the feeling of sublimity itself.[55] The exposition of the judgement of sublimity, in contrast to that of beauty, is, then, in itself adequate as a deduction of the judgement:

> For when we analyzed the reflection of the power of judgement [in judgements on the sublime], we found in them a purposive relation of the cognitive faculties, which must ground the faculty of ends (the will) *a priori*, and hence is itself purposive *a priori*, which then immediately contains the deduction, i.e. the justification of the claim of such judgement to universally necessary validity.[56]

With regard to the distinction between beauty and sublimity in terms of their different grounding, it does not very much matter at this stage whether or not we feel Kant's grounding of the beautiful is adequate. (Kant himself is clearly far more satisfied with his grounding of the sublime.) Even if we do not feel that the *content* of the two analyses can be contrasted there is clearly a contrast between the sublime and the beautiful in the very fact that the former can, apparently, be given a clearly comprehensible grounding while the latter cannot.

These three points (form, feeling, and grounding) are, then, the premises of Kant's distinction between the beautiful and the sublime, and thus of his division of aesthetic judgement into four fundamental kinds: the agreeable, the beautiful, the sublime, and the good.[57] The question now is whether these points do actually justify such a fundamental distinction.

THE SUBLIME AS DEPENDENT BEAUTY

Kant's analysis of the sublime is a masterpiece of criticism. He begins with a certain class of objects in connection with which he feels a certain kind of effect, and moves by plausible stages to an explanation for the grounds of that effect which link it firmly to the properties of the objects, account for the precise tenor of the feeling, and almost explain why we might reasonably expect what appears to be a 'disinterested' pleasure to arise from that effect. What he does not achieve, however, is the establishment of the sublime as a category fundamentally separate from the category of beauty in the way in which the agreeable or the good can be said to be fundamentally separate.

Kant, as we have seen, divides the beautiful (as the object of judgements of taste) into two forms: free and dependent. To distinguish sublimity from free beauty (or 'beauty' in the modern sense), according to Kant's criteria for such a distinction, is an easy matter. It is an easy matter, however, only because in the case of free beauty Kant finds himself unable to go beyond the mere apprehension of the phenomena. The distinguishing characteristic of free beauty, even among judgements of taste, is exclusively a matter of its *appearing* self-subsisting, in the sense of belonging necessarily to an object independently of any concept of that object which we might be conscious of entertaining. The feeling involved in free beauty, then, does not appear to contain a 'mental movement' of any kind. (The case of the bird song, though it casts doubt on the immediacy of free beauty, does not effect the fact that free beauty, nevertheless, appears to the subject to be free.) Any judgement, then, which does not appear to the subject to be one of free beauty *must* be distinguished from free beauty. However, distinguishing between sublimity and dependent beauty (which is the object of every judgement of taste that is not cognized as a judgement on free beauty) is quite a different matter.

Judgements upon both free and dependent beauty are judgements of taste and so share such formal properties as belong to that kind of judgement, that is, their object appears to the subject as a source of disinterested, necessary, or immediate satisfaction. Dependent beauty (or 'aesthetic merit' in a non-Kantian sense) differs from free beauty in that it is discerned when the subject is conscious that a concept has been active in the process of cognizing the object which is the object of the judgement of taste. This involvement of concepts in the cognition of the object makes the experience of dependent beauty qualitatively different from the experience of free beauty, and it is this qualitative difference, that is, the difference in the way it feels, that is, ultimately, the only thing that allows us to distinguish it from free beauty. (Though, since dependent beauty is, in fact, a range of feelings, it might be better to place the emphasis on our distinguishing free beauty from it.) That we perceive there is some concept involved in the judgement does not, however, mean that the judgement is the outcome of a logical deduction: we still feel that the end point of that process is an object of disinterested, that is, necessary satisfaction. Dependent beauty, then, appears to involve concepts but not to be absolutely determined by concepts. An object is judged a free beauty if the judgement feels like a bare reflection upon a given intuition; an object appears as a dependent beauty if we feel that our judgement is somehow attributable to a concept.

Insofar as it does appear attributable to concepts, dependent beauty can be divided into kinds according to the kind of concept or mental movement that we discern is involved; for example the graceful, moving, profound, dramatic, erotic, lyrical, picturesque, tragic, and so on. Moreover, as this list demonstrates, because dependent beauties are linked to concepts/processes, we can, most obviously in the case of art, discern an intention or potential for effects even in those cases when we do not actually feel the effect; so that it is possible to speak not only of the dependent beauty we feel (the *aesthetic effect*), but also the properties of an object that we cognize merely as intended to be, or potentially, productive of such effects (the *aesthetic properties*), and even, in some highly conventionalized cases, which particular customary way of organizing potentially dependent beauties the object exhibits (*genre*).

The kind of concept that we discern in our attribution of dependent beauty (as felt, rather than merely cognized) takes the form of an aesthetic idea: 'that representation of the imagination that occasions much thinking though without it being possible for any determinate thought, i.e. *concept*, to be adequate to it, which, consequently, no language fully attains or can make intelligible'. In dependent beauty, then, though reason is, as Kant says, put into 'motion' in the form of imagining, this motion does not culminate in a definite concept. We may be able to point to the general ideas that are at play in the object insofar as we believe these ideas have a constitutive role in our judgement of taste on the object, but we cannot show how any judgement is absolutely determined by the concept or concepts involved, or, consequently, use such concepts to establish the objectivity of that judgement.

If we review the way in which Kant sought to distinguish the sublime from beauty we find that, in fact, sublimity is quite compatible with his concept of dependent beauty. Moreover, the differentiation, both in terms of relationship to form, and in terms of the feeling involved, rather than being a premise that leads to the proposed grounding is rather, at least insofar as these qualities are made to stand as a contrast to beauty, deduced from that grounding.

Form: While, according to Kant, the beautiful is always a question of form, the sublime is to be found even in an object devoid of form. Kant does, of course, give several examples of *forms* that are, let us say for the moment, 'involved' in the instance of sublimity – the pyramids, the interior of St Peter's, overhanging rocks, high waterfalls, and so on.[58] Moreover, mere vagueness of form, that is, the difficulty of distinguishing between the object of the effect and its context, of establishing, on reflection, that the ostensible object of the judgement really is the object that gives rise to the judgement, seems to be a distinguishing characteristic of judgements upon beauty (both dependent and free), rather than a condition that would disqualify a judgement from being such. Even the highly abstract objects involved in the mathematically sublime – as, for example, the thought of the size of the universe – are, indeed, no more abstract than our idea of the 'content' of a poem, or even whatever that idea is which makes such a decisive difference between the sound of a bird singing and a perfect reproduction of a bird singing.

Kant, however, means something more radical than this; specifically, that, although a form is involved in the sublime, in reality sublimity 'is not contained in anything in nature, but only in our mind':

> For the beautiful in nature we must seek a ground outside ourselves, but for the sublime merely one in ourselves and in the way of thinking that introduces sublimity into the representation of nature.[59]

In order to put forward this as a characteristic that distinguishes the sublime from the beautiful, however, he would have to prove that the grounds of free or dependent beauty do lie outside the subject, that, for example, a play really is moving *in itself* whether I am moved or not, a bird's song really is beautiful whether I find it so or not: that the mind is introducing nothing into the representations it finds beautiful. But this, as we have seen, he does not do.

Yet, because dependent beauties are, necessarily, linked to concepts, it is possible to discern, on the basis of experience, an intention to produce, or a potential for, such effects in objects, on the basis of experience, even without feeling the effect; as for example, when we cognize a scene as intended to be moving, though (and, indeed, because) it strikes us as merely melodramatic, or when we cognize a view as picturesque, even if we have no taste for the picturesque. In this sense, then, the grounds of dependent beauty may appear 'external to ourselves' (that is, lying in what we now sometimes call 'aesthetic properties'), but they are so only in the same sense that the grounds of sublimity are external. You may be unmoved by the film that holds me spellbound, I may find your sublime mountains altogether oppressive. Moreover, if I know your 'feeling' for this kind of sublimity I will be able to predict with a fair degree of accuracy what you will find sublime, before the fact. For, if one is at all familiar with the meaning of the word 'sublime', it is possible to recognize the intention to inspire it – as for example with Milton, the Gothic novel, the painting of George Martin or Caspar David Friedrich, the music of Wagner, the *Rambo* series, the Alps (in their role as scenery), and so on – even without any satisfaction necessarily accompanying this recognition. There are, then, *sublime properties* which I may or may not have a feeling for, or, as we would say with dependent beauty, which I may or may not have a taste for.

It might still be possible to rescue the distinction in terms of form if it could be shown that the form of the sublime differs in the way it appears in connection with the subject's judgement. Free beauty, for example, is specifically distinguished in this way: insofar as the judgement appears to defer to no concept whatsoever, but merely to an object considered in itself, the ineffability of the grounds of the judgement strike us at once. (In dependent beauty, by contrast, we may feel we have good 'reasons' for our judgement, over and above a mere pointing to the object *in itself,* and it is only in the process of linking these 'reasons' to the judgement that we hit upon the real ineffability that makes the judgement one of taste.) We could, then, distinguish between dependent beauty and the sublime, if we could show that they strike us differently, that there is something in the very cognizance of the sublime that makes us feel we must seek its ground not in what is external to ourselves, but 'merely in ourselves'. Indeed, Kant does appear to make such a distinction on the grounds of appearance when he says that a stormy ocean is not itself sublime but only inspires sublimity in the subject. Yet most would feel that it is as proper to speak of 'sublime scenery' as of a 'beautiful flower', or a 'moving poem'. The distinction on these grounds is a deduction from the proposed grounds, and these grounds were not only not given to all other lovers of the sublime aside from Kant, but are not even given to the subject in Kant's own characterization of the sublime.

For a judgement on the sublime to be such, and not some other form of judgement, says Kant, it must arise from regarding the object not on the basis of a concept of the understanding, but rather 'as we see it', 'in accordance with what its appearance shows'.[60] That the eye does not reveal the grounds Kant has proposed is something he himself concedes when, at the end of the exposition of these grounds, he remarks that although the explanation will doubtless seem 'far-fetched and subtle', observation of the conditions surrounding such judgements, and reflection on one's own experience, will prove that his proposed grounding is justified.[61] Though the sublime is constituted by the revelation of the subject's superiority to the sensuous, a superiority which is, as Kant says, 'of quite another kind' to a sensuous superiority, yet it is our measuring ourselves against the sensuous that gives rise to this feeling.[62]

> [The] feeling of the sublime in nature is respect for our own vocation, which we show to an object in nature through a certain subreption (substitution of a respect for the object instead of for the idea of humanity in our subject), which as it were makes intuitable the superiority of the rational vocation in our cognitive faculty over the greatest faculty of sensibility. . . . [The mind] thereby acquires an enlargement and power which is greater than that which it sacrifices, but whose ground is hidden from it, whereas it *feels* the sacrifice or deprivation and at the same time the cause to which it is subjected. The *astonishment* bordering on terror . . . [is] not actual fear, but only an attempt to involve ourselves in it by means of the imagination, in order to feel the power of that very faculty, to combine the movement of the mind thereby aroused with its calmness, and so to be superior to nature within us, and thus also that outside us, insofar as it can have an influence on our feeling of well-being. [63]

The feeling, then, must attach itself to a form, that is, attribute itself, 'by a certain subreption', to an object, in order to exist at all.

This last is well brought out by an instance not from Kant but from Francis Jeffrey's review of Alison's *Essays on the Nature and Principles of Taste*:

> The noise of a cart rolling over the stones is often mistaken for thunder; and as long as the mistake lasts, this very vulgar and insignificant noise is actually felt to be prodigiously sublime. It is so felt, however, it is perfectly plain, merely because it is then associated with ideas of prodigious power and undefined danger; – and the sublimity is accordingly destroyed, the moment the association is dissolved, though the sound itself, and its effect on the organ, continue exactly the same.[64]

The characterization of the sublime in this passage is quite consistent with Kant's, insofar as it posits the idea of prodigious power, rather than the object itself, as the true object of the sublime. It shows, moreover, that, as Kant has said, such a concept is essential to the form of the object of the judgement of sublimity. (That we cannot attach such a concept to a cart is the reason why the impression of sublimity disappears.) However, in doing so, it also undermines Kant's distinction between the beautiful and the sublime on the grounds of form, for, if the instance shows that the concept is an indispensable condition, it also shows that the object, as it exists external to the subject's judgement, is no less an indispensable condition. The mere idea of the thunder – which we may get from the sound of the cart that so perfectly imitates it – is not sufficient to inspire the sublime. The sublime, then, is, in this sense, no less or more 'self-subsisting' than the beautiful. That it is no more 'self-subsisting' than the beautiful can be seen from the obvious parallel between this passage and Kant's own instance of the bird's song that loses its beauty when it turns out that it is not being produced by a bird. For, as was mentioned earlier, Kant's grounding of taste, the exposition of which still lies ahead of him at this stage, does not show that beauty, even in its 'free' form, really is self-subsisting. Nor does he posit dependent beauty as being apparently self-subsisting in any way that would make the appearance of the sublime at all different.

Feeling. The sublime should, of course, appear different, since its objects are, for the most part, objects that we would, at least in the case of the dynamically sublime, normally regard as naturally fearful. Hence Kant's assertion that the pleasure involved must be a 'negative pleasure'. Yet this distinction in terms of the quality of the feeling – the beautiful is attended with a feeling of the furtherance of life, the sublime is 'something serious in the activity of the imagination', the pleasure of the one is almost akin to charm, the pleasure of the other arises only indirectly from the discharge of vital forces after a momentary check, one presupposes restful contemplation, the other 'mental movement', and so on – while it would certainly serve to distinguish the sublime from free beauty, will not distinguish it from dependent beauty.

Distinguishing any kind of aesthetic judgement (Kantian) from a judgement on free beauty is, as we have seen, not only an easy procedure but also an inevitable one. For it is free beauty that is, by definition, the odd one out among such judgements, and even among judgements of taste: whatever its object the feeling is uniform, and even that element which allows us to discern dependent beauty, and to divide it into kinds, that is, the role of the conceptual in the process of our attribution, appears, in free beauty, conspicuously absent. Dependent beauty, by definition, does not denote one kind of feeling: it is a group of feelings/effects, all of which are qualitatively different from one another. To say that the sublime is qualitatively different from all dependent beauty would, then, be equivalent to saying that the sublime is the 'most unique' of dependent beauties.[65] Neither can it be distinguished from taste in general in the way that free beauty can, that is, by its relationship to concepts in themselves, for Kant has himself demonstrated the role of reason, that is, the presence of an aesthetic idea, in feeling the sublime. All dependent beauties must involve 'mental movement'.

It might still be said that, in comparison with the sublime, all other dependent beauties have something in common – charm, or a tendency to inspire,
or be inspired by, restful contemplation. Yet it must be remembered that the
category of 'dependent beauty' is intended to cover every judgement of taste
that is not a judgement on free beauty ('beauty' in the modern sense). Charm,
or a tendency to inspire, or be inspired by, restful contemplation will obviously not do as a characterization of the conditions of every judgement of
taste. Many dependent beauties, or potential sources of dependent beauty –
as, for example, the tragic, horrific, grotesque, wistful, sentimental, and even,
in certain forms, the comic – have, indeed, certain fundamental properties
(the reception of a pleasure 'that is possible only by means of a displeasure',
for example) that are more compatible with the sublime than with other
dependent beauties.[66] While it must be allowed that the sublime of the eighteenth century did include, for some, certain examples of tragedy and horror,
there also existed examples of the same form that were judged to possess merit
by virtue of that form and yet were still not considered sublime. It might be
said that the sublime is, nevertheless, distinct in that its objects are overwhelming, except that the object of the sublime is not what is actually overwhelming but rather what in other circumstances would be overwhelming.
Yet, if we were in those other circumstances, says Kant, the object would not
be sublime but merely terrifying.

Kant, then, does not succeed in justifying the distinction he makes between
the beautiful and the sublime.[67] This should not surprise us, since many of
Kant's contemporaries, and most since his time, have felt that the sublime is
not a fundamental form of judgement, separate from judgements of taste, but
rather a *particular taste*.

To call a thing 'sublime' is to make a judgement of taste. Kant, apparently,
does not wish to say this, but neither does he ultimately justify the fundamental distinction between the sublime and the beautiful (as the object of judgements of taste) that he proposes. For the only thing that ultimately
distinguishes the sublime from dependent beauty in Kant's scheme is his provision of a detailed grounding for the former. The sublime lacks form only in
the light of this grounding. It is an essentially 'negative' pleasure only in the
light of this grounding. This grounding is not, however, given in the sublime,
nor is it part of the experience of the sublime, though Kant's account of it may
strike one as not only logical but also, intuitively, just: no irony was intended
in my comment that his account is a masterpiece of criticism. And herein lies
its importance for the subject of taste.

Kant's teleology of the sublime is the analysis of a particular aesthetic idea,
and, thus, may carry us further towards the grounds of taste *per se*. That it does
appear in the light of an aesthetic idea, that is, an idea/mental movement connected with an object that we feel, albeit obscurely, accounts for the pleasure
we feel in that object, is born out by Kant's own account. For, while the subject
might seem naturally to take an interest in having the absolutely great located

in itself, there is still a hiatus between this thought and the satisfaction, a hiatus the presence of which is principally signalled by the sublime's *necessarily* appearing the property of an object. It is for this reason that I said, again without any intended irony, that, thorough as it is, Kant's grounding of the sublime only 'almost' explains why we might reasonably expect the sublime to be a source of pleasure. It is, indeed, this 'almost' that, even in the light of Kant's teleology, marks the sublime's membership of the category of judgements of taste.

The sublime is, of course, different from every other dependent beauty (aesthetic merit in the modern sense): every dependent beauty is different from every other dependent beauty – that is part of our cognizance of the beauty as dependent. We cannot, then, expect every aesthetic idea to have the same content. Nevertheless, it seems reasonable to suppose that they will all have a similar form, that is, they must be distinguishable from ideas of logic, or desires, they must be in some way connected to the subject's discernment of the object as an object of 'disinterested' pleasure, and yet be ultimately unintelligible to that subject: the subject must feel that they somehow justify the judgement but must be unable to show how they do so.

Most important, perhaps, is to discover how the aesthetic idea can be entertained as a ground of the pleasure, while yet that pleasure also appears to be a pleasure *in* the object. This last is most obvious in the case of free beauty, for free beauty, as we have seen in the example of the bird's song, may involve subreption, no less than, as the examples of the partial poet and the fake thunder show, does dependent beauty. For in all three cases the subject, on discovering the 'mistake', cannot simply transfer the feeling elsewhere – rather the feeling disappears, though it must originally have had a merely mental object. That the object should appear external seems, then, to be an essential condition of judgements of taste: the mere idea of thunder, or a bird singing, is not enough. Curiously, then, taste will respond to an illusion but not to an idea. The feeling, even if it is in the subject, as Kant explicitly claims it is in the case of the sublime, must somehow be sustained by, and, indeed, attributed to, the object itself in order to exist at all.

These, then, are the problems of the aesthetic idea that we must solve. To do so we shall return to Kant's analysis of the sublime, bearing in mind that we are now dealing not with a separate aesthetic category (Kantian) but rather with a particular form of dependent beauty, that is, a particular taste.

5

Reason and Morality in the Sublime

REASON IN THE SUBLIME

It is Kant's contention, as we saw in the last chapter, that his exposition of the sublime is at the same time a complete deduction of its grounds.[1] Certainly the way in which he describes the cause of the feeling would seem to imply a satisfaction of the subject's interests, and thus account for the pleasure involved. The 'point of excess' towards which the imagination is driven in its attempt to comprehend the intuition of the object is, according to Kant, 'as it were an abyss in which it fears to lose itself'. Yet, at the very moment the abyss opens beneath our feet, we find ourselves soaring above it: the attempt to comprehend imaginatively what exceeds the power of the imagination 'reveals' to us the fact that there exists in the rational faculty a 'nonsensible standard, which has . . . infinity under itself as a unit against which everything in nature is small'. In the experience the forces of the soul are raised above the height of the commonplace, the mind, on finding 'the entire power of the imagination inadequate to its ideas', feels itself elevated in its own estimate of itself, and the subject 'recognizes' that the 'absolutely great' is located not without but within.

> Thus the feeling of the sublime in nature is respect for our own vocation
> . . . which as it were makes intuitable the superiority of the rational voca-
> tion in our cognitive faculty over the greatest faculty of sensibility. The
> feeling of the sublime is thus a feeling of displeasure from the inadequacy
> of the imagination in the aesthetic estimation of magnitude for the estima-
> tion by means of reason, and a pleasure that is thereby aroused at the same
> time from the correspondence of this very judgement of the inadequacy of
> the greatest sensibility faculty in comparison with ideas of reason, insofar
> as striving for them is nevertheless a law for us.[2]

In short, it is a pleasure to find every standard of sensibility falling short of the ideas of reason.[3] Not, that is, because in doing so the imagination actually fastens upon something beyond the sensible, but rather because the mind suddenly feels its ability to 'eliminate the limits of sensibility'.[4] It is this thrusting aside, this mental movement, rather than the satisfaction of any end or inter-est, that is, according to Kant, 'subjectively purposive', and thus makes the sublime a pleasure.[5]

Moreover, the grounds of the sublime have universal validity, for, accord-ing to Kant, it is 'a law (of reason) for us and part of our vocation to estimate everything great that nature contains as an object of the senses for us as small in comparison with ideas of reason'; so that whatever 'makes intuitable the superiority of the rational vocation of our cognitive faculty', whatever 'arouses the feeling of this supersensible vocation in us', will be in harmony with this 'law'.[6] Yet, as a matter of fact, not everyone appears to appreciate the sublime, or at least not everyone will find that it is inspired by what Kant feels should, *reasonably*, inspire it. (Indeed, Kant himself asserts that we can more readily predict that others will find the same things beautiful than that they will find the same things sublime.[7])

It might be argued that what strikes the subject as 'great' must be a func-tion of that subject's standards of greatness. (Huysman's, for example, found trains sublime – a judgement that only very small children could be expected to concur with today.) This is not, however, the line that Kant takes. The 'absolutely great', he asserts, is not a matter of magnitude: no comparison with other things is required.[8] It is enough, in the case of the mathematically sublime, that the object (the size of the universe, the interior of St Peter's) cannot be measured in a single intuition by the subject from that subject's vantage point and thus conveys the impression of infinity, or that, in the case of the dynamically sublime, resistance to the force expressed by the object should appear to the subject to be futile. This would appear to make the sublime, in one sense, an individual matter. This is not, however, the line Kant takes. Rather he accounts for different perceptions of what is sublime, or different judgements, from the same vantage point, of objects that may inspire the feeling of sublimity, in terms of the subject's deference to 'the moral law':

> The pleasure in the sublime in nature, as a pleasure of contemplation involving subtle reasoning, also [like beauty] lays claim to universal parti-cipation, yet already presupposes another feeling, namely that of its super-sensible vocation, which no matter how obscure it might be, has a moral foundation. But that other human beings will take regard of it and find a satisfaction in the consideration of the brute magnitude of nature . . . is not something that I am justified in simply presupposing. Nevertheless, in con-sideration of what should be taken account of in those moral predisposi-tions on every appropriate occasion, I can still require even that satisfaction of everyone, but only by means of the moral law, which for its part is in turn founded on concepts of reason.[9]

The sublime, then, according to Kant, presupposes another feeling, which feeling has a 'moral foundation'. For to feel the sublime, and not merely terror, we must be susceptible to certain ideas: we only feel sublimity insofar as our reason exercises a dominion over our sensibility, letting it look out beyond itself into the infinite, which for it is an 'abyss'. For this reason, Kant says, only the individual who has developed moral ideas will experience the sublime – the untutored will merely experience terror. A stormy ocean is only sublime if we bring to it 'all sorts of ideas', enabling the mind to abandon sensibility (which would react with horror) for 'ideas that contain a higher purposiveness'.[10] He contrasts this prerequisite with the accessibility of beauty:

> [A] far greater culture, not merely of the aesthetic power of judgement, but also of the cognitive faculties on which that is based, seems to be requisite in order to be able to make a judgement about this excellence of the objects of nature. The disposition of the mind to the feeling of the sublime requires its receptivity to ideas; for it is precisely in the inadequacy of nature to the latter . . . that what is repellent for the sensibility, but which is at the same time attractive for it, consists, because it is a dominion that reason exercises over sensibility only in order to enlarge it in a way suitable for its own proper domain (the practical) and to allow it to look out upon the infinite, which for sensibility is an abyss. In fact, without the development of moral ideas, that which we, prepared by culture, call sublime will appear merely repellent to the unrefined person. He will see in the proofs of the dominion of nature given by its destructiveness and in the enormous measure of its power, against which his own vanishes away to nothing, only the distress, danger, and need that would surround the person who was banished thereto.[11]

It is a matter of common observation, he asserts, that 'a feeling for the sublime in nature cannot even be conceived without connecting it to a disposition of the mind that is similar to the moral disposition'.[12] (Such an association was certainly commonplace enough in Kant's century.[13]) However, it is the grounding of the sublime itself, rather than such observation, that Kant feels justifies the assertion that the sublime must be 'grounded in the feeling of a vocation of the mind that entirely oversteps the domain of [nature]'.[14] He is quite categorical in insisting that sublimity is not a product of culture, not something 'introduced into society merely as a matter of convention'.[15] Rather its foundations lie in humanity's 'native capacity' for *feeling* moral ideas, a product of our moral birthright. Hence, he continues, our judgement on the sublime always implies the necessity of others' agreement, and just as we say someone who does not appreciate beauty has no taste, so we say that someone unaffected by the sublime has 'no *feeling*'. For the necessity of the judgement of sublimity arises from a connection between the imagination and reason, based, according to Kant, on a warranted subjective presupposition of moral feeling.[16] To understand why Kant links the feeling for the sublime with our 'moral birthright', and thus, ultimately, concepts of reason, we must here turn to Kant's account of morality. For what Kant has to say about the latter is intimately connected with his proposed grounding of the sublime, and bears particularly upon what can be legitimately postulated concerning the relationship between the feeling experienced (which issues in the attribution of sublimity to an object) and that proposed grounding. For, as we shall see, the appeal to the rational obligation of the moral law not only does not lessen the ideality of Kant's sublimity, but even points us towards the very different grounding for the sublime which will be developed in the next chapter.

THE MORAL LAW AND ITS SUBLIMITY

For Kant morality is a rational obligation, insofar as, undetermined by any interest, it gives itself the laws which it obeys. What guarantees the universality, and hence the rationality, of the categorical imperative ('I ought never to act except in such a way *that I can also will that my maxim should become a universal law*') is precisely its negative relation to any possible personal inclination.[17] If one performs a dutiful action because one is inclined to do so, or even for the sake of its result, to say the action was 'performed out of duty' is meaningless.[18] Thus morality, for Kant, is wholly comprehended by the concept of duty; not, that is, merely acting out of duty, but rather acting *for the sake of duty*, that is, acting out of respect for the law *per se*, which is also, necessarily, respect for ourselves as free, rational beings.[19]

The subject, then, must 'make every possible conscious effort to ensure that no *motive* derived from the desire for happiness imperceptibly infiltrates his conceptions of duty'.[20] For morality, according to Kant, is not a matter of learning how to be happy but rather how to be 'worthy of happiness'.[21] Kant does, of course, concede that our goal is happiness, but observes that reason is inadequate to the task of discovering 'the whole series of predetermining causes which would allow it to predict accurately the happy or unhappy consequences of human activities as dictated by the mechanism of nature; it can only hope that the result will meet with its wishes'.[22] By contrast, reason, as expressed in the categorical imperative, can, he asserts, 'at all times shows us clearly enough what we have to do in order to remain in the paths of duty, as the rules of wisdom require, and thus shows us the way towards our ultimate goal'.[23]

It is in this way, then, that Kant grounds his moral theory in reason. That it should be so grounded is of the utmost importance to him, for, if moral laws are to hold for every rational being as such, the principle underlying them must be derived from 'the general concept of a rational being as such'.[24]

All moral concepts must have their seat and origin in reason completely *a priori*, and indeed in the most ordinary human reason just as much as in the most highly speculative: they cannot be abstracted from any empirical, and therefore merely contingent knowledge. In this purity of their origin is to be found their very worthiness to serve as supreme practical principles, and everything empirical added to them is just so much taken away from their genuine influence and from the absolute value of the corresponding actions.[25]

Kant's formula presupposes that the will and the reason are inevitably in conflict in any situation where morality comes into play. Not, that is, because an action cannot be good if it is motivated by inclination as well as duty, but because any action is only exemplary of a good will *insofar as* it is motivated by duty, and duty only emerges as such by its contrast with inclination or self-interest. It is only meaningful to speak of the triumph of reason, which is also the emergence of morality, in such instances as also demonstrate the subordination of inclination. Acting in accordance with the law, then, according to Kant, inevitably means displeasure, the constraint of the 'sensuously affected subject'. However, since this constraint is exercised only through the legislation of the subject's reason, the experience also contains 'something elevating, and the subjective effect on feeling, in so far as pure practical reason is its sole cause, can also be called self-approbation . . . for one knows himself to be determined thereto solely by the law and without any [sensuous] interest; he becomes conscious of an altogether different interest which is subjectively produced by the law and which is purely practical and free'.[26] This would be very well if the subject could ever actually be sure that it is this 'altogether different interest' that is the motive of the action, but in practice, of course, the subject can be sure of no such thing.

Indeed, Kant willingly concedes that the subject cannot, in practice, conclusively separate out the motives that have led to an act, and thus cannot achieve 'a certain awareness of *having fulfilled* his duty completely unselfishly'.[27] We may be aware, 'with the utmost clarity', that we ought to fulfil our duty completely unselfishly, and that in order to do so we must totally separate our desire for happiness from the concept of duty, in order to preserve the purity of the latter, but this does not mean that the psychological state involved carries its own guarantee of authenticity.[28] Careful self-examination will reveal a certain amount – we can be aware of what seems a feeling of self-denial with respect to many motives in conflict with the idea of duty – but that our motivation is ultimately a matter of neither inclination nor self-interest is not something that can be verified. It is sufficient, according to Kant, that we should be aware of 'striving towards moral purity' in order for us to follow our duty, though in fact it may be that 'no recognised and respected duty has ever been carried out by anyone without some selfishness or interference from other motives', and, indeed, 'perhaps no-one will ever succeed in doing so, however hard he tries'.[29]

Despite, then, what Kant says about the 'elevation' the subject may experience in believing they are acting from duty, this subject is, in reality, cut off from the possibility of deriving pleasure from the idea that they have done their duty, have acted virtuously, for, in practice, 'it is absolutely impossible for experience to establish with complete certainty a single case in which the maxim of an action in other respects right has rested solely on moral grounds and on the thought of one's duty'.[30]

A little introspection certainly confirms that this last is especially so in just those cases in which the categorical imperative should emerge most clearly, that is, those cases in which the strongest inclinations are apparently overcome. (This is perhaps another aspect of what Kant describes as the unavoidable difficulty of maintaining that 'merely negative element' which is reason's self-legislation.[31]) The *lure* of duty is obvious; as a 'higher' imperative it removes us from the infinite pain of choosing between what is merely relative, and absolves us from the more absolute forms of regret. Moreover, it is hardly possible to read Kant's account of the 'elevation' that accompanies the thought of doing one's duty without being reminded that self-denial can be one of the most pernicious forms of egoism.

What, then, of this 'elevation'? According to Kant, we cannot claim to be acting morally if we are acting from either inclination or desire, and yet, as he himself concedes, since the subject is, ineluctably, a 'sensuously affected being', in order to will an action for which reason by itself prescribes an 'ought', it is necessary that reason should have 'a power of *infusing* a *feeling of pleasure* or satisfaction in the fulfilment of duty, and consequently that it should possess a kind of causality by which it can determine sensibility in accordance with rational principles'.[32] It is this 'power' which we shall now examine, though it will be well to state at the outset that Kant declares that it is, in fact, 'wholly impossible to comprehend – that is, to make intelligible *a priori* – how a mere thought containing nothing sensible in itself can bring about a sensation of pleasure or displeasure'.[33]

Despite this disclaimer Kant does offer the following answer to the question of how a rational principle can in itself be the incentive for a sensuous being. The incentive in the case of the moral law, he asserts, does not belong to the private, sensuous side of our being, that is, is not based on any sensuous impulse, but rather belongs to the workings of the moral principle itself, which though objective are nevertheless subjectively conditioned insofar as they are located in, and thus in part depend upon, the constitution of the subject:

In the subject there is no antecedent feeling tending to morality; that is impossible, because all feeling is sensuous, and the incentives of the moral disposition must be free from every sensuous condition. Rather, sensuous feeling, which is the basis of all our inclinations, is the condition of the particular feeling we call respect, but the cause that determines this feeling lies in the pure practical reason; because of its origin, therefore, this particular feeling cannot be said to be pathologically effected; rather, it is practically effected. Since the idea of the moral law deprives self-love of its influence and self-conceit of its delusion, it lessens the obstacle to pure practical reason and produces the idea of the superiority of its objective law to the impulse of sensibility; it increases the weight of the moral law by removing in the judgement of reason, the counterweight to the moral law which bears on a will affected by the sensibility. Thus respect for the law is not the incentive to morality; it is morality itself, regarded subjectively as an incentive, inasmuch as pure practical reason, by rejecting all the rival claims of self-love, gives authority and absolute sovereignty to the law.[34]

Consciousness of the law, then, necessarily entails respect for the law, that is, knowledge of the law and respect or reverence for it (irrespective of whether it is obeyed) are identical.[35]

This effect of the consciousness of the law on sensuous feeling is, according to Kant, what we call 'moral feeling' and is the basis of the interest we can take in moral laws; though he stresses that this feeling cannot itself be the 'gauge of our moral judgements'.[36] The moral law is not binding because it arouses our interest; rather it arouses our interest because we recognize it as binding. Indeed, Kant claims that the *only* proper object of respect or reverence is the moral law or whatever expresses it, since only something 'which is conjoined with my will solely as a ground and never as an effect – something which does not serve my inclination, but outweighs it or at least leaves it entirely out of account in my choice . . . can be an object of reverence and therewith a command'.[37]

Respect or reverence, then, is to be regarded as a '*subjective* effect exercised on our will by the law and having its objective ground in reason alone.'[38] This grounding, according to Kant, is what distinguishes respect from incentives based on inclination or desire. For, though reverence is a feeling, it is, in contrast to those feelings, reducible to inclination or fear, which are '*received* through outside influence', one that is '*self-produced* by a rational concept':

> Reverence is properly awareness of a value which demolishes my self-love. Hence there is something which is regarded neither as an object of inclination nor as an object of fear, though it has at the same time analogy with both. . . . All moral *interest*, so-called, consists solely in *reverence* for the law.[39]

What are we to make of this assertion that reverence is neither inclination nor fear, and yet analogous to both? At different points in his exposition Kant emphasizes the analogy with either the one or the other. Respect, he says, is so far from being a pleasure, is, indeed, so 'humiliating' and contrary to sensuous interest, that one only reluctantly gives way to it; one endeavours to keep oneself from yielding that respect to the moral law which 'so severely shows us our own unworthiness'.[40] Yet there is also, according to Kant, a pleasurable component, that is, something analogous to inclination, in respect. For while on some occasions he describes this respect as an incentive for obedience to the law only in the sense that it 'weakens the hindering influence of the inclinations through humiliating self-conceit', on other occasions it becomes something far more positive:[41]

> [There is] so little displeasure in [respect for the law] that, when once we renounce our self-conceit and respect has established its practical influence, we cannot ever satisfy ourselves in contemplating the majesty of this law, and the soul believes itself to be elevated in proportion as it sees the holy law as elevated over it and its frail nature.[42]

The object of this contemplation must, of course, be the moral law itself, not our own virtue in respecting the moral law. The danger of the latter masquerading as the former was one that Kant was well aware of. Virtue, he asserts, is an ideal of perfection that we use as a rule and a standard, but, he continues, it is overreaching to believe, as the Stoics did, that mere consciousness of our own 'strength of mind' guarantees the real presence of that perfection.[43] By contrast he praises the Gospels for being more suited to 'the limitations of finite beings', insofar as they advance the concept of duty in a way that 'does not permit [us] to indulge in fancies of moral perfection; and [sets] bounds of humility (i.e., self-knowledge) to self-conceit as well as to self-love, both of which readily mistake their limits'.[44]

Acting out of respect for the law, then, is, according to Kant, different from attempting to gratify an emotion. Indeed he specifically rejects the notion (to be found, for example, in Hutcheson) of a special moral sense which is gratified by the moral, not only because such a sense could not serve as a basis for establishing what morality is, but also because the notion itself 'bases morality on sensuous motives which rather undermines it and totally destroys its sublimity, inasmuch as the motives of virtue are put in the same class as those of vice'.[45] Nevertheless, Kant adds, the idea of moral feeling still remains related to morality in that 'it does virtue the honour of ascribing to her *immediately* the approval and esteem in which she is held, and does not, as it were, tell her to her face that we are attached to her, not for her beauty, but only for our own advantage'.[46] Though, of course, if we are attached to morality for 'her beauty', then it is not morality that we are attached to.[47]

This last is an important point, for though Kant's 'respect' or 'reverence' does appear at times similar to what we might now call an 'aesthetic response', he is nevertheless at pains to argue that the feeling we have in contemplating the moral law, though it is a disinterested satisfaction, is, nevertheless, not identifiable with the contemplation of beauty. (He specifically contrasts the 'intrinsic value' of the dignity that results from following the moral law both with those inclinations and needs which have a 'market price', and with that which satisfies 'the mere purposeless play of our mental powers', that is, that which possesses what he terms an *Affektionspreis*.[48]) The contemplation of morality, he argues, involves a merely 'negative presentation', though this is, in effect, remarkably positive.[49] Writing apropos the trappings of religion, for example, he asserts that

> It is utterly mistaken to worry that if [the moral law and our predisposition to morality] were deprived of everything that the senses can recommend it would then bring with it nothing but cold, lifeless approval and no moving force or emotion. It is exactly the reverse: for where the senses no longer see anything before them, yet the unmistakable and inextinguishable idea of morality remains, there it would be more necessary to moderate the momentum of an unbounded imagination so as not to let it reach the point of enthusiasm, rather than, from fear of the powerlessness of these ideas, to look for assistance for them in images and childish devices.[50]

At the same time, it is the purely negative character of this presentation which, he asserts, preserves respect for the moral law from turning into enthusiasm or fanaticism, since these abnegations of reason always involve, according to Kant, '*a delusion of being able to see something beyond all bounds of sensibility*, i.e. [they would] dream in accordance with principles (to rave with reason)'.[51]

Yet, for all this, there is palpably some kind of image involved in Kant's account of the moral; the concept of dignity is inseparable from some *picture* of the human condition. Moreover Kant himself cannot resist the draw of images in his own exposition of the moral law. Thus he describes one who bases virtue on contingent grounds rather than on the moral law as like Ixion 'embracing' the cloud in mistake for Juno.[52] Sexual intercourse may not seem like the most appropriate metaphor to convey the idea of an incentive that stands in contrast to both inclination and need, yet in a footnote to the same passage we find the following:

> To behold virtue in her proper shape is nothing other than to show morality stripped of all admixture with the sensuous and of all the spurious adornments of reward or self-love. How much she then casts into the shade all else that appears attractive to the inclination can be readily perceived by every man if he will exert his reason in the slightest – providing he has not entirely ruined it for all abstractions.[53]

If this is not a continuation of the sexual metaphor introduced by the reference to Ixion then it is at least an appeal to *Affektionspreis*, that is, that value which beauty (the 'mere purposeless play of our mental powers') has for us.

In fact, though Kant rejects the possibility of basing morality on an appeal to beauty, he does identify respect with another form of taste, though, as we have seen, a form that he denies is a matter of taste, that is, the sublime:

> [No] idea can so greatly elevate the human mind and inspire it with such enthusiasm as that of a pure moral conviction, respecting duty above all

else, struggling with countless evils of existence and even with their most seductive temptations, and yet overcoming them – for we may rightly assume that man can do so. The fact that man is aware that he can do this just because he ought to discloses within him an ample store of divine capabilities and inspires him, so to speak, with a holy awe at the greatness and *sublimity* of his own vocation.[54]

And again:

What is it in me that makes it so that I can sacrifice the most inner allurements of my drives and all the desires that proceed from my nature to a law that promises me no advantage as a replacement and threatens no loss if it is transgressed: indeed, a law that I honor all the more inwardly the more strictly it bids and the less it offers in return? The question stirs up the entire soul through the astonishment over the greatness and sublimity of the inner disposition of humanity and at the same time the impenetrability of the secret that it conceals . . . One cannot become tired of directing one's attention toward it and admiring in oneself a power that yields to no power of nature.[55]

And again:

Duty! Thou *sublime* and mighty name that dost embrace nothing charming or insinuating but requirest submission and yet seekest not to move the will by threatening aught that would arouse natural aversion or terror, but only holdest forth a law which of itself finds entrance into the mind and yet gains reluctant reverence . . . a law before which all inclinations are dumb even though they secretly work against it: what origin is there worthy of thee, and where is to be found the root of thy noble descent which proudly rejects all kinship with the inclinations and from which to be descended is the indispensable condition of the only worth which men can give themselves?[56]

In such passages, as in his evocation of the naked charms of true virtue, we must make allowance for the distortion of meaning which rhetoric inevitably introduces. The idea that duty is admirable because it is aristocratic, like the idea that following virtue is like having sex with a goddess, is not a tenet of Kant's philosophy on the same level as, for example, the proposition that only the will can be unconditionally good. One might set his apostrophization of duty as sublime against his own assertion that 'The mind is disposed to nothing but blatant moral fanaticism and exaggerated self-conceit by exhortation to actions as noble, sublime, and magnanimous.'[57] Indeed Kant was well aware of the potential for, at best, striking the wrong tone, or, at worst, intellectual confusion, in the use of such rhetorical devices; he himself elsewhere characterized

Enlightenment as a distinguishing between the symbolic and the intellectual, and held that, fundamentally, 'all philosophy is prosaic'.[58] While an aesthetic mode of representation may be useful to 'enliven' an idea that has already been set out logically, he writes in 'On a Newly Arisen Superior Tone in Philosophy', nevertheless, such a mode of representation 'always runs the danger of falling into an exalting vision, which is the death of all philosophy'.[59] Attention is drawn here to the above passages on the sublimity of the moral law not in order to suggest that they undermine Kant's central thesis but rather to illustrate one aspect of that thesis: specifically his own contention that self-conceit and self-love 'readily mistake their limits'.

THE OCCASION FOR SUBREPTION

Since it is crucial for Kant that the categorical imperative be a rational obligation, giving rise to, at the most, the 'negative pleasure' of respect, it is important that this respect *should not* become love of the law, for, if it does, then the actions it gave rise to, being now based on inclination, would no longer qualify as moral.[60] It is for this reason that when Kant speaks of the nature of respect he defines it almost as a contrast with love. The might of the moral law over all antecedent motives of the mind is, he writes, an 'object of a pure and unconditioned intellectual satisfaction', and, since it is only through sacrifices or deprivation that this might make itself known to us 'aesthetically', it follows that the satisfaction, looked at from the 'aesthetic' side (that is, in reference to sensibility) is negative, in the sense of opposed to any interest, but from the intellectual side, it is positive and 'combined with an interest':

> From this it follows that the intellectual, intrinsically purposive (moral) good, judged aesthetically, must not be represented so much as beautiful but rather as sublime, so that it arouses more the feeling of respect (which scorns charm) than that of love and intimate affection, since human nature does not agree with that good of its own accord, but only through the dominion that reason exercises over sensibility.[61]

This ascription of sublimity rather than beauty to the moral law does not however allow us to escape from the possibility that, in practice, we are following inclination rather than the moral law. Nor, as we shall see, does Kant claim that a feeling of sublimity in the subject guarantees the integrity of that subject's motives.

In the relationship between the moral law and pleasure in the moral law, writes Kant, there is always 'an occasion for a subreption . . . and, as it were, for an optical illusion in the self-consciousness of what one does in contradistinction to what one feels, which even the most experienced person cannot entirely avoid'.[62] Since a 'consciousness of a determination of the faculty of desire is always a ground for satisfaction in the resulting action', and, since the

moral disposition is necessarily connected with a consciousness of the determination of the will directly by law, some form of satisfaction must follow
from performing an action which we believe to have been determined by the
law.[63] This 'optical illusion' may result in our believing that, since the determination involved 'produces the same inward effect, i.e. an impulse to activity, as does a feeling of agreeableness which is expected from the desired
action', the real determining ground of the action was a sensuous one.[64] The
important point about this 'illusion of the inner sense', in respect to the
present context, is the aesthetic status that Kant accords it:

> It is a very sublime thing in human nature to be determined to actions
> directly by a pure law of reason, and even the illusion wherein the subjec-
> tive element of this intellectual determination of the will is held to be sen-
> suous and an effect of a particular sensuous feeling (an 'intellectual feeling'
> being self-contradictory) partakes of this sublimity.[65]

An illusion, then, may also be sublime. Moreover the subreption that Kant
describes may cut both ways. For we have already seen, in Kant's rhapsodies
on 'elevation' and 'dignity', how there might be the strongest incentive for the
subject to mistake sensuous interest for obedience to the moral law.

A consciousness of virtue, according to Kant, is necessarily accompanied by
'self-contentment', a term which, unlike 'happiness', does not indicate a
gratification, since 'in its real meaning [it] refers only to negative satisfaction
with existence in which one is conscious of needing nothing'.[66]

> Freedom and the consciousness of freedom, as a capacity for following the
> moral law with an unyielding disposition, is independence from inclina-
> tions, at least as motives determining (though not affecting) our desiring;
> and, so far as I am conscious of freedom in obeying my moral maxims, it
> is the exclusive source of an unchanging contentment necessarily connected
> with it and resting on no particular feeling. This may be called intellectual
> contentment. Sensuous contentment (improperly so called) which rests on
> the satisfaction of inclinations, however refined they may be, can never be
> adequate to that which is conceived under contentment. For inclinations
> vary; they grow with the indulgence we allow them, and they leave behind
> a greater void than the one we intended to fill. They are consequently
> always burdensome to a rational being, and, though he cannot put them
> aside, they nevertheless elicit from him the wish to be free of them. Even
> an inclination to do that which accords with duty (e.g. to do beneficent
> acts) can at most facilitate the effectiveness of moral maxims but not
> produce any such maxims. . . . Inclination, be it good-natured or otherwise,
> is blind and slavish; reason, when it is a question of morality, must not play
> the part of mere guardian of the inclinations, but, with regard to them, as
> pure practical reason it must care for its own interest to the exclusion of all

else. Even the feeling of sympathy and warmhearted fellow-feeling, when preceding the consideration of what is duty and serving as a determining ground, is burdensome even to right-thinking persons, confusing their considered maxims and creating the wish to be free from them and subject only to law-giving reason.[67]

Potentially, then, there is a sensuous interest in being able to believe that one is following the moral law: escape from the burden of one's contingent inclinations. This I may achieve, according to Kant, insofar as I am 'conscious of freedom in obeying my moral maxims'. Such consciousness, however, as Kant himself has said, is impossible to achieve. At most I can be conscious of self-denial with respect to certain inclinations, though whether this self-denial is ultimately made in the name of the moral law or in the interests of some secret spring of self-love is something I cannot know. Moreover, not only can I not be conscious of being virtuous, neither can I be conscious of intending to be virtuous, for, if a good will is the manifestation of the moral law, then the two things – the intention and the result – are, in fact, identical, and compromised by the possibility of interest in the same way. Not only is any form of self-contentment unwarranted, then, but the attitude that could derive such contentment from the perception of one's own intention to be virtuous would also seem to border too closely on complacency.

If reverence, as a feeling of sublimity, was an effect only of the moral law, then its presence should ensure that the moral law is being followed. But nothing, says Kant, will ensure this. Therefore there must be fake reverence/sublimity just as there is a fake doing-for-the-sake-of-duty. Morality, as Kant conceives it, is 'the only condition under which a rational being can be an end in himself', and, therefore, the only thing which has that *dignity* ('intrinsic value') which makes it the proper object of *reverence*.[68] This provides us with a strong incentive to interpret our own sensuous interests as expressions of the law, to substitute, albeit unconsciously, reverence for the self as lawgiver, for reverence for the law-giving potential of the self. Hence the common observation that humility is often the apotheosis of pride.

None of the above is intended as criticism of Kant. As we have seen, he often alludes to the ways in which self-conceit and self-love 'readily mistake their limits', and he himself insists on the impossibility of our verifying when we are truly acting with what he holds to be a good will. The main point to be established here, however, is that his claim that the feeling of respect which the law inspires (or is) is 'purely negative in character' must be read as the statement of an ideal, deduced from the form of the moral law, rather than a description of something which can be directly experienced. According to Kant, since the subject is a 'sensuously affected being', in order to will an action for which reason by itself prescribes an 'ought', it is necessary that reason should have 'a power of *infusing* a *feeling of pleasure* or satisfaction in the fulfilment of duty, and consequently that it should possess a kind of causality by which it can determine sensibility in accordance with rational principles'.[69] The perception of the law as sublime is this 'power', though, as we have seen, neither the experience of sublimity, in itself, nor, indeed, anything else, guarantees that sensibility, on any particular occasion, is being determined by rational principles.

In the *Critique of Aesthetic Judgement*, however, Kant does speak of the 'pure, elevating, merely negative' character of the sublime presentation of morality as being, by virtue of this character, a safeguard against the delusion of 'visionary rapture', insofar as the positive presentations of such *Schwärmerei* are 'brooding and absurd' and thus incompatible with sublimity.[70] Such an assertion, however, presupposes that in any particular case where a thing is taken as sublime the subject can have a clear consciousness that the feeling arises from reason's domination of sensibility (in the interest of reason): a form of consciousness, the possibility of which Kant has ruled out in discussing the moral imperative. Kant seems to suggest here that, apparently in contrast to what happens in attempting to follow duty, consciousness is capable of distinguishing its own perceptions of what is sublime (as the dominance of sensibility by reason) from its own perceptions of what merely strikes it as such (but which for others, or if the subject itself were capable of cognizing the grounds of its own perceptions, would be ridiculous). Clearly this is an impossible requirement. (Even granting Kant's grounding does not allow us to verify, in practice, that any particular experience that feels like sublimity is so grounded.) Indeed, it is difficult to think of two other effects so closely allied as the sublime and the ridiculous. Other people's sublimity is commonly either silly or brutal.[71] Kant's own example of a sublime character – the disappointed philanthropist who has isolated himself from society, and who is 'interestingly' rather than 'tediously' sad – is more likely to strike us now as an instance of posturing self-deception than sublimity.[72] Moreover, we can hardly suppose that the visionary, or fanatic, perceives the object of their fanaticism as ridiculous, rather everything points towards its appearing to them as sublime: as evidence of their own reverence for a principle they consider greater than themselves.

By contrast Kant makes no claim about sublimity guaranteeing the absence of the 'delusion of sense' of enthusiasm, though he discusses this alongside the 'delusion of mind' of visionary rapture in the passage referred to above.[73] Enthusiasm, as an affect in which 'the imagination is unreined', is, he avers, 'a passing accident, which occasionally affects the most healthy understanding'.[74] Moreover, one of the most pernicious forms of enthusiasm is one which, as we have seen, is inextricably bound up with the sublime, that is, that enthusiasm which manifests itself in a belief that we are acting out of reverence for reason when, in fact, we are motivated by a desire we have merely 'elevated' out of its proper sphere by attributing it to reason.

6

The Anatomy of an Aesthetic Idea

Because of the reciprocity between the sublime and the moral, because they arise from the same deference to reason over the demands of sensibility, it follows, according to Kant, that what gives evidence of the moral law will also be sublime. It is important to note that this is not a point he tries to make in connection with taste in general. Indeed, he asserts that the beautiful can only be a 'symbol' of the morally good.[1] This symbolic relationship, as he is at pains to explain, is one of an analogy resting on the following similarities between their operations:

1. Both please immediately (beauty in its intuition, morality in its concepts).
2. Both please apart from any interest, for while pleasure in the moral seems bound up with interest, it is an interest which the judgement itself for the first time calls into existence.
3. Both are free, in the sense of undetermined by moral, utilitarian, or cognitive ends (the imagination is free in estimating the beautiful, the will is free in estimating the moral).
4. Both appear to the subject as universally valid.[2]

There is, then, apparently no question of the moral and the beautiful being identical, revelatory of one another, or even in anyway interdependent; they merely share, or appear to share, the same *formal conditions*.

By contrast the sublime actually depends, according to Kant, upon the capacity for moral feeling. Since 'that which we call sublime in nature outside us or even within ourselves (e.g. certain affects) is represented only as a power of the mind to soar above *certain* obstacles of sensibility by means of moral principles', we should be able to discern in each instance of sublimity that the sensuous interest is being overcome be reason alone.[3] He illustrates this with reference to four areas of feeling: affect, passion, sentimentality ('over-sensitivity'), and enthusiasm.

Affect and passion. According to Kant only affects can be called sublime, never passions, since in passion there is not that freedom of mind that would allow us speak of choosing against sensible interest:

[Affects] are related merely to feeling; [passions] belong to the faculty of desire, and are inclinations that make all determinability of the faculty of choice by means of principles difficult or impossible. . . . [Thus] indignation, as anger, is an affect, but as hatred (vindictiveness), it is a passion. The latter can never, in any circumstances, be called sublime, because while in the case of an affect the freedom of the mind is certainly *hampered*, in the case of passion it is removed. [4]

Sentimentality. Sentimentality, or 'oversensitivity', is likewise debarred from being sublime since, by definition, it is an abrogation of choice:

Every affect of the *courageous sort* (that is, which arouses the consciousness of our powers to overcome any resistance . . .) is *aesthetically sublime*, e.g. anger, even despair (that is, the *enraged*, not the *despondent* kind). Affect of the *yielding* kind, however (which makes the effort at resistance itself into an object of displeasure . . .) has nothing *noble* in it, although it can be counted as belonging to beauty of the sensory kind. Hence the *emotions* that can reach the strength of an affect are also quite diverse. We have *brave* as well as *tender* emotions. The latter, if they reach the level of an affect, are good for nothing at all; the tendency toward them is called *oversensitivity* [sentimentality]. A sympathetic pain that will not let itself be consoled, or with which, when it concerns invented evils, we consciously become involved, to the point of being taken in by the fantasy, as if it were real, proves and constitutes a tenderhearted but at the same time weak soul, which reveals a beautiful side, and which can certainly be called fantastic but not even enthusiastic. Novels, sentimental plays, shallow moral precepts, which make play with (falsely) so-called noble dispositions, but in fact enervate the heart and make it unreceptive to the rigorous precept of duty and incapable of all respect for the dignity of humanity in our own person and the right of human beings (which is something entirely different from their happiness), and in general incapable of all firm principles . . . [5]

However, melancholy, so long as it is grounded in moral ideas (as for example when it is the result of disappointed philanthropy) is still, according to Kant, a vigorous affection, and therefore sublime. [6]

Enthusiasm: The case of enthusiasm – the 'idea of good with affect' – is more complicated. [7] Enthusiasm, says Kant, may appear to be sublime, yet it should not, for every affect, he continues, is 'blind', in the sense that affect is 'that movement of the mind that makes it incapable of engaging in free consideration of principles, in order to determine itself in accordance with them', so that enthusiasm, which presupposes affect, 'cannot in any way merit a satisfaction of reason'. [8] Yet Kant nevertheless claims that the first impression – that enthusiasm is sublime – is justified, on the grounds that, though reason cannot approve, yet 'enthusiasm is aesthetically sublime, because it is a stretching of the powers through ideas, which gives the mind a momentum that acts far more powerfully and persistently than the impetus given by sensory representations'.[9] Enthusiasm may be sublime, then, insofar as it demonstrates a dominion over the sensuous, not because but rather despite the fact that this dominion is exercised by affect.[10] As we have seen, Kant holds that insofar as the freedom of the mind is 'impeded' by affect, affect itself should not, though it does, appear sublime. Indeed,

> *affectlessness* . . . in a mind that emphatically pursues its own inalterable principles is sublime, and indeed in a far superior way, because it also has the satisfaction of pure reason on its side. Only such a mentality is called *noble* . . . [11]

What emerges, then, from this analysis of the different objects of sublimity is an implicit distinction between 'the sublime' and 'the justifiably sublime': between those things (or states of mind) which people mistakenly believe, through the influence of affect, passion, sentimentality, or enthusiasm, to be sublime, and those things (or states of mind) which really are sublime. Tumultuous movements of the mind, asserts Kant, 'can in no way claim the honor of being a *sublime* presentation, if they do not leave behind a disposition of mind that, even if only indirectly, has influence on the consciousness of its strength and resolution in regard to that which brings with it intellectual purposiveness (the supersensible)'.[12] In the absence of this effect, the emotion is mere *motion*: the feelings aroused take the form not of vigorous exercise but rather of massage.

> Now any a person does believe himself to be edified by a sermon in which, however, nothing (no system of good maxims) has been erected, or improved by a tragedy when he is merely glad about a lucky escape from boredom. Thus the sublime must always have a relation to the *manner of thinking*, i.e. to maxims for making the intellectual and the ideas of reason superior to sensibility. [13]

However, Kant is here engaging in persuasive definition, for the sermon *is* sublime to the one who feels edified by it, the tragedy *is* sublime to one who feels improved by it. (Indeed, were such 'mistakes' not possible, Kant's discussion here would serve no purpose.) Moreover affects, which 'impede' the freedom of mind requisite for morality, are also, on occasion, sublime for some. The sublime is not, then, always compatible with the moral, though Kant has said that it presupposes a capacity for the moral, and does so because it is grounded not upon the appearance but upon the reality of reason's dominion over sensibility.[14] There must be, then, something more in the grounds of the sublime, in the 'aesthetic idea' that is sublimity, than Kant has hitherto given us.

THE 'TRUE' AND 'FALSE' SUBLIME

We saw in Chapter 4 that the sublime cannot be distinguished from dependent beauty on the grounds either of the form that it takes or the feeling that it gives rise to: it is only within Kant's proposed grounding of the sublime that this distinction arises. We have now seen how this grounding, if it is justified, lifts the sublime entirely out of the sphere of taste and attributes it, ultimately, to reason. If this deduction is justified then there can be no question of the sublime providing us with an example of an aesthetic idea. An aesthetic idea, let us recall, is a 'a representation of the imagination, associated with a given concept, which is combined with such a manifold of partial representations in the free use of the imagination that no expression designating a determinate concept can be found for it, [one] which therefore allows the addition to a concept of much that is unnameable, the feeling of which animates the cognitive faculties'.[15] Though such *ideas* are representations of the imagination, they may still, according to Kant, be termed *ideas* insofar as they 'at least strive toward something lying beyond the bounds of experience, and thus seek to approximate a presentation of concepts of reason (of intellectual ideas)'.[16] Moreover such ideas must also, somehow, lead us to attribute what we feel purely to the quality of the object; for though it would appear that the *idea* is in some way an interpretation of the object as symbolic, nevertheless the interpretation and the object are inseparable.[17]

It is because the object and the idea are inseparable, that is, because the subject is not conscious of symbolically interpreting the object but merely of *feeling* the result together with a sense that some ultimately vague idea is part of what is responsible for this feeling, that the aesthetic idea (though as an idea it 'approximates' to the intellectual) can still be posited as belonging to the realm of taste. (Indeed, Addison, at the beginning of the eighteenth century, very neatly summarized the case when he described the 'Pleasures of the Imagination' as 'not so gross as those of Sense, nor so refined as those of Understanding'.[18]) It is unnecessary to argue that ideas may have a role in taste, for we have tastes in objects (as, for example, works of art) that are clearly incognizable without the use of concepts.

Even within Kant's description of the moral tenor of the sublime, it emerges that the feeling for the sublime still behaves as if it were a taste: it is a disinterested satisfaction in an object, its attribution is an individual matter, and we are unable to regulate its perception by principles. Kant, as we have seen, attributes this to a mistake – some things are only apparently sublime, or are sublime only in some sense (as for example when the overcoming of sensibility takes place through affect rather than a deference to the moral law). If Kant is correct, and there is a true and a false sublime, or a sublime and another feeling that is merely taken for sublime, then this in itself will show that the former, at least, does not belong to the sphere of taste. In order to do this, however, he must show that it is possible to distinguish between a true and a false sublime, that is, to show that the sublime is not a mere matter of taste. The circularity here is only apparent: if he can demonstrate how we can infallibly know when reason, rather than affect, or desire, is dominating sensibility, then he will have given us a true, justifiable sublime.

Before continuing, however, it must be noted that Kant does not in fact use the terms 'true' and 'false' in connection with judgements of the sublime. The distinction he draws is between 'proper' judgements on the sublime, that is, those that arise from the domination of sensibility by reason, and other judgements that feel the same to the subject, but which are not grounded in this way. In his account, then, a judgement that does not arise from the domination of sensibility by reason is simply not a matter of sublimity at all, rather than an instance of 'false' sublimity. Nevertheless, insofar as the mental states involved are, even in Kant's account, indistinguishable from one another except on the presupposition of his own grounding – a grounding that cannot itself be an object of experience – drawing the distinction in this 'true/false' way (even if it turns out, as I believe it does, that such a distinction is invalid) is simply a matter of not begging the question as to whether Kant is justified in presupposing such a grounding.[19]

So far we have been dealing with abstractions – *the* mind, *the* reason, interests of sensibility, and so on – and on the level of abstraction it is a simple matter to state that reason, in the form of the moral law, may exercise a dominion over sensibility. (Such a thing, as Kant shows in his treatment of morality, is certainly implied by any consistent use of the word 'good'.) But whether this may ever be so is not germane to the present purpose, rather what we wish discover is whether I, or you, or Kant, could ever *know*, on any particular occasion, that what we were experiencing within us was exemplary of this dominion, rather than merely something else which feels like it (as, for example, enthusiasm). Kant's own answer to this question is, as we have seen, negative:

> I willingly concede that no-one can have a certain awareness of *having fulfilled* his duty completely unselfishly. For this is part of inward experience, and such awareness of one's psychological state would involve an absolutely clear conception of all the secondary notions and considerations which, through imagination, habit, and inclination, accompany the concept of duty. And this is too much to ask for. Besides, the non-existence of something (including that of an unconsciously intended advantage) can never be an object of experience.[20]

And again:

> In actual fact it is absolutely impossible for experience to establish with complete certainty a single case in which the maxim of an action in other respects right has rested solely on moral grounds and on the thought of one's duty. It is indeed at times the case that after the keenest self-examination we find

nothing that without the moral motive of duty could have been strong enough to move us to this or that good action and to so great a sacrifice; but we cannot infer from this with certainty that it is not some secret impulse of self-love which has actually, under the mere show of the Idea of duty, been the cause genuinely determining our will. We are pleased to flatter ourselves with the claim to a nobler motive, but in fact we can never get to the bottom of our secret impulsions . . .[21]

Such a concession does not, of course, effect the applicability of the moral law itself; such a necessary agnosticism, says Kant, should not stop us from striving towards moral purity, and, even if we cannot ensure that 'some selfishness or interference from other motives' is not present, we are at least left with the yardstick of perceived 'self-denial' with respect to what is in conflict with the idea of duty.[22] The concession is, however, of crucial importance to Kant's attempt to assert that the sublime lies outside the realm of taste.

The sublime is supposed to be evidence of the reason's capacity to dominate sensibility, that is, to be the pleasure we derive from feeling that this is what our mind has done in finding the object sublime rather than merely terrifying. Yet how do we know that this is what the mind has done? Kant himself denies that the experience of one's reason exercising a dominion over sensibility is transparent, or self-guaranteeing. Moreover, he provides examples of what can be taken for sublime but does not satisfy, even in the abstract, the conditions he lays down for sublimity.

There may, then, indeed be a true and a false sublime (or a sublime and what merely appears sublime to the subject), but such a distinction is not, and cannot be, part of our experience. (Except, perhaps, in retrospect and merely negatively: 'I can't understand why I ever felt that was sublime!') There is only the sublime we feel, and this may not rest on the pleasure we feel in experiencing every standard of sensibility falling short of the ideas of reason. For we cannot know that it is not rather the expression of some 'secret impulse of self-love', arising from affect (providing it is not cognized as such), that would appear to another subject enthusiasm, or even sentimentality, that is, that which implies an interest, and therefore desire.[23] We cannot, in short, ever be sure that what we are experiencing is not merely the result of a weaker interest of sensibility giving way to a stronger one. If, then, we wish to keep as much as is tenable of Kant's own grounding of the sublime we must alter its terms to take account of this potential for self-love. By doing so, we shall begin to see the nature of the *idea* involved in sublimity, and to get some inkling of what an aesthetic idea may be in itself.

SELF-LOVE IN THE SUBLIME

On first view Kant's characterization of the grounds of the sublime – a sudden elevation accompanying the realization that the absolutely great resides solely in the subject's reason – will almost certainly smack not so much of evidence of moral feeling, but rather of that most ubiquitous and invidious begetter of illusion: pride.[24] The same charge has often been levelled against Kant's theory of morality itself. The notion that morality is a matter of duty, of rising above affection, has appeared to many to be too closely tied to the ethos of Frederick's Prussia. Yet it is to Kant's own account that we should turn for a description of the difficulty of avoiding that very overreaching, introduced by the secret impulses of self-love, between ideal and practice which Prussianism exemplifies.

The case of Kant's perception of the sublime, however, is quite different. In connection with the concept of duty, Kant argues that, although we can never verify when we are acting morally, we have at least the rough, if occasionally deceptive, yardstick of perceived self-denial against which to measure our intentions. By contrast the sublime, for all that it arises in connection with objects that in other circumstances would be terrifying, is a pleasure. To take pleasure in the thought of reason's dominion over sensibility is, as we saw above, almost a contradiction in terms. Indeed, the one false note, from a Kantian point of view, in the account Kant gives of the moral law *per se* is his admiration of that law as sublime, his invocation on the goddess virtue stripped of her spurious adornments. (We could argue that this admiration is 'purely aesthetic', but not, of course, in the present context – where it is the nature of the aesthetic itself that is in question.)

Yet there are many reasons why we might take pleasure in the thought of reason's dominion over sensibility – providing that dominion were exercised on behalf of the interests of sensibility, without appearing to us as such. 'We are pleased to flatter ourselves', as Kant says, 'with the claim to a nobler motive.' For we cannot pretend to achieve the indomitable state of ruling sensibility, or entertain the feeling, given us by the sublime, that we are capable of anything, so long as we are conscious that we are doing so out of a desire that arises in sensibility. It is precisely because this is so obviously the case that Kant warns against love of the law, and concedes the impossibility of knowing when reason is dominating sensibility even in the case of the most obvious self-denial. Reverence for the law is a mere step away from the abnegation of reason that is enthusiasm, and, though there is a world of difference between the two in principle, it is impossible to know in any practical instance whether we have made this step or not. The most outrageous illusions of enthusiasm, too, will appear to raise the forces of the soul above the height of vulgar commonplace, will allow us to soar over the abyss of our quotidian finitude – on wings not of reason, however, but of desire.

It is precisely because Kant discovers in the sublime a pleasure in finding every standard of sensibility fall short of the ideas of reason that he should hesitate to ascribe those ideas to reason. The test that Kant proposes for discerning the true sublime, that is, that it should leave behind 'a disposition of mind that, even if only indirectly, has influence on the consciousness of its strength

and resolution in regard to that which brings with it intellectual purposiveness', will not, of course, help to distinguish between a sublime born of reason
and one born of affection, for if the latter can generate the sublime it must
already have taken the form of unacknowledged sensuous interest.[25]

For some time now we have been considering the sublime almost as if it
were something we *do*. There is, as we have seen, some justification in this way
of looking at the phenomenon; certainly in Kant's account the subject must
be active, and active in a very specific way, to create the sublime out of the
potentially overwhelming. But in an equally justified sense the sublime, like
beauty and all aesthetic effects, is something that *happens to us*. As Kant
himself says, sublimity must arise merely from regarding the object 'as we see
it', just as it strikes the eye.[26] We find the sublime in objects only 'by a certain
subreption', that is, by attributing the sublimity to the external world.[27] We
do not consciously choose whether or not to find an object sublime, but rather
experience a certainty – '*This* is sublime!'. (Indeed it is just this spontaneity
that would have made the sublime so useful to Kant as evidence of the mind's
capacity to overcome sensible interest.)

The sublime is an action that is experienced as a reaction, as a state we are
thrown into by the mere appearance of the object in itself. (In Kant's own
account there is already this much of subreption.) We might at this point ask
why a sudden intuition of 'the superiority of the rational vocation of our cognitive faculties over the greatest faculty of sensibility' should have to remain
itself incognizable, that is, why it should appear, or rather fail to appear, in just
this way. To which Kant might reasonably answer that, given the nature of this
supremacy, there is no other way for it to be intuited. But in fact such a question would, as we have seen, be presuming what we cannot know, that is, that
what we are experiencing is the exhibition of such a superiority. On the contrary, what is hidden in the certainty of the experience of the sublime is not a
type of intuition but rather the inability to have such an intuition. It is in this
light that we should examine what Kant describes as the subreption by which
we attribute sublimity to the external world.

As noted above, the reason we cannot ever be sure about our motivation in
apparently following the moral law is precisely because there are certain forms
of self-love (enthusiasm being the prime example) which not only take the
form, for the deluded subject, of deference to a categorical imperative, but
actually must take this form in order to exist at all. That is, there are certain
desires, certain impossible dreams of power or purity (the enemies of
Enlightenment), that cannot be acknowledged by the subject without their
power or purity being compromised for that subject by the admixture of a subjective element, without, that is, their impossibility becoming manifest. If the
sublime were an intuition of the possibility of the fulfilment of this kind of
desire, that is, if it were motivated by self-love, there would appear to be every
reason for the subject to ascribe the feeling to the merely sensible qualities of
the external world, to feel the elevation of the soul not as an action performed

but rather as a revelation from without, to feel *moved* rather than simply in motion.

This possibility alone does not, of course, establish that it must be self-love, rather than moral feeling, that lies at the heart of the sublime. Indeed, though Kant himself offers examples of what can be characterized as 'false' sublimity, of what must both feel like the sublime to the subject, and yet be grounded in self-love, nevertheless, merely noting the fact that we must remain sceptical about what does and what does not arise from truly moral feeling, still, apparently, leaves us free to assert that sometimes what we take to be sublime may be, as Kant would have it, a 'rationalizing contemplation', or 'really' sublime.

However, if the pleasure that is the sublime is supposed to arise from the feeling of reason's superiority over sensibility then that pleasure presupposes either an instance of the demonstration of this superiority, or at least an instance of the demonstration of the potential for such superiority. But the subject's experience of sublimity is neither of these things; indeed, even according to Kant, no instance of what appears to the subject to be sublimity can ever be proved to be grounded otherwise than in the domination of one interest of sensibility by another. If, then, we are to concede to Kant that it is this general feeling of superiority that is involved – a concession that seems justified by the subreption involved in the sublime, that is, by the very fact that it is the attribution of a quality to an object, rather than an intuition of some sense of potency with regard to a specific obstacle – the grounding that Kant gives must be qualified. For if we allow that the pleasure involved does arise from the *feeling* of reason's superiority over sensibility, then this pleasure presupposes that sensibility has (in its own interests) set aside the requirement (of reason) that the instance in question be distinguishable from instances of one interest of sensibility dominating another, and has done so *for the sake of* entertaining the pleasurable feeling of reason's superiority. The pleasure, then, can be said to be grounded in a feeling of the superiority of reason to sensibility, but only on the condition that it is allowed that this feeling is a delusion.[28] For the *feeling* that reason is dominating sensibility could only be the result of a state of mind in which sensibility was dominating reason.

The logic of the case could hardly have escaped Kant, and, as with his *prima facie* rejection of a psychological explanation for judgements of taste, what seems to be here pushing his thesis concerning the grounding of the sublime both beyond what the argument will tolerate, and even beyond what can be born by his own phenomenology, is the *a priori* requirement that the grounding of the experience accommodate the possibility of subjective universal validity. The consequences of this *a priori* requirement are, however, far more drastic in connection with the sublime than they were with beauty. With the analysis of beauty the effect of this aspiration to demonstrate the possibility of universal validity was merely the rejection of certain theses on insufficient grounds (insufficient, that is, from the viewpoint of Kant's own phenomenology), and the ultimate necessity of a grounding for the feeling (in the free play of the faculties), the only strength, and the prime weakness, of which is its irrefutability. With the analysis of the sublime, on the other hand, this same concern with demonstrating the possibility of a subjective universal validity leads to the supposition of a grounding for the feeling (in an *intuition* of the necessary superiority of reason over imagination) that is simply untenable. In order, then, to salvage what is tenable in Kant's grounding of the sublime, all concern for the legitimacy of the claim to universal validity must be, at least temporarily, set aside.

THE AESTHETIC IDEA IN THE SUBLIME

The immediacy/certainty of the sublime, like that of all tastes, is of a peculiar nature. Kant does not say, in so many words, that when he looks at overhanging rocks, waterfalls, and so on, he finds himself congratulating himself on the superiority of his rational vocation, on his own capacity for moral feeling. Indeed, despite the grounding he proposes, he concedes that it is no part of sublimity to make us directly conscious that this is the case, and that, consequently, his own explanation may appear to others to be far-fetched: others may experience the sublime and yet not immediately see the justice of his account. The exposition and the deduction of the sublime, may be, as he says, the same, but the grounds of sublimity are, nevertheless, something that must be deduced from the feeling itself.

What Kant does, then, is look at the mountain, or the waterfall, or whatever, and find it sublime. This, I would argue, is the subreption that allows us to simultaneously entertain and disavow a sense of absolute potency: the mind's necessary deference to the reality principle contravened by this sense. Such a hypothesis, of course, runs directly counter to what Kant demands of a true judgement on sublimity: a judgement that conforms to that stipulative definition that also contains, as a necessary condition, a legitimate claim to universal validity. At the same time it is a necessary hypothesis if, having set aside what is merely *a priori* in that definition, we are to preserve the rest of Kant's theory of the sublime. It may be, of course, that Kant has quite mistaken the grounds of his sublime. Not, that is, in the sense that his explanation is, as we have seen, inconsistent, but simply in the crude sense that he may be barking up the wrong tree. Recourse to other theorists on the sublime would not, however, help us very much here; while there are several different characterizations of the sublime, there are much fewer theories of the grounds of sublimity, fewer still that are developed enough to stand comparison with Kant's, and none, among these last, which could ultimately stand as a counter thesis to Kant's account.[29] We might also attempt to ignore Kant's account altogether by recourse to unconscious motives we believe we can see operating on his judgement, to the workings of repressed sexuality, or, more promisingly, repressed religion.[30] But this is not the kind of trick to play on the living, let alone the dead. His own proposed grounding for the sublime, in the light of his own theory of morality, itself highlights, though we can hardly say explicitly, what might be unconscious in his idea of the sublime. Moreover, this grounding appears justified, insofar as, inconsistent though it ultimately is, it yet closely follows the contours of the feeling – amazement, vertigo, and a sudden rush of undirected yet palpable potency that appears to lift me pleasurably above the accidentals of my life – which most of us would call 'sublimity'.

What we set out to discover was the nature of an aesthetic idea, and Kant, in his account of what he discerns as the grounds of the sublime gives us just such an idea. It is not that the ground of the sublime is given to us, or even to Kant, in the form of a rational concept in the experience of sublimity itself, but rather that Kant, in trying to identify the various circumstances of sublimity, both in the object and the subject, works up his impression into something resembling a rational concept. (Just as with all of what Kant calls 'dependent beauties', we feel the effect, have some intimation of what we believe are its grounds in this or that quality of the object, but only occasionally, unless we are professional critics, do we try to work up a systematic idea from this intimation.) The aesthetic idea in the sublime is, naturally, similar for all who experience the sublime; having a word 'sublime' signifies as much. The exposition Kant provides, of the mind almost plunging into the abyss of its own impotence, only to find itself soaring above that abyss in the sudden security of a feeling that the absolutely great resides solely within, is part of what the word 'sublime' means. That part of his exposition that is also the deduction of the sublime, and which grounds it on a moral/rational foundation, is Kant's rationalization of the experience, and as such constitutes the working out of his personal aesthetic idea. (Though the supposition of a moral foundation can also be said to follow fairly faithfully the common features of the experience of sublimity for many of his contemporaries.[31]) That it is, perhaps, personal is no drawback to our present purpose. For even those very characteristics which Kant gives the sublime, and which lead him to believe what perhaps another might not, namely that the sublime is not a taste, are, after all, part of somebody's (Kant's) aesthetic idea. And all that we require for the present is one, preferably well-developed, aesthetic idea.

In fact Kant's description of the sublime not only fulfils the kind of conditions that an aesthetic idea, as he describes such ideas, should fulfil, it also illuminates why there might be such a thing as an 'aesthetic idea' at all. For the aesthetic idea arises when a representation of the imagination strains after something lying out beyond the confines of experience, and so seeks to approximate to the presentation of a rational concept:

> [In] this case the imagination is creative, and sets the faculty of intellectual ideas (reason) into motion, that is, at the instigation of a representation it gives more to think about than can be grasped and made distinct in it

(although it does, to be sure, belong to the concept of the object). . . . [The] aesthetic idea is a representation of the imagination, associated with a given concept, which is combined with such a manifold of partial representations in the free use of the imagination that no expression designating a determinate concept can be found for it, which therefore allows the addition to a concept of much that is unnameable, the feeling of which animates the cognitive faculties . . . [32]

That we entertain a 'given concept' of the object in the case of the sublime is shown by the very fact that we distinguish the sublime from other effects/objects. There is, as with other examples of dependent beauty, a distinct kind of 'mental movement' involved. In the case of the sublime this movement involves the cognizance of the vast or apparently infinite, a feeling of being overwhelmed, and an intimation of transcendence – albeit that these 'stages' may appear simultaneous. Thus, though the judgement is, in no sense, the outcome of a logical deduction, it appears not merely, as is the case with free beauty, to be attributable to the object, but also to involve an activity of thought that is, in some way, exemplary of a concept.[33]

That the idea Kant entertains in relation to the sublime only approximates to the presentation of a rational concept, rather than actually being one, is sufficiently demonstrated by the inconsistency of that idea. Moreover, the fact that Kant allows this inconsistency to pass, that is, that he manages to entertain the deduction as consistent, might very well be taken for an illustration of what is intended by the figure of a representation 'striving' to become a rational concept.[34]

Even in the form that Kant gives his proposed grounding of the sublime there is still some vagueness as to why the faculties should be quickened in the experience, that is, why the contemplation of the sublime should be a pleasure. (He does not, after all, say that feeling sublimity is an experience identical to entertaining a rational concept.) The difficulty would not disappear even if we accepted the moral/rational basis he posits. For despite his assertion that there is pleasure in contemplating the moral law within, the problem remains that not only is the pleasure contemplative (thus throwing us right back to the beginning of our enquiry: 'How is pleasure in mere contemplation possible?'), but he also specifically describes the experience as one of sublimity. An explanation of the pleasure of sublimity that had to rely on its being produced by the contemplation of the moral law within would, then, be viciously circular.

One of the principal ways in which an examination of Kant's account of the sublime illuminates the concept of aesthetic ideas is by showing how such an idea may be connected to pleasure without *appearing* to belong to interest. (For, as we have seen, the feeling of transcendence that we enjoy in the sublime is, and must be, based on an interest that is unacknowledged as such.) If we allow that pleasure must arise from the satisfaction of some desire, then merely positing the sublime as an expression of the desire to transcend the conditions of one's finitude does not explain why the sublime is a pleasure, since there is, apparently, no satisfaction involved. However, the sublime is more than this: it is the entertaining of the idea that one can so transcend one's condition. This idea is not, of course, entertained as a rational concept; the pleasure we feel is the only indication of the presence of the idea, and this pleasure itself is attributed to the mere representation of the object, is pleasure 'in the object'. Yet it is in allowing oneself to desire the impossible that this pleasure lies, for in so doing one is not only implicitly entertaining the impossible as a possibility, that is, as a legitimate object of desire, but also dwelling on an image of the fulfilment of that desire.

It is essential to the pleasure of the sublime, then, that the transcendence involved is *not* cognized as a real possibility. It is only when the absolute potency is entertained as an impossibility that the sublime occurs. It is in this sense, then, that the suppression of the question of whether the sublime is a revelation of the transcendence of one's finitude or merely the desire for such a transcendence, that is, sensibility's setting aside of the requirement (of reason) that we should be able to distinguish between these, though it takes place in Kant's account of sublimity, cannot, in a sense, be said to take place in the experience of the sublime. For the experience of the sublime is necessarily constituted by both an entertainment of what would constitute the fulfilment of the desire (the 'revelation') and recognition that this fulfilment is impossible (that it exists *only as* an object of desire). It is in not sundering these two contradictory orientations that the pleasure of the sublime lies. (The deference to reason, as a reality principle, is signalled by the necessity of attributing sublimity to an object in the world; this is what distinguishes the experience of the sublime from an outright 'delusion of grandeur'.) Indeed, it is for the sake of this pleasure – the pleasure of entertaining a transcendently desirable impossibility – that the sublime exists. For it is not that the sublime and this form of entertaining the desire are separate matters, rather the sublime *is* this form of entertaining the desire.

This view of the sublime allows us to see why a leading characteristic of the aesthetic idea should be its internal mobility, its lack of definable limits: why 'no expression designating a determinate concept can be found for it'. The true grounds of the sublime cannot be entertained as such, for the sublime could not exist for the subject who was conscious of the mechanism that produced it: the sublime strikes the subject neither as a rational concept, nor an exhibition of, for example, enthusiasm. (Though the latter is precisely how other people's sublimity is likely to strike us.) It cannot exhibit itself to the subject as, simultaneously, both sublime and the product of what produces sublimity. The aesthetic idea, then, no matter how closely it comes to corresponding to the real ground of the feeling can never actually be a complete representation of that ground.

In the light of this last we can see how the revised grounding of the sublime proposed here will also account for the subreption involved in our cognizance of the sublime, that is, will explain why we should tend, despite what we know, to attribute sublimity to the object itself. For even when we are conscious of entertaining a fairly comprehensive, or even 'precise', aesthetic idea in connection with an object, we still feel as though our pleasure is, paradoxically, attributable to the object itself. For though it would appear that the *idea* is in some way an interpretation of the object, or our relationship to the object, as symbolic, nevertheless the interpretation and the object also appear inseparable: despite what reflection may inform us, we cognize the sublime as a revelation from the object rather than a projection onto the object. This resistance to acknowledging the grounds of the feeling is, as we have seen above, an essential part of the feeling itself. Despite what we may believe about beauty being in the eye of the beholder we cannot simultaneously see an instance of beauty and *feel* that it is merely in our own eye.

CONCLUSION

The form of the idea discerned in the sublime does, then, conform to that required by the concept of the aesthetic idea: it is not identifiable with an idea which can be cognized *by the subject* as grounded in either logic, or desire, it accounts for the subject's discernment of the object as an object of 'disinterested' pleasure, and it is ultimately unintelligible to that subject, that is, the subject may feel that the idea somehow justifies the judgement but is unable to show how it does so. Most importantly, the form that the idea takes will also account for the way in which the aesthetic idea can be entertained as inextricable from the pleasure, while yet that pleasure also appears to be a pleasure *in* the object, rather than in the idea itself.

In §40, where Kant is discussing the *sensus communis*, he gives the following three 'maxims of the common human understanding'; to think for oneself, to think from the standpoint of everyone else, to always think consistently.[35] It is these three habits of thought which he claims are essential to the process of enlightenment; the first, 'the maxim of a reason that is never *passive*', could, indeed, be taken as the very motto of that era which goes by the name 'Enlightenment'. The greatest danger to thought, the abnegation of that in which thinking consists, arises, according to Kant, through failure to observe this first maxim, that is, in effect, the abandonment of the mind to prejudice. Yet such a passivity of reason is, in practice, something active:

> One readily sees that while enlightenment is easy *in thesi*, *in hypothesi* it is a difficult matter that can only be accomplished slowly; for while not being passive with his reason but always legislative for himself is something that is very easy for the person who would only be adequate to his essential end and does not demand to know that which is beyond his understanding, nevertheless, since striving for the latter is hardly to be forbidden . . . it must

be very difficult to maintain or establish the merely negative element (which constitutes genuine enlightenment) in the manner of thinking . . .[36]

The way in which desire may cause understanding to run ahead, as it were, of itself is illuminated by a footnote to the Introduction of the *Critique of the Power of Judgement*, where Kant is discussing the place of the third *Critique* in his system as a whole. Desire, he there writes, is that faculty '*for being through one's representations the cause of the reality of the objects of these representations*'.[37] That one cannot, however, wish objects into existence only proves that 'there are . . . desires in a human being as a result of which he stands in contradiction with himself'. Such consciously 'fantastic desires', he continues, manifest themselves in those instances where we seek the production of an object by means of representation alone, without any hope of succeeding, and with the full knowledge that success would be impossible; as, for example, when we wish to undo the past, or to annihilate the interval that divides us from a wished-for moment. Though we are conscious, he continues, of the inefficiency of our representations as causes of their objects, every wish or longing still involves a reference to cause, and is not deterred from 'striving' (*Bestrebung*) to achieve its object by this consciousness. Why this should be so, why we should have this propensity to consciously vain desires, is, he believes, a question for anthropology, though he does offer the following suggestion:

> It appears that if we were not determined to the application of our powers until we had assured ourselves of the adequacy of our faculties for the production of an object, then these powers would remain largely unemployed. For ordinarily we learn to know our powers only by first trying them out. This illusion in empty wishes is therefore only the consequence of a beneficent arrangement in our nature. [38]

Aesthetic ideas, too, though they are, like desires, mere representations of the imagination, can be called 'ideas', according to Kant, because they 'at least strive [*streben*] toward something lying beyond the bounds of experience, and thus seek to approximate a presentation of concepts of reason'.[39]

This coincidence of vocabulary arises, I would suggest, not merely from an analogy but from an at least partial identity. What both the 'fantastic desire' and the aesthetic idea strain against in their striving is understanding, and the effort, in both cases, is produced by the action of desire. The result of this striving must, of course, in the case of free and dependent beauty, take on a peculiar character in order to give rise to a feeling that is, predominantly, one of pleasure.[40]

We might speculate that one difference between the aesthetic idea and the consciously vain wish is that in the latter the desire is the avoidance of a specific pain (a particular humiliation), and whatever pleasure may arise is of a character that the subject is not prepared to acknowledge (the self-indulgent pangs of romantic yearning, the self-righteousness of the bigot), while in the aesthetic idea the desire is the avoidance of a general sense of pain (the sense of our human finitude) by the production of a specific pleasure (free or dependent beauty), and it is the pleasure itself, albeit mixed, as it often is, with a certain sense of sadness, or yearning, a partial acknowledgement, in the domain of feeling, of the pleasure's source, which is our only cognizance of what has taken place. In both cases, of course, it is not a matter of substituting a pain for a pleasure; rather the latter arises from the avoidance of the former and takes its character both from the means of the avoidance employed, and from the necessity of preventing these means from becoming fully conscious.

*

The last two chapters have been almost exclusively concerned with the sublime. To some extent this represents the balance, at least in terms of analysis, between beauty and sublimity in the *Critique* itself. (A balance that also reflects the general tendency in eighteenth-century aesthetics.) The reason why this should be so, why it should be easier to enlarge on the grounding of the sublime than on that of beauty, is suggested by one of the ways in which Kant distinguishes between the two. In excluding emotion from the determining grounds of the pure judgement of taste Kant remarks that, by contrast, 'the feeling of emotion' is necessarily combined with sublimity.[41] (Hence Kant's exclusion of the sublime from the realm of taste, and the necessity for a separate grounding.) Indeed Kant at this point defines an emotion as 'a sensation in which agreeableness is produced only by means of a momentary inhibition followed by a stronger outpouring of the vital force'; a definition that could make sublimity almost the type of emotion, insofar as the inhibition takes place on a symbolic level (the object is not a real threat), and the outpouring is correspondingly abstract (the pleasure involved signifies the furtherance of no *particular* goal of the subject).[42] I do not wish, however, to categorize the sublime (or any aesthetic affect) as an emotion, for reasons that have been indicated above but which there is not space here to enlarge upon. The instance of sublimity nevertheless has this much in common with an emotion, that it implies a narrative (an interest and its potential advancement or thwarting) that connects it with the general life of the subject. Kant's grounding of beauty is, by contrast, relatively autistic: there is, of course, a sequence of events, but they immediately relate only to the indeterminate play of the understanding and imagination. While not denying that this play could be of general significance for the subject (Hutcheson, as we saw in Chapter 3, suggests how it might), it can be granted that an existential situation is more directly implied by the sublime, even in Kant's account. It is for this reason that Kant's sublimity is, among the aesthetic categories he deals with, the most amenable to further analysis. Moreover, it was necessary, to establish that, once we have suspended the *a priori* requirement that its grounding legitimize a claim to subjective universal validity, the sublime can be seen as belonging to the domain Kant assigns to taste, despite his assertion to the contrary. Nevertheless the object of our enquiry here is the realm of taste as a whole, and we must now turn to the way in which the foregoing analysis of the sublime might bear on the (non-Kantian) aesthetic in general. For just as a particular form of what Kant calls 'fantastic desire' can be discovered as a constitutive moment in the creation of sublimity, so also, I will argue, can it be seen as essential to the grounding of judgements of taste (aesthetic experience) in general.

7

Fantastic Desires I: Dependent Beauty

In Chapter 4 it was suggested that though we cannot expect every aesthetic idea to have the same content – since we distinguish between different kinds of dependent beauty – we might nevertheless expect the aesthetic idea always to take something like the same form, to have an essential dynamic. The present chapter and the following will offer two further examples, taken from Kant, of the operation of taste, in which the form of the aesthetic idea so far distinguished appears to recur. We will not be returning to the example of the partial young poet, or to Kant's cognizance of the moral law itself as sublime. Our examination of sublimity has made an analysis of the latter example redundant, while the former is not sufficiently developed by Kant for us to see the grounds of the taste involved. (To say that the poet finds the poetry beautiful because it is his own would be to say precisely nothing apropos that beauty.) The two examples we will use are the fragment of a poem by Frederick the Great that Kant quotes during his exposition of the aesthetic idea, as an example of what inspires such an idea in him, and the example of the bird song, already mentioned in Chapter 2.

Kant himself says that it is 'the art of poetry in which the faculty of aesthetic ideas can reveal itself in its full measure'.[1] It is for this reason that the second example, of the bird song, is the more crucial; for we have yet to justify both Kant's remark that all forms of beauty depend upon the expression of aesthetic ideas, and, more importantly, the very link which Kant makes between free beauty (modern 'beauty') and dependent beauty (modern 'aesthetic merit') in calling them both forms of 'beauty'. Dependent beauty is, however, as the preceding treatment has made clear, by far the more accessible of the two forms, and it is to an example of dependent beauty that we shall first turn. First, however, it is necessary to offer some explanation for the change of pace that follows. The first part of this chapter will consist of an analysis (possibly *ad nauseam*) of the poetry that Kant quotes in §49; poetry generally considered so embarrassingly bad that the majority of commentators simply pretend it is not there. This polite deference, by the secondary literature, to the principle of *de gustibus non est disputandum* is odd in a context where, in a sense, that is precisely what is in dispute. It is the most developed example of a judgement of taste that Kant gives in the *Critique*, and, more importantly, his key illustration of the concept of aesthetic ideas. The attention it receives below, however, is not a matter of making the soundness of Kant's theory dependent on the details of his tastes. On the contrary I wish to follow Kant here, that is, to use the poem precisely in order to illustrate the concept of the aesthetic idea. That our tastes radically diverge over the example is what makes it so valuable: a fundamental aesthetics must cover every instance of what is an aesthetic judgement for any subject.

This last requirement runs, of course, directly counter to any positing of an ideal judgement of taste, such as is found in Kant. So long as one feels free to pick and choose among what counts as an aesthetic judgement, irrespective of the feelings of the subject (that is, all subjects at all times), the construction of an aesthetic theory presents no great difficulties – or rewards. Such ideality is, however, by no means a peculiarity of Kant. Aesthetics has, traditionally, been grounded in admiration, and its function has been to justify this admiration. Hence the positive value invariably ascribed to aesthetic experience; value, that is, over and above the actual pleasure which constitutes that experience. In apparently dealing with the aesthetic *per se* what such theories have actually dealt with is the theorist's response to that class of objects that represent their own aesthetic preferences. This may either be done explicitly, by discounting some tastes as errors, or implicitly, by sustaining a degree of abstraction that renders the theory similar to a skilful horoscope – it could not fail to 'particularly' cover one's preferences.[2] In both cases a philosophical distortion enters in not because the theory bases itself upon personal response (which is, indeed, the only 'fixed' point in aesthetics), but because this initial discrimination produces both a tendency for the theory to become too object-led, and, perhaps more importantly, a tendency, since we start from our own admiration rather than admiration *per se*, to set ourselves the task of *justifying*, rather than *accounting for*, aesthetic value.

Cassirer both exemplifies the above tendency in aesthetics, and brings us back to the present instance, when he writes that there is a 'pre-established harmony' between Kant's aesthetics and the poetry of Goethe, and that this harmony shows how, in eighteenth-century Germany, the critical and the productive 'converted . . . directly' into each other.[3] For Cassirer, Goethe is sufficiently great, and Kant sufficiently abstract, for the one to support the other in the exaltation of the aesthetic. (Support, as it were, on each other's shoulders.) It is, however, the poetry of Frederick the Great, not Goethe, that Kant brings forward to illustrate his aesthetics. In justice to the aesthetic, then, albeit in defiance of Kant's own idealistic tendency in this matter, we should grant that this poetry is beautiful for Kant, just as the young poet's poetry was beautiful for the young poet. Moreover, I believe that it does successfully illustrate the aesthetic idea that is constitutive of aesthetic experience.

Given what is said above, it should not be necessary to justify in detail the other aspect of the change of pace, and contravention of academic practice, to be found in this chapter, that is, the consistent use of the personal pronoun.

Although one could be fairly confident of a contemporary consensus on the value of Frederick's poem, any use of 'we' in the discussion would have to particularly exclude Kant. In dealing with examples of the aesthetic nothing could be less philosophical than the pretence that one is not dealing, first and foremost, with a matter of personal feeling. To proceed on any other presumption is to run the risk of entirely losing sight of the object.[4]

ILLUSTRATION OF THE AESTHETIC IDEA

Kant does not give a specific name to the species of dependent beauty possessed by the lines by Frederick the Great he quotes, beyond the late eighteenth-century catch-all title of 'genius':

> Oui, finissons sans trouble, et mourons sans regrets,
> En laissant l'Univers comblé de nos bienfaits.
> Ainsi l'Astre du jour, au bout de sa carrière,
> Répand sur l'horizon une douce lumière,
> Et les derniers rayons qu'il darde dans les airs
> Sont les derniers soupirs qu'il donne à l'Univers;[5]

> [Yes, let us end without disorder and die without regrets,
> Leaving the universe filled with our blessings.
> Thus the daystar at the end of its course,
> Sheds on the horizon a gentle light;
> And the last rays that it beams into the air,
> Are the last sighs that it gives the universe;[6]]

According to Kant, the poet here 'animates his idea of reason of a cosmopolitan disposition even at the end of life by means of an attribute that the imagination (in the recollection of everything agreeable in a beautiful summer day, drawn to a close, which a bright evening calls to mind) associates with that representation, and which arouses a multitude of sensations and supplementary representations for which no expression is found'.[7] The basic concept (*Oui, finissons sans trouble, et mourons sans regrets*) is thus, according to Kant, supplemented in thought by much that is 'unnameable', for while the imagination, when it is employed on behalf of cognition, is subject to the constraints of understanding, in 'an aesthetic respect' it is 'free to provide, beyond that concord with the concept, unsought extensive undeveloped material for the understanding, of which the latter took no regard in its concept, but which it applies, not so much objectively, for cognition, as subjectively, for the animation of the cognitive powers, and thus also indirectly to cognitions'.[8] It is, then, the way in which the 'basic concept' is presented which animates that concept, and makes the lines exemplary of genius.

What makes the instance exemplary of the aesthetic idea, according to

Kant, is that the way in which the concept is supplemented is impossible to put into words, over and above, that is, Kant's own pointing towards the analogy involved: crudely, that our dying blessings are to our death, as the last rays of the sun are to its setting.[9] It is this analogy that Kant identifies as the grounds of the 'soul' (*Geist*), or merit, of the lines. It will be well to point out before starting to examine this analogy that, with respect to the analysis of its creation of an aesthetic idea, I enjoy a distinct advantage over Kant in finding the lines without merit. Pointing out the workings of bad poetry (meaning poetry one does not like) is a relatively straightforward affair. Indeed the contrast between the ease with which we can discover how bad poetry intended to move us, compared with the difficulty of discovering how good poetry (meaning poetry one likes) does move us, is so great that one might be tempted to make this contrast the very distinction between good and bad poetry. Indeed, this is precisely what we might expect, given that the aesthetic idea, as we saw with the sublime, cannot exist as such if the 'fantastic desire' that it contains is directly cognized as desire. It would, of course, be impossible to cognize an effect as a (failed) attempt to inspire an aesthetic idea outside of a context in which we are cognizant of the intention to make such an attempt. (Anything, after all, may inspire an aesthetic idea, yet we do not cognize every object in the world that fails to do so as a failure.) As we have seen in dealing with the sublime as a dependent beauty, such a context may be provided by nature if we have 'gone to nature' in the expectation of some form of aesthetic experience, but it is invariably provided by art. Even in the absence of Kant's claim that Frederick's lines express an aesthetic idea, we must cognize them, in recognizing the lines as belonging to a poem, as the attracting of our attention towards an aesthetic idea.

In what way, then, do the lines 'animate' the concept (*Oui, finissons sans trouble, et mourons sans regrets*) for Kant? What is the ultimately indefinable supplement that the imagination provides through the image of the setting sun? The answering of these questions is greatly facilitated by the fact that death is not actually comparable to any other experience. Thus the words *finissons* (end) and *laissant* (leaving) in connection with death, though this connection is by no means peculiar to the present context, or even any recognizably poetic context, are themselves, in a weak sense, figurative. To end or finish something implies that what is involved is a circumscribed task, an activity which must necessarily be bordered by other activities, or at least a potential for activity. Likewise to leave (to 'pass on') implies a transition, and thus, necessarily, a continued existence elsewhere. Both words, then, describe death as if it were precisely what it most emphatically is not, that is, a temporal activity. It is this suggestion – that death is something in experience rather than merely the cessation of experience – which makes such expressions, as implicit mollifications of the reality of death, suitable everyday euphemisms.

These observations, in themselves, confined as they are to just two words, do not, of course, account for that supplement which is the genius/badness of the whole fragment. Indeed there are a great many poems that I find intensely moving, yet which are overtly based on the premise that death is a transition from one kind of existence to another. Henry Vaughn's 'They are all gone into the world of light' is a good example.[10] I do not, however, find the implication that death is a transition at all troublesome in an avowedly Christian context. The reason why this should be so is, perhaps, best expressed by the obvious unsuitability of the word 'implication' here. I can read, or at least I believe I can read, the very context itself as the expression of a desire that death should be a transition, which allows the lines to express for me not the certainty that death is such, but rather the regret that it is not, or, at least, that I cannot be certain that it is. I am vaguely conscious, however, that it is not as a meditation on death that I enjoy Vaughn's poem, and it is referred to here not as a comparison with the poem Kant quotes, but simply in order to qualify the point being made about the way in which that poem, too obviously (for me), attempts to draw the sting of death.[11] For it is this last that constitutes the 'genius' of the poem for Kant.

This too obvious attempt to draw the sting of death can be seen in the extended metaphor of the setting sun. The further the lines push the euphemistic description of death, the more obvious becomes the evasion. It might, of course, be possible to cognize this as the line's intention: precisely the intention to convey the futility of such an evasion along the lines that it is ostensibly taking. One of those many commentators on art who, unaccountably, identify artistic merit with truth, might, perhaps, admire the lines if they believed such was the case; even though the premise of such admiration – that we should be pleased by having nothing more than the absolute loss of ourselves in death brought forcibly home to us – would be nonsensical. Yet another commentator might enjoy the irony in itself, that is, the intellectual pleasure – whatever such pleasure may signify – of decoding the utterance, regardless of the content; though I do not feel the lines, if they were ironical, to be ultimately worth such trouble, since they imply no interesting standpoint from which, were they ironical, they would be mocking the attitude to death expressed. The only difference, then, an ironical reading would make would be the experience of a different kind of failure; for the consequent meaning would be just as uninteresting as the meaning that seems to be intended. Moreover it is the grounds of Kant's pleasure, insofar as he formulates what he believes these to be, which are our present object.

Kant, it seems safe to presume from his own comment on the lines, does not read them as ironical: he does not pause over the justice of such words as *finissons* and *laissant*, as we are doing here, nor ask in what precise sense we can claim to be able to fill (*comblé*) the universe with our benefactions. This is as it should be, for Kant is enjoying a poem, and poetry is what cannot be paraphrased, what is lost in translation, and so on. These familiar aphorisms contain an important truth about the phenomenology of the aesthetic, but it should be noted that they use the word 'poetry' in an evaluative sense, and the lines by Frederick are not 'poetry', in that evaluative sense, to this reader.[12]

It is specifically the casting of the 'cosmopolitan disposition' into the image of the last rays of the setting sun that Kant singles out for praise, and it is this conceit that annexes to the basic concept the crowd of inexpressible sensations and secondary representations (the wealth of undeveloped material that the understanding did not regard in its concept, but which it can make use of subjectively for animating the cognitive faculties, and, indirectly, for cognitions) that constitutes the aesthetic idea. We shall now turn, then, to a more detailed examination of this positing, albeit as a matter of poetical conceit (*Ainsi*), of the 'cosmopolitan attitude' on the point of death in terms of the setting sun.

> Ainsi l'Astre du jour, au bout de sa carrière,
> Répand sur l'horizon une douce lumière,
> Et les derniers rayons qu'il darde dans les airs
> Sont les derniers soupirs qu'il donne à l'Univers;

This, as was noted above, is a development of the euphemism (*finissons, laissant*) of the opening lines. (Once again we have a parallel – 'twilight years' – in everyday use.) Its being thought in terms of a temporal event, and particularly an event that, like the setting of the sun, is cyclical in character, must, as we have seen, mollify the reality of death.[13] However, there is obviously more to this simile than the mere softening of extinction into 'setting'. The presence of *l'Astre du jour* introduces a host of 'supplementary representations' which would be lost were it replaced by sun; for the former, unlike the latter, can evoke the night that will follow, and thus a temporal succession beyond the setting, not to mention (or at least not in detail) the host of uplifting and comforting associations which the 'eternal firmament' once had for the West. The notion that the stars were the abode of the soul after death was, in the eighteenth century, a mere archaism, yet that the sublimity of nature was evidence that the soul was bound for some abode after death was a notion that Deism's rejection of scriptural revelation made especially attractive. Thus Addison:

> What though in solemn silence, all
> Move round this dark terrestrial ball?
> What though nor real voice nor sound
> Amidst their radiant orbs be found?
> In Reason's ear they all rejoice,
> And utter forth a glorious voice,
> Forever singing as they shine:
> 'The hand that made us is divine!'[14]

Kant, as we shall see, did not hold, as a matter of reason at least, that the stars proclaimed any such thing, though he did describe them as one of the two things (the other being the moral law) that 'fill the mind with ever new and increasing admiration and awe, the oftener and more steadily we reflect on them'.[15] It is not, however, necessary, nor would it be justifiable, to follow such passing evocations to the very limits of their sources, for it is not as rational concepts that they operate in the poem. Rather, they are part of the 'multitude of sensations and supplementary representations' that remains beyond the grasp of formulation for one who is enjoying the poem.[16]

There is, likewise, much in the fact that the subject should identify with the sun, that is, with what is both unique and, in a literal sense, super-human, that which will rise tomorrow on the world without us, and which does, indeed, fill that world with its light in the way that the subject hopes to *fill* the world with their benefactions, but it would be churlish, not to say redundant, to spell out what this much might be. What is more interesting is the anthropomorphization of the sun itself, merely prepared for in the thoroughly dead metaphors of *carrière*, *douce*, and *darde*, but fully realized in the last line.

> Et les derniers rayons qu'il darde dans les airs
> Sont les derniers soupirs qu'il donne à l'Univers;

What is striking, and what might be effective, in this final line, is the way that it reverses the basic simile that the preceding lines have established. The dying *philosophe*, says the poem, should be (that is, can be) like the setting sun, yet in the final line it is the sun that, like a dying *philosophe*, bequeaths the world its last sighs (*soupirs*). This is the folding back, or final securing knot, of the aesthetic idea: the image that, in assuming the identity of dying man and setting sun, implicit in the ability to reverse the terms of the simile, should hold in place that idea as an aesthetic one. A mere comparison, exclusively of dying *philosophe* in terms of sun, might very easily, unless it was found completely convincing, allow such an idea to escape. On the other hand, it is only necessary to try to imagine the effect of a poem which set out to say that the setting sun was like a dying *philosophe*, in that it ends without disorder and dies without regrets, to realize how palpably absurd, and unpoetic, the comparison would be if drawn from that direction.

This lack of equivalence does not, however, indicate that there was anything faulty in the structure of the original analogy; analogies, after all, are only supposed to work in one direction, to provide us with the illumination of one situation in terms of another, to express the intangible by the tangible, the obscure by the clear. But, for this reader, it is absurd for the sun to sigh, especially to give precisely that resigned, 'philosophical', sigh that echoes through the late eighteenth century; the sigh of Rousseau's Savoyard priest, of Radcliffe's La Luc, of Clarissa Harlowe resignedly dying of a broken heart, of Kant's hypothetical disappointed philanthropist who has isolated himself from all society, of all those who despair of the world being as reasonable as they are themselves, the sigh of all the eighteenth-century's voluptuaries of 'reason' and regret.[17] Now, if the sun were required to kowtow, or to shrug its shoulders, or to burp appreciatively, it could not more obviously cease to be the sun, than it does by sighing in this all-too-eighteenth-century way. The effect, then, of the final line, is of an unravelling, rather than a securing, of the aesthetic idea that might be inspired by thinking of the dying *philosophe* in terms of the setting sun. (In another poetic context, of course, the image might become more effective by the very same means.) It will not work if the setting sun has to become a dying *philosophe* in order for this to happen.

But it is not because death is just death, and the dying *philosophe* is nothing like the setting sun, that this poem is bad. All that does not matter at all. It is because I cognize the lines as trying, and failing, to say otherwise, that it is bad. It is bad because it insults my intelligence. Not, of course, that it had to gratify my intelligence in order to appear good. If I had thought it good there would have been no question of intelligence or its gratification, rather I would simply have been moved; and if I had sought to analyse it, I would have found it a profound evocation of the transience of life, a brilliant fusion of sound and sense, or something else that could only be expressed by one of the customary non-sequiturs of criticism. But in *appearing* to me as merely an attempt to sway my feelings, I must cognize it as bad. As Kant himself says, 'beautiful art must be *regarded* as nature, although of course one is aware of it as art'.[18] If it had succeeded (unknown to myself) in mollifying my sense of death I would, no doubt, have thought it brilliant. As it is, all I see is the artfulness of its attempt.

This is not, of course, the way in which Kant saw the lines: he saw them, and in particular the simile of the setting sun, as exemplary of 'genius'. They roused in him a host of supplementary impressions, for which he could find no expression, which kindled the basic concept into something poetic. By contrast, it is precisely because I find these supplementary impressions too explicit, that they do not 'animate' the basic concept for me. Moreover, it is because they do not animate the basic concept for me, that I can see the way in which they might supplement the concept for another; for we always identify a taste, as a specific taste, in terms of what we can perceive as its blind spots. (It is these blind spots that we discern in the old as 'characteristic limitations', in the recent as what is 'dated', and in the contemporary as what is merely 'trendy'.) We may, then, suppose Kant to have found the lines exemplary of genius because they allowed him to entertain a quasi-religious sense of death as a transition, coupled, rather paradoxically, with an (almost literally) uplifting stoicism, and a sense of the universe itself both as animated and sympathetic. This is the aesthetic idea expressed by the lines.

It is, moreover, crucial to the form of the aesthetic idea that none of the elements of the idea outlined above are beliefs that Kant would entertain as philosophically meaningful. Apropos religion, he may have regarded the Deity as a 'warranted supposition' (though warranted, as we shall see in the next chapter, only by a contemplation of our own inner nature), but he was certainly conscious of the fatuous aspect of stoicism, that is, precisely that aspect discernible in the poem, and the animation of the universe is a sup-position which he specifically calls 'absurd'.[19] As we saw with the sublime, however, it is one of the essential characteristics of a taste that it is not only an entertaining of certain ideas; it is also a way of *not* entertaining the same ideas as rational concepts. For the beliefs described above are all ones that Kant, or indeed anyone, might have an interest in entertaining: they imply the satis-faction of interest. Yet they are gratifications, or the entertaining of gratifica-tions, which Kant finds he must, intellectually, deny himself.[20] Given that these are the notions evoked by what he calls the 'supplementing' of the basic concept presented in the poem, there is an aptness in his judgement that this supplement is inexpressible, that, in the aesthetic idea, '*understanding*, by means of its concepts, never attains to the complete inner intuition of the imagination which it combines with a given representation'.[21] Were this understanding able, or rather, willing to reduce the intuition to definite con-cepts, the too explicit presence of wishful thinking would preclude any pos-sibility of pleasure.

For, as we are now in a position to see, the crowd of supplementary impres-sions that the subject leaves consciously undeveloped are not, in fact, a sup-plement to the poetry of the lines, rather they are the poetry of the lines: they are what give the lines what Kant perceives as their indefinable suggestiveness, their force. (There may also have been certain personal associations that, for Kant, contributed to this force, but there is no way to recover these.) It is only by interpreting the simile of the sun literally that it is possible to make it sustain an assertion of our triumph over death, yet it is only because the asser-tion is made through a simile that it can exist in the first place. In enjoying the lines, then, Kant must at once take what is said as simultaneously literal and figurative, that is, he must receive the assertion as if it were true, and as if it were not asserted at all. The entertaining of the idea in this way constitutes an aesthetic idea, and it is because it is entertained in this way that it must, necessarily, appear ineffable (not amenable to paraphrase) to the subject. What enables, or rather impels, the subject to entertain such an idea is desire: the desire that what is expressed should be so, coupled with the recognition that either it is not so, or that we cannot be certain that it is so. In short, the pleasure is grounded in what Kant calls a 'fantastic' or 'vain' wish.

Kant provides a far simpler example of the same mechanism at work in a footnote to his treatment of Frederick's poem:

> Perhaps nothing more sublime has ever been said, or any thought more sublimely expressed, than in the inscription over the temple of *Isis* (Mother *Nature*): 'I am all that is, that was, and that will be, and my veil no mortal has removed.'[22]

The ostensible meaning of the words relates, of course, to a topic in which Kant was deeply interested, that is, the extent to which we can know the world. We have seen in Chapter 3 the limits that he fixes, through the concept of the noumenal, to what can conceivably be known. The concept is intended to be employed merely negatively, as a curb to the pretensions of sensibility, and nothing can be positively affirmed about the nature of the noumenal in itself. It is presumably this limit of sensibility that is evoked, for Kant, by the words of Isis. ('Presumably' because there is another way of reading the lines which we shall deal with in a moment.) This idea, then, if properly understood, should not appear so terribly impressive in itself. The words are obviously not, however, simply a statement of the idea, they are, rather, a 'sublime' poetical rendering of it; and, for this reason, we must look at what is conveyed in excess of the literal, must examine the 'supplementary' impressions involved.

The first thing to note is that the evocation of the idea takes the form of words; words, moreover, that are spoken from the *other side* of the limit that is asserted to be the absolute limit of what is knowable. It seems, then, that the basic concept is principally supplemented by an image that runs counter to what is cognized in that concept: by an implicit denial of its truth. The unknowable is that about which we can assert nothing, and yet here it is; 'it' addresses words (with distinct Judaeo-Christian overtones) to us, it has a veiled (that is, potentially unveiled) face, and the face itself is other than mortal (divine).[23] This 'denial' is hardly one that can be cognized as such in the context of the assertion of the basic concept, and yet it is only in the form of this 'denial' that the basic concept is given. The resulting paradox, instead of unravelling into a contradiction in terms (cognized either as irony or nonsense), is allowed, by the suitably impressed subject, to hold in place both assertions – that there is an absolutely unknowable, and that it is potentially an object of knowledge. As with the sublime in general, and the image of the setting sun, it is the idea of the satisfaction of a desire for transcendence, cognized as impossible, yet, at the same time, too desirable to completely relinquish, that is entertained by the subject in finding the words of Isis beautiful or sublime.

By a happy chance Kant himself returned to this most sublime image of Isis in a piece, published six years later, intended as an attack on philosophers who claim, and promise, 'the presentiment (*praevisio sensitiva*) of that which is absolutely not an object of the senses: that is, the *intimation* of the supersensible'.[24] Kant pours scorn on this 'Platonizing philosophy of feeling' that claims that, though it 'cannot lift up the veil of Isis', it can, nevertheless, 'make it so thin that one can *intimate* the goddess under this veil'.[25] In a gesture of conciliation towards such philosophers he suggests, towards the end of the essay, that in fact his veiled goddess, 'before whom we both parties bend our knees', is in fact the moral law.[26] He nevertheless warns against the dangers of substituting figurative language for clear concepts:

[The] procedure whereby the law is personified and reason's moral bidding is made into a veiled Isis (even if we attribute to her no other properties than those discovered according to [a logical methodology]), is an *aesthetic* mode of representing precisely the same object; one can doubtless use this mode of representation backward, after the first [logical] procedure has already purified the principles, in order to enliven those ideas by a sensible, albeit only analogical, presentation, and yet one always runs the danger of falling into an exalting vision, which is the death of all philosophy.[27]

The danger arises, of course, because such an exalting vision is tempting. The sublime (and, indeed, the aesthetic in general) is a means of giving way to this temptation without involving the intellect in self-immolation.

I mentioned above that there was another way of reading the words, yet this reading, though it finds some support in the context in which Kant quotes the words, strikes me as so much less impressive than that which renders Isis as a personification of the noumenon, that I prefer to give it a subordinate position in this account. For the lines can also be read as an invocation of the division not between the knowable and the unknowable, but simply between the known and the unknown within science. The rest of Kant's footnote runs as follows:

Segner made use of this idea [that is, the inscription from the temple of Isis] by means of a vignette, *rich in sense*, placed at the beginning of his theory of nature, in order at the outset to fill his pupils, whom he was ready to lead into this temple, with the holy fear that should dispose the mind to solemn attentiveness. [28]

We are talking here, let us note, not about a work on metaphysics or theology, but plain old physics.[29] To invoke the division between the known and the simply not yet known, by a suggestion of divine mystery, strikes me as ludicrous, and whereas I find in myself sufficient sympathy for the previous reading to render the image, in certain moods, impressive, I baulk at ascribing to Kant the naivety, even unconsciously entertained, that this second reading requires. As with the example of Frederick's poem, however, this reading does square with the spirit of the age; specifically with its quasi-religious sense of science.

In a writer who held that to discover the secrets of nature was, at the same time, to uncover the design discernible in creation, the image of the pupil entering the 'temple' of science with 'holy fear' would be, in the context at least, justifiable. But Kant is not such a writer. Indeed, the metaphor of the temple and its inscription is explicitly posited by Kant as merely analogous, that is, as disposable in terms of the meaning intended, when he says that its function is rhetorical: it serves to dispose the pupil's mind to 'solemn attentiveness'. That the metaphor should work, however, that is, that it should impress (be aesthetic) rather than being simply cognized as a contradiction in terms (as nonsense), does depend on the partial impressions aroused answering the subject's desire.

Moreover, even a reading of the lines which took them as a reference merely to the division between the known and the unknown would ultimately only find them impressive insofar as that reading was grounded in the first reading given above: that the words refer to the division between the knowable and the unknowable. It is often remarked that particular solutions to problems in science and mathematics do indeed, on occasion, appear beautiful or sublime. The frontispiece to Segner's book may illuminate why this is so: for when what seemed impossible, or unknowable, suddenly becomes possible, or known, it can, by virtue of this fact, for a brief time at least, allow the particular instance of knowing to be symbolic of absolute knowledge, the particular capability to be symbolic of absolute potency. It is because, however, this symbolizing depends upon the experience of *feeling* the previous, apparently insuperable, ignorance or impossibility, that the achievements of science and technology, even when they are not surpassed, invariably become, as objects of taste, dated. Though art, too, may become dated, such a process is not inevitable; for, providing we have some blind spots in common with the age in which it was produced, we will cognize it as being, at least in some aspects, 'of timeless value'.

Having dealt with the aesthetic idea in an example of dependent beauty we must now look at the more problematic question of how free beauty may be grounded in such an idea. Before doing so, however, we shall turn to Kant's discussion of rhetoric, not only for its direct relevance to the subject of this chapter, but also for the light it throws on Kant's assertion that art, to fulfil for us the function of art, must appear as if it were nature.

POETRY AND RHETORIC

In the preceding argument much has turned upon the relationship between poetry and rhetoric. Since, as we have seen, the 'supplementary' impressions involved in the aesthetic idea function rhetorically to *allow* us to entertain a notion that intellectually we cannot, it is not surprising that where we are aware of the work attempting to do this we should cognize it as directly rhetorical, that is, as an attempt to *persuade* us to entertain the notion involved. Kant himself deals with the relationship between the poetic and the rhetorical in dealing with the division of the fine arts:

> The arts of *speech* are *rhetoric* and *poetry*. *Rhetoric* is the art of conducting a business of the understanding as a free play of the imagination; *poetry* that of carrying out a free play of the imagination as a business of the under-standing. The *orator* thus announces a matter of business and carries it out as if it were merely a *play* with ideas in order to entertain the audience. The *poet* announces merely an entertaining *play* with ideas, and yet as much results for the understanding as if he had merely had the intention of carry-ing on its business.[30]

Yet, though Kant makes poetry and rhetoric mirror images of one another, he considers the inversion involved to produce a corresponding reversal in merit. For while he holds, as we have seen, that poetry is first among the arts, his estimate of rhetoric is much closer to that made in our own time than to eighteenth-century orthodoxy. Rhetoric, he writes, is the 'art of . . . deceiving by means of beautiful illusion', that is, in effect, the art of depriving the subject of their freedom to arrive at a just verdict on the question in hand.[31] Even when it is employed for praiseworthy ends, then, rhetoric is still reprehensible, according to Kant, since it necessarily entails an abatement of the subject's freedom: '[For] it is not enough to do what is right, but it is also to be performed solely on the grounds that it is right.'[32]

Kant's disapproval is not, however, merely a theoretical one – it is also a matter of taste. In a footnote that serves as a conclusion to the discussion of the relative merits of poetry and rhetoric he reports his own, for the time, rather unusual feelings in the matter:

> I must confess that a beautiful poem has always given me a pure enjoyment, whereas reading the best speech of a Roman popular speaker or a contemporary speaker in parliament or the pulpit has always been mixed with the disagreeable feeling of disapproval of a deceitful art, which understands how to move people, like machines, to a judgement in important matters which must lose all weight for them in calm reflection. Eloquence and well-spokenness (together, rhetoric) belong to beautiful art; but the art of the orator (*ars oratoria*), as the art of using the weakness of people for one's own purposes (however well intentioned or even really good these may be) is not worthy of any *respect* at all.[33]

In the case of rhetoric, then, art cannot, for Kant at least, take on the aspect of nature because he finds that he can never completely free himself of the consciousness of the practicality of its occasion, that is, its intentionality. Yet, as we saw in the last chapter, so ubiquitous was the elevated rhetorical mode at this time that Kant himself resorts to it even in his discussion of that most weighty of subjects: the moral law.[34] Indeed, as Kant must have been aware, the sublime, since its revival at the beginning of the century, had been discussed in terms of rhetoric. Even those outside of the Longinian tradition (which treated the sublime principally as a rhetorical figure rather than an attribute of, or response to, objects) tended to take over their descriptions of the effect of the sublime from that tradition. Burke, for example, whose discussion of the influence of words on the passions is, to a great extent, the model of Kant's treatment of the subject here, describes how in sublimity the mind is 'so entirely filled with its object, that it cannot entertain any other, nor by consequence reason on that object which employs it', so that the sublime 'hurries us on by an irresistible force'.[35] Something of this moral ambivalence in sublimity can, indeed, be found in Kant's own treatment of the relationship between the moral and the sublime, in, for example, his discussion of the potential sublimity of passions.

Kant's objection to rhetoric is that sensibility and understanding cannot be united without 'constraint and mutual harm'.[36] Yet this union is common to both rhetoric and poetry. How, then, does poetry, which is also a matter of 'semblance' and 'force', escape the strictures he applies to rhetoric? Poetry, he asserts, 'plays with the illusion which it produces at will, yet without [in contrast to rhetoric] thereby being deceitful; for it itself declares its occupation to be mere play'.[37] This 'play', however, is one that, according to Kant, understanding may employ 'for its own business'.[38] Thus while the orator fails to come up to his promise to engage the understanding in 'purposive occupation', the poet, by contrast, though he appears to offer merely a play with ideas, 'accomplishes something that is worthy of business, namely providing nourishment to the understanding in play'.[39]

Strangely, then, poetry is acquitted of being deceptive, after the manner of rhetoric, on the grounds of appearance, that is, of semblance. In a passage reminiscent of Sidney's defence of poetry against the charge of falsehood – that the poet 'nothing affirms and therefore never lieth' – Kant asserts that

> In poetry [in contrast to rhetoric], everything proceeds honestly and uprightly. It declares that it will conduct a merely entertaining play with the imagination, and indeed concerning form, in concord with the laws of the understanding, and does not demand that the understanding be deceived and embroiled through sensible presentation.[40]

Yet Kant himself has said that poetry provides 'nourishment to the understanding', that it performs more than it promises. Moreover, far from being above board it is, in Kant's own description, even less direct than the oratory he criticizes, for, as he says, the combination of understanding and sensibility in poetry 'must *seem* to be unintentional'.[41] It could be argued that at least when faced with a lawyer, or a politician, or a preacher, we know what to expect, whereas poetry engages the understanding without even announcing that it will do so. Considered in this way poetry would appear to be potentially the most insidiously rhetorical form of discourse. (Hence perhaps those 'misunderstandings' of art: from such mild eccentricity as confusing actors with the characters they play, to the outright derangement of believing that literary criticism can be an act of moral or political engagement.) How is this to be squared with the common opinion, affirmed by Kant, that fine art is 'free', in the sense that 'while the mind is certainly occupied, it must feel itself to be satisfied and stimulated (independently of remuneration) without looking beyond to another end'?[42] This question of satisfaction independent of reward is, of course, the central concern of the present work, and we have already seen what may constitute such a satisfaction. The form of this satisfaction, as hitherto described, reconciles the antinomy in Kant's thesis, though hardly in a way that would satisfy Kant.

In dealing with the fragment of Frederick's poetry we saw how, in enjoying art, we must receive what is asserted both as if it were true, and as if it were not asserted at all. It is the entertaining of the idea in this way that constitutes an aesthetic idea, and it is because it is entertained in this way that it must, necessarily, appear ineffable to the subject, in the sense that no paraphrase can exhaust what it 'communicates'. What prompts the subject to entertain such an idea is desire: the desire that what is expressed should be so, coupled with the recognition that either it is not so, or that we cannot be certain that it is so. Yet the fact that in poetry we allow ourselves to entertain what we would reject intellectually will not, in itself, serve to distinguish poetry from rhetoric; 'being persuaded' to hold a notion, and 'allowing oneself' to entertain a notion are hardly, from the point of view of the outcome, distinct actions.

It would be convenient if we were able to distinguish poetry and rhetoric in terms of a difference in the kind of ideas they respectively deal with. But though there is obviously some difference here – rhetoric is often concerned with the issues of the hour, poetry often with the more enduring verities, the concerns of rhetoric are local, those of poetry universal – we would have to be very selective in our examples of the two to ultimately justify such a distinction. Moreover, was not the problem with Frederick's poem that it turned out to be 'too much of its time'? Yet it was fine art for Kant. We might still distinguish poetry and rhetoric on the grounds that rhetoric is always an incitement to action, while poetry inspires no more than reverie, that rhetoric deals with the inculcation of *beliefs*, while poetry merely invites us to assume certain *moods*. Again, not only will this distinction not cover every case that might be advanced, but the difference between a general orientation and a specific action, a mood and a belief, is merely one of relative diffusiveness.

There is, however, some truth in both of the previous two proposed grounds of distinction: that the concerns of poetry are very unlikely to be 'local', and, for connected reasons, that poetry deals more in moods than specific beliefs. Moreover one can hardly carry on indefinitely implying the identity of two modes of discourse when the very terms in which one does so presuppose that they are in some way separate. Though I was prepared to suspend the distinction when faced with the lines by Frederick, it does not mean that I did not cognize those lines as poetry. They are intended to be poetry, and so that is what they are. Failed poetry is rhetoric, but it is no less poetry for that; it is merely poetry with the mechanism showing. The desire that it appeals to is directly cognized as desire, and the means by which it seeks to satisfy/persuade are directly cognized as persuasive. Hence the fact that there is almost no way, aside from the supposition of dullness, in which one can describe the badness of a work of art that is not, at the same time, implicitly a description of why somebody else would think it was good.

By contrast, when we enjoy a poem we do not, indeed cannot, cognize it as rhetorical, since we cannot be conscious of our grounds for entertaining an aesthetic idea. Good poetry is not amenable to exhaustive interpretation because good poetry is rhetoric that has not failed. (With the added proviso, of course, that it appear intended as poetry, in the sense of occupying a space analogous to the space occupied by what has hitherto been called 'poetry'.[43]) The distinction between good and bad poetry here – the former being rhetoric that conceals itself, the latter being merely rhetoric – is obviously not a description of the inherent properties of either considered separately from the perception of a particular subject: it is, rather, a matter of taste. To have no taste for a thing is either to be entirely deaf to its rhetorical appeal (in which case it will appear merely boring or aesthetically redundant), or to find that appeal too overt (as was my own experience with Frederick's poetry); conversely, to have a taste for a thing is to have a strong desire to entertain the impossibility it expresses – a desire strong enough to allow it to express the possibility of that impossibility.[44]

8

Fantastic Desires II: Free Beauty

It is Kant's contention that dependent beauty does not present us with a 'pure' example of the judgement of taste. Given that he has begun by defining judgements of taste in terms of their freedom from any dependence on concepts, either of use or perfection, this assertion of the impurity of dependent beauty seems justified. However, while concepts are involved in dependent beauty, nevertheless, they are not (and, for reasons we have seen, *cannot* be) cognized as playing an absolutely determining role in the judgement. It is this apparently *ultimate* lack of determination that justifies Kant's identifying such judgements, along with judgements on free beauty, as judgements of taste.

The word 'pure', like 'higher' and 'natural', is almost always dubious in a philosophical context. Nevertheless, it is Kant's free beauty that, in appearance at least, conforms immediately, and without qualification, to the fundamental definition of 'taste' he gives at the beginning of the *Critique*. For this very reason, however, it is the more puzzling of the two basic expressions of taste he posits. In dependent beauty, as we have seen, we are conscious of an ability to refer our judgement to some concept of the object, even to the extent of being able to classify the kind of concept involved, and to argue plausibly, though not decisively, about the merit of the object in relation to others in which we discern a similar conceptual element. Free beauty, by contrast, is, according to Kant, 'self-subsisting': the object we attribute it to is cognized as devoid of intrinsic meaning, representative of nothing, and the judgement itself appears as a bare reflection upon a given intuition.[1] This is not, of course, to say that things are free beauties in themselves: anything may be cognized either in terms of a definite concept of usefulness, goodness, or agreeableness, or, indeed, as symbolic, and, therefore, dependently beautiful. Conversely even an object that possesses a definite internal end can be judged as a free beauty providing, as Kant says, 'the person making the judgement either had no concept of this end or abstracted from it in his judgement'.[2] Both the beauty, and its freedom or dependence, then, depend not on the properties of the object, but rather on the way in which the representation of the object is, on any particular occasion, cognized by the subject.

It would seem impossible, therefore, to give an example of a free beauty in itself, since, despite Kant's provision of a list of free and dependent beauties, the distinction he is drawing is, in effect, not a distinction between different kinds of objects, but rather between different orientations of the subject: it depends on whether or not the subject refers, or is conscious of referring, the beauty to a concept (albeit in the form of an aesthetic idea) of the object. The flower, for instance, which at one point Kant uses as exemplary of free beauty, is only such in a particular subject's particular cognizance of a particular flower. I could not take you now and show you a 'beautiful flower', not only because you might not find the last one I saw beautiful, but also because I cannot be certain that I will now find it so myself. The example of flowers in the abstract would, moreover, serve equally well to illustrate dependent beauty, since there are numerous aesthetic merits a flower may potentially possess aside from beauty: it may be restful, gay, pathetic, companionable, grotesque, comic, decorative (as part of a larger form), moving (in the context of a human action – though it is the flower itself which is perceived as moving). In addition, though in some instances, as, for example, in many uses of the word 'flower' in a literary context, an invocation of free beauty is part of the effect, in many other instances the flower may assume a symbolic function, that is, may *embody* the aesthetic idea, irrespective of any reference to a cognizance of free beauty.[3]

What is required here, then, is an example not of free beauty in itself, since, even strictly following Kant's stipulative definition, it is something that cannot be exemplified, but rather a specific example of somebody's cognizance of a free beauty. Given, however, that it is part of the definition of free beauty that it should appear self-subsisting, that the subject should be conscious of entertaining no concept in connection with the object, and, therefore, should have no inkling of the grounds of the judgement over and above a cognizance of the limits of the object to which the beauty is ascribed, even a particular judgement must still leave us merely with an object in itself. What is further required, then, though the requirement would seem self-contradictory, is an example of a subject's cognizance of free beauty that yet, in some way, did involve an inkling of the determining conditions of the particular judgement.

THE MISTAKE

Despite the apparent impossibility of finding an example that would fulfil these requirements, we have actually encountered just such a situation in the instance, already mentioned in Chapter 2, of Kant's feelings about the bird's song:

> Even the song of the bird, which we cannot bring under any musical rules, seems to contain more freedom and thus more that is entertaining for taste than even a human song that is performed in accordance with all the rules of the art of music: for one grows tired of the latter far more quickly if it is repeated often and for a long time. But here we may well confuse our sym-

pathy with the merriment of a beloved little creature with the beauty of his song, which, when it is exactly imitated by a human being (as is sometimes done with the notes of the nightingale) strikes our ear as utterly tasteless. . . . [There] have been examples in which . . . some jolly landlord has tricked the guests staying with him, to their complete satisfaction, by hiding in a bush a mischievous lad who knew how to imitate this song (with a reed or a pipe in his mouth) just like nature. But as soon as one becomes aware that it is a trick, no one would long endure listening to this song, previously taken to be so charming . . .[4]

The case is, of course, only hypothetical: Kant imagines a bird's song, and imagines the effect of discovering that what he heard was artificially produced. We may, however, allow that Kant advances the example in good faith. Certainly there is nothing in the instance that serves his theoretical purposes at this point (the very end of the 'Analytic of the Beautiful'). On the contrary, in the context, the concession that the song, if reproduced, would not be beautiful, introduces a difficulty which, in the event, he chooses to pass over by half-suggesting that perhaps it was only a 'confusion' that led him to believe the bird's song was a suitable example of free beauty in the first place.

Moreover, to describe the instance as 'merely' hypothetical would be misleading. For the remembered song must sufficiently evoke beauty for him to light on it as exemplary of beauty, while the very idea of the artificial imitation is sufficient to check his sense of the beauty of the imagined sound. (Whether or not the effect would be the same for anyone else is irrelevant, since it is a particular judgement that is required here.[5]) Even if, however, we wanted to argue that Kant has no proof that he would not find a perfect imitation of bird's song beautiful, we may justify his supposition from our own experience: it is relatively easy to discover, on reflection, analogous situations, where what seemed, if not accidental, then, at least, inessential, to the beauty of an object, that is, not actually part of that object *qua* beautiful object, was revealed, by the passage of time, or, what is really the same thing, a change of context, to be essential: the beauty no longer existed without this 'inessential' component. For, it must be noted, it is the song, and not the bird singing that Kant originally cognizes as the beautiful object.

Alison, whose *Essays on the Nature and Principles of Taste* was published in the same year as the *Critique of Aesthetic Judgement*, advances numerous instances of just such a phenomenon as Kant describes – how the revelation of the artificial provenance of what was perceived as a natural sound affects our judgement of that sound – as evidence for the central contention of his work: that beauty and sublimity depend upon association.

That the beauty of such sounds arises from the qualities of which they are expressive, and not from any original fitness in them to produce this emotion, may perhaps be evident from the following considerations: 1. To those who have no such associations, or who consider them simply as sounds, they have no beauty. . . . 2. It is further observable, that such sounds are beautiful only in particular tempers of mind, or when we are under the influence of such emotions as accord with the expressions which they possess. If, on the contrary, such sounds were beautiful in themselves, although in different states of mind, we might afford them different degrees of attention; yet in all situations they would be beautiful, in the same manner as in every state of mind the objects of all other senses uniformly produce their correspondent ideas. . . . 3. When such associations are dissolved, the sounds themselves cease to be beautiful. If a man of the most common taste were carried into any striking scene of an ornamented garden, and placed within the hearing of a cascade, and were told, in the midst of his enthusiasm, that what he takes for a cascade is only a deception, the sound continues the same, but the beauty of it would be irrevocably gone.[6]

With regard to bird's song itself he proposes the following explanation of the significance that makes it beautiful:

1st, Such notes approach much nearer than any other, to the tones of the human voice, and are therefore much more strongly expressive to us of such qualities as we are affected by. 2dly, These animals are much more than any other the objects of our interest and regard; not only from our greater acquaintance with them, and from the minuteness and delicacy of their forms, which renders them in some measure the objects of tenderness; but chiefly from their modes of life, and from the little domestic arrangements and attachments which we observe among them so much more strongly than among any other animals, and which indicate more affecting and endearing qualities in the animals themselves, than in any others we know. That we have such associations with birds is very obvious, from the use which is made of their instincts and manner of life, in the poetical compositions of all nations.[7]

Kant's 'sympathy with the merriment of a beloved little creature' indeed!

One last point that might be put forward to justify using Kant's original contention (despite his tentative reservations) that the example is one of free beauty is the distinction that he makes between free and dependent beauty in terms of nature/art. He does not, as we have seen, justify such a division theoretically, but we should, nevertheless, note that this is, at least, how the matter struck him. He is presumably voicing his own feelings when he declares that 'nature . . . subject to no coercion from artificial rules' provides 'lasting nourishment' to taste, and that it is only what is natural, or 'taken to be nature', that can arouse an immediate interest in its beauty.[8] The fact that he retrospectively throws doubt on how immediate this interest was in the case of the bird's song, that is, that he concedes, in the light of what the imitation reveals to him, that he may have 'confused' a feeling of sympathy (and, therefore, perhaps, a judgement on either the merely charming or on dependent beauty) with a judgement on free beauty, is, indeed, rather a reason for pursuing the example than otherwise. For if we agree that, since the judgement on the sound turned out to be, at least vaguely, determined by a concept (a bird singing), it cannot really have been a judgement on free beauty, this still leaves us with the interesting question of how such a confusion is possible, that is, how a judgement can be cognized as a judgement on free beauty without actually being one. For, as we have seen, a judgement on free beauty is only such insofar as it appears to be such to the subject.

There are, then, apparently three possible interpretations we can give to the instance.

1. Kant felt he was experiencing a free beauty, though, in fact, what he was experiencing was 'sympathy with the merriment of a beloved little creature', or at least some other kind of pleasure, possibly in the form of a dependent beauty.
2. Kant was experiencing free beauty, but, though he was unconscious of the fact, this free beauty depended upon a concept of the object.
3. Kant was experiencing free beauty, but he misattributed that beauty to the form of the sound of the song rather than the bird's singing of it.

It might be most tempting, in the light of these alternatives, to declare that what Kant experienced was in fact dependent beauty, though he was unaware of the fact. This solution would account even for interpretation 3, since there is, as we have seen, considerable space for vagueness in the cognition of the grounds of the pleasure in any particular instance of dependent beauty: a vagueness that can easily lead us, in attempting to account for that beauty, to light on, as significant, irrelevant formulations of the object itself.[9] On the basis of this supposition we might also solve the problem of free beauty, by asserting that, in fact, it is always no more than 'confused' dependent beauty. This last, however, is out of the question, since, as we have seen, the distinguishing characteristic of dependent beauty is the subject's awareness of dependence, and this kind of awareness is conspicuously lacking from all three possibilities.

Circumstances may force upon Kant the knowledge that his judgement on the sound was in some way dependent on a concept, but this is quite a different matter from this dependence being cognized in the experience of the beauty itself. Likewise, the feeling that one is experiencing free beauty is, by definition, an indistinguishable phenomenon from actually experiencing free beauty. (Though, of course, Kant's requirement that the sufficient conditions of a judgement of taste include a legitimate claim to universal validity means that, for him, even though they are empirically indistinguishable, they nevertheless *cannot* be the same phenomenon.) Even, then, if we concede that free beauty may be dependent upon concepts this does not justify our abandoning the distinction between free and dependent beauty, since this distinction, though it appears to be an assertion concerning the grounds of the two judgements, actually can only be, in practice, a reflection of the way in which the subject cognizes the experience of the two kinds of judgement.[10]

It is not, then, possible to formulate the first of the three interpretations of the instance in the way that it is formulated above – 'Kant felt he was experiencing a free beauty, though, in fact, what he was experiencing was something else'. Rather we would have to say that whatever this 'something else' was it was a determining factor in what was, nevertheless, an experience of free beauty. This would appear to leave us with one of two possibilities: that the experience of free beauty was, unconsciously, determined by a concept, or that what was involved was a simple misattribution of the beauty to the sound of the song rather than to the bird's singing of it. This second possibility, however, will not do in this form, for whatever kind of misattribution may be involved it is not a 'simple' one. Such a misattribution in itself implies the presence of a concept: the concept, made conspicuous by the discovery that it is erroneous, that this object (the sound) is the cause of what appears to be a 'bare reflection on a given intuition'.

Whichever way we interpret the instance, then, the fact remains that being natural, that is, being produced by a bird, is a determining condition of Kant's judgement on an object (the sound) which he, nevertheless, cognized as a free beauty, that is, a beauty which appears undetermined by any concept. Moreover, as we saw in Chapter 2, it is not possible to posit that while the ostensible free beauty is, in fact, dependent, it may nevertheless, in some way, ultimately rest on a genuinely 'free' beauty. We cannot, for example, say that although the form of the sound itself is not a free beauty, nevertheless, the idea of the bird's singing of it is a free beauty, or, if it turned out that this apparently free beauty was, in fact, in some way, conceptually determined, simply again postpone what we designated as the free beauty of the 'bird's song'. Aside from the general unsatisfactoriness of accounting for free beauty in terms of free beauty, there are two further problems: not only would this leave unexplained why it was the sound itself that was cognized as a free beauty, but it would also entail us ascribing beauty to some object, or context as object, which the subject did not even cognize as an object, let alone an object of beauty. We would then, confusingly, be using 'beauty' to describe both cause and effect. (In the case of dependent beauty, as we have seen, though it is possible to give the grounds which render the object beautiful – providing it is not beautiful for oneself – there is no question of these grounds themselves, if they could be cognized as grounds, appearing beautiful even to the subject who makes the judgement.)

There can be no doubt that what Kant cognized as a judgement on free beauty was, in fact, determined. It now remains to discover both how it was determined, and why it was not cognized as determined. Before doing so, however, we shall turn to the way in which Kant himself attempts to deal with the problem that the instance of the bird's song creates.

KANT'S TREATMENT OF THE MISTAKE

Kant responds to the discovery that the apparently free judgement on the form of the sound of the bird was, in fact, determined by conjecturing that he was mistaken in believing his original judgement was of free beauty. This is in the 'General Remark', succeeding §22, and concluding the 'Analytic of the Beautiful'. In §42, that is, in the 'Deduction of Pure Aesthetic Judgements' that succeeds his treatment of the sublime, there is, however, another reference to the same phenomenon that appears to account for it in quite a different way. His purpose in this later section, perhaps as a response to what he has deduced from his analysis of the sublime, is to find to what extent we may be justified in asserting, as did many people at the time, a necessary connection between a '*feeling* for beautiful nature', or even beauty in general, and a 'good moral disposition'.[11] Kant himself maintains that 'to take an *immediate interest* in the beauty of *nature* (not merely to have a taste in order to judge it) is always a mark of a good soul'.[12] This question is not, in itself, however, our main concern here; for it is only the expression 'immediate interest', and the implied distinction from some other kind of interest, that is directly relevant to the problem that the instance of the bird's song presents.

In order to demonstrate what he means by 'immediate interest' Kant asks us to imagine a man who has taste enough to judge fine art yet who nevertheless prefers nature, where he finds 'an ecstasy for his spirit in a line of thought that he can never fully develop'.[13] In point of taste we cannot say that any one taste is superior to another, yet nature, according to Kant, is more attractive than art because there is an additional, intellectual, interest in nature:

> Someone who . . . considers the beautiful shape of a wildflower, a bird, an insect, etc., in order to marvel at it, to love it, and to be unwilling for it to be entirely absent from nature, even though some harm might come to him from it rather than there being any prospect of advantage to him from it, takes an immediate and certainly intellectual interest in the beauty of nature. I.e., not only the form of its product but also its existence pleases him, even though no sensory charm has a part of this and he does not combine any sort of end with it.[14]

This is not, of course, to say that the judgement of taste in itself is cognized as being anything other than indifferent to the real existence of the object (it could not be a judgement of taste otherwise), but rather that the beauty of the natural forms 'arouses' an interest in their real existence.

Finding an object beautiful and having an interest in that object are not, of course, incompatible states of mind. In this case, according to Kant, the very autonomy of beauty is responsible for the interest:

> [Since] it . . . interests reason that the ideas (for which it produces an immediate interest in the moral feeling) also have objective reality, i.e. that nature should at least show some trace or give a sign that it contains in itself some sort of ground for assuming a lawful correspondence of its products with our satisfaction that is independent of all interest (which we recognize *a priori* as a law valid for everyone, without being able to ground this on proofs), reason must take an interest in every manifestation in nature of a correspondence similar to this; consequently the mind cannot reflect on the beauty of *nature* without finding itself at the same time to be interested in it.[15]

It is in this way, according to Kant, that nature 'figuratively speaks to us in its beautiful forms'.[16] Because, then, the beauty does not depend on the interest, there is no question of the frustration of this interest – the discovery that we have mistaken the provenance of the object – reacting on the beauty itself. In the present context, then, though Kant gives a situation analogous to that of the bird's song – the subject suddenly discovers that the flowers and birds he has been taking an intellectual interest in are artificial – the outcome is nevertheless different:

> The thought that nature has produced that beauty must accompany the intuition and reflection, and on this alone is grounded the immediate interest that one takes in it. Otherwise there remains either a mere judgement of taste, without any interest, or only one combined with a mediate interest, namely one related to society [that is, we may consider how these things could decorate our room for the eyes of others] . . . [17]

In the present instance Kant specifies that the original judgement is made on the bare form of the object, whereas in the previous instance he conjectured that the judgement, though it appeared to be on the bare form, must, in fact, have been on the charm of the idea of the object.

Indeed, in order to isolate precisely what constitutes an 'immediate interest in the beauty of nature', Kant contrasts it to both an interest in the beautiful in art (including the use of nature for the purposes of art) and a feeling for the 'charms' of nature. It is, according to Kant, impossible for art to arouse the interest of reason, that is, to answer the desire for an objective reality beyond us that, nevertheless, defers, as it were, to our taste. It is impossible because to defer to our taste is precisely the avowed purpose of art. In art, he asserts, we can see (unless it deceives us into believing it is nature) that it is 'intentionally directed toward our satisfaction'.[18] (Moreover, it remains, contra-Romanticism, entirely within the sphere of human intention.) In both nature and art, then, though the satisfaction is immediate, that is, belongs to taste, in the latter case the interest in the 'cause that lay beneath' would only be mediate interest, that is, aroused by the effect of the cause and therefore not an interest in the existence of that cause itself. It is for this reason, as we saw in Chapter 2, that art appears, theoretically at least, to be confined exclusively to the sphere of dependent beauty. (Kant does say that in 'genius', 'the faculty of *aesthetic ideas*', it is nature rather than a particular set purpose that gives the rule to art.[19] This 'nature' is, however, human nature, which, though, as Kant says, it cannot be comprehended under rules or concepts, cannot ultimately be credited with the production of the superhuman. However, as I have said elsewhere, where the 'rules' of the art are, from a conceptual point of view, arbitrary – as with music – the beauty is potentially as 'free' as if it were produced by nature. This may be the point that Kant is making with the list of free beauties discussed in Chapter 2 above.)

The charm of nature, too, seems to take the form, in Kant's account of it here, of dependent beauty.[20] For nature is charming, according to Kant, when it interests us because we link its objects to moral ideas.[21] It is in discussing such links that he returns to the case of the bird's song that suddenly ceases to be beautiful with the discovery that it is not being produced by a bird. Such charms which, he says, are frequently to be found 'as it were melted together with the beautiful form', are yet distinct from such beauty insofar as they are the result of our 'interpreting' nature as symbolic: our sensations 'as it were contain a language that nature brings to us that seems to have a higher meaning'.[22] So, for example, a bird's song appears to the subject as an expression of the bird's joyousness and contentment with existence.[23] (Beauty of form, by contrast, is here simply beauty of form.) It is the interest aroused by this kind of 'beauty' which he asserts is absolutely determined by our belief that the object we attribute it to really is natural: 'It disappears entirely as soon as one notices that one has been deceived and that it is only art, so much so that even taste can no longer find anything beautiful in it.'[24] This he illustrates with the account, quoted above, of the trick played by the host upon his guests.

It is immediately after giving this illustration that Kant asserts that a thing 'must be nature, or taken to be nature by us, for us to be able to take . . . an immediate *interest* in the beautiful'.[25] The placing of this generalization appears, at first sight, odd, since Kant's discussion of the charm (expressiveness) of nature seemed to be advanced here with the purpose of establishing that our interest in such charm was, in contrast to our interest in the beautiful bare forms of nature, *not* immediate. At the beginning of §42 he explicitly states that, in considering intellectual interest in the beautiful, he means to refer 'strictly [to] the beautiful *forms* of nature, and by contrast [to] set to one side the *charms* that it usually combines so abundantly with them, since the interest in them is to be sure also immediate, but nevertheless empirical'.[26] Nevertheless he has left open the possibility that the charms of nature could arouse immediate interest, not as charms, but as the beauty that qualifies them to be charms. For in distinguishing between the beauty of art and the charm of nature, he writes, apropos the fact that we can only be interested in the grounds of art as means rather than ends in themselves:

> One will perhaps say that this is also the case if an object of nature interests us through its beauty only insofar as a moral idea is associated with it [that is, insofar as it is charming]; but it is not this, but rather the quality inherent in it by means of which it qualifies for such an association, which thus pertains to it internally, that interests immediately.[27]

This is consistent enough, but it is noteworthy that, rather than simply justifying the contrast between the charms of nature, as Kant conceives them in connection with the bird's song (not itself beautiful), the above passage actually introduces a third kind of judgement into the discussion: charms of nature which are only charming by virtue of their beauty. Such a judgement, then, would involve, 'as it were melted', both an immediate interest in the beautiful bare form of nature, and a mediate interest inspired by the charm (expressiveness) of this beauty.

The preceding may perhaps explain why Kant makes his general remark about immediate interest in the context of the discussion of charm, though it does not, of course, justify his making it in connection with the particular example of the bird's song. For if the charm of the bird's song depends upon its essential beauty there is no reason why that beauty itself should disappear, as Kant says it does, with the discovery that the 'song' is artificially produced. A change in the provenance of the object should have two effects: first, insofar as the object is a bare beauty, the cessation of our immediate interest in the existence of that beauty, and second, insofar as the object is charming, a cessation of that charm. This should, of course, still leave us with a residue of beauty, that is, that form which was responsible for the charm (the expressiveness of the object). Yet this is not what happens with the case of the bird's song. This would seem to indicate that the remark about immediate interest was indeed misplaced. There are a number of rather tangled variables involved here, and the below table lays them out in some sort of provisional pattern.

Two things should be clear from these distinctions: first, that, as Kant's reference to the loss of 'beauty' in the case of the bird's song indicates, if we are to make sense of the distinction between charm and beauty here we must do so in terms of the former being dependent beauty, and the latter free. Second, it should become clear that the fundamental condition that beauty must fulfil in order to arouse an intellectual interest is that it should be free, that is, what he calls elsewhere 'self-subsisting' beauty. For although he talks of the bare forms of nature inspiring 'an ecstasy for [the] spirit in a line of thought that [we] can never fully develop', this is yet not identifiable with the aesthetic idea, which it so obviously echoes, for it is not, according to Kant,

Type	Ground	Interest in existence of	Result of change in provenance
art	idea expressed	mediate because know it is intended	not given
natural form	form itself (i.e. beauty)	immediate because of interests of reason (in beauty itself)	loss of interest though not beauty
charm of nature	idea expressed	mediate because expressive of moral ideas	loss of interest and 'beauty'
charm and beauty of nature	idea expressed by its beauty	mediate insofar as it is charm; immediate insofar as it is beauty	loss of interest and charm; effect on beauty not given

part of the cognizance of the beauty itself, but rather of the interest which that beauty arouses.

Though §42 is obviously concerned with establishing the nature of our 'intellectual interest' in the free beauty of nature, the way in which Kant here seeks to define that free beauty, by contrasting it with the charm of nature, demonstrates how difficult it is to explain the beauty of a thing by reference solely to its beauty. For, though the point is essential to his purpose, he, nevertheless, does not manage to show how charm and free beauty are to be distinguished by the subject in the act of judging. Certainly, if charm can be taken as a form of dependent beauty, then the two experiences should be different, since a qualitative difference in terms of feeling separates the two kinds. But in the case of nature, according to Kant's account, not only are they to be found 'as it were melted' together, but also the one, as the example of the bird's song demonstrated, may even be mistaken for the other. Not, that is, that we may mistake one kind of feeling for another, but rather that we can believe our judgement is free when in fact it is determined. For, however we look at it, if the beauty of free beauty depends solely upon beauty (as form), a change in provenance, though it may change the interest we feel, should not affect the judgement.

What the instance of the bird song demonstrates, however, is that, despite Kant's conviction that his judgement was one of free beauty, there was, for him, no 'inherent character' of the beauty of the form of the song *in itself*. It was not purely a judgement on a self-subsisting beautiful form, nor was it the beauty of the song that qualified that song for partnership with moral ideas, rather it was an apparently unconscious partnering, by Kant, of the song with moral ideas that qualified it to be beautiful. While he believed he was responding immediately to the 'beauty of an object', in fact he was making a conceptual reconstruction of that 'object', projecting all that a bird's singing might be made to imply into a sound which, in itself, he would find dull. In this sense, then, what struck him as the 'inherent' properties of the object were properties that he *made* inherent in the object. In short, the free beauty was a matter of subreption.

What has been so far said about the active nature of the judgement is, however, only a repetition of what was established in Chapter 2. It was, nevertheless, necessary to rehearse the problem as it appears in §42, not only in order to establish that Kant does not actually there solve (on the phenomenological plane) the problem which his confusion over the bird's song gives rise to, but also because his analysis in this section gives some hint as to what kind of determination may be involved.

THE DETERMINATION OF FREE BEAUTY

Kant, as we have seen, initially perceived his judgement on the bird's song as a judgement upon a free rather than a dependent beauty: it felt to him, at the time, that he was making a bare reflection upon a given intuition. (His subsequent suggestion of 'confusion' only makes sense on such a supposition.) The experience, then, was qualitatively different from an experience of dependent beauty, insofar as the determining role of the concept (of naturalness) involved was not apparent to him at the moment of making the judgement: the form *appeared* bare to reflection. It is only when a recognition of the true object of his judgement is forced upon him, by the demise of the beauty, that he concedes that the form, as cognized, was in some way dependent upon a context or provenance, that is, upon a concept: it appears, in retrospect, to have been a dependent beauty. It was, however, a dependent beauty of a very peculiar kind, for the presence of the aesthetic idea, whatever it may have been, was, in some way, hidden from the subject. This precludes our saying that the free beauty was, unconsciously, a dependent beauty, since it is only our cognizance of the kind of judgement that we are making that can, in practice, distinguish the two kinds. Rather what the instance presents us with is a free beauty that is perceived as such, and is yet dependent. It would appear, moreover, that it is essential to the beauty that this dependence should *not* be part of our cognizance of the judgement, that is, not only is the beauty dependent on the provenance of the object, but it is also dependent on not appearing dependent.

We have seen, in connection with the sublime and with the poetry that Kant offered as exemplary of 'genius', how a certain kind of interest can lead to the concealment of the grounds of an effect for the sake of that effect. How, that is, the subreption serves the interests of sensibility. It now remains to be seen if we can discern the action of a similar 'fantastic desire' in the present instance.

We must presume that the song was, for Kant, expressive of the notion of a bird singing, and that this notion, in turn, was interpreted, by him, as an expression of a joyousness, or something similar, into which he could, sympathetically, enter. This raises two questions. Why was the sound not cognized, by Kant, as expressive, that is, why did it seem, to him, to be a free beauty? Why does it cease to be expressive (become 'wholly destitute of taste'), though he can conjecture in what way it was expressive (that is, the feeling he had mistaken for beauty), once he becomes aware that this was the grounds of its beauty for him? These two questions are closely connected, for they both point to an answer that must lie in whatever makes the difference, for Kant, between the object being expressive (though not cognized as such) and beautiful, and being 'merely' expressive and 'destitute of taste'. It is, of course, perceived naturalness that makes this difference and it is in whatever extra significance being natural lends to the object that we shall find the answer.

Kant himself, as we have seen, has proposed a significance peculiar to natural objects: the object, insofar as it is beautiful, will, if natural, satisfy reason's interest in nature showing, or at least suggesting, that it 'contains in itself some sort of ground for assuming a lawful correspondence of its products with our satisfaction that is independent of all interest'.[28] Thus beauty, if it is natural, satisfies, or gestures towards the satisfaction of, reason's desire that nature should manifest a harmony with our judgements of taste. It is this satisfaction, says Kant, that nature expresses 'figuratively . . . in its beautiful forms'.[29]

This significance, this suggestion of the satisfaction of an interest of reason, however, only belongs to the form insofar as it is already beautiful: it is an interest, says Kant, which is aroused by the beauty. There is no question, then, in Kant's account, of this interest of reason actually being responsible for the beauty, that is, of the beauty being, in any way, determined by this interest. It must be conceded, however, that this does leave room for an interest in a beautiful object being cognized as an object of nature, and, consequently an interest in *not* cognizing the song merely as expressive of an, albeit aesthetic, idea (which cognizance renders the beauty of the object relative to ourselves), but rather in cognizing it as a free, 'self-subsisting' beauty of nature, that is, a beauty which will satisfy what Kant calls the 'interests of reason'. This would suggest the following process at work in the instance of the fake bird's song:

1. Kant perceives the sound, insofar as it is the song of a bird, as, potentially, expressive of joyousness.
2. He is aware that this can be interpreted as a projection of his own feelings.
3. He wishes to feel, in the 'interest of reason', that it is really nature that is expressing 'herself'.
4. In order to entertain the idea that nature really is expressing 'herself' he must suppress the consciousness of this wish by suppressing the consciousness that his response depends upon the idea that the sound is the expression of joyousness.
5. He cognizes the sound, in itself, as a free beauty. (A beautiful *bare form* of

nature.) This feeling being the only way in which consciousness registers the preceding process.

6. He suddenly learns that what he is hearing is not the song of a bird.
7. He realizes that if the sound is not coming from a bird then it is not even expressive, and he cognizes it as, in itself, devoid of taste.
8. He conjectures that, since a change in the provenance of the object should make no difference to a free beauty, that, in fact, the sound itself had never struck him as a free beauty, but rather that what he had previously felt was the charm, now lost, of what the sound, as a bird singing, might express.

(Naturally, the above process is not posited as the necessary aesthetic response to any perceived change in the provenance of an object, but only as Kant's response on this occasion.) This ordering necessitates the inversion of the relationship that Kant posits between beauty and 'intellectual interest', for there is no question of a cognizance of any kind of beauty – free or dependent – until the fifth stage; up until that point there is merely the desire to interpret nature as symbolic: at first in the particular (1), and then in general (3). (The interpretation of the song (1) must, of course, take place against the general background of the interest (3). The presence of this interest is implied throughout the instance, just as the interest involved in the sublime, though it was necessary to speak of it emerging at a certain point in the process leading to an ascription of sublimity, is, nevertheless, an enduring one.) It is not, then, that the beauty arouses the interest, but rather that the interest, in combination with the potentially symbolic properties of nature, or our relationship to it, arouses/constitutes the beauty.

We have seen, in dealing with the sublime and with Frederick's poem, how the kind of concepts that give rise to the interest that is responsible for dependent beauty are such that they cannot be entertained by the subject as concepts. We have also seen how dependent beauty is a way of entertaining the idea of the satisfaction of the interest *without* entertaining the concept, upon which this satisfaction depends, as a concept. It now remains to be seen if the concept implied by the 'interest of reason' is comparable to those we have discovered at work in dependent beauty, that is, whether it is entertainable, by Kant, as a concept, and whether the interest which it implies is sufficiently strong to account for a repression of its entertainment should it turn out that it is not entertainable as a concept. If it turns out that it is such a concept, then it is at least plausible that the structure of the instance of the bird's song outlined above is viable.

Kant is quite clear about the concept that the 'interest of reason' implies: that nature should be adapted to our 'wholly disinterested satisfaction', should not only appear, but actually be, addressed to our taste. He puts this in a different way, in connection with his contention that an immediate interest in the beauty of nature indicates 'at least . . . the predisposition to a good moral disposition':

[Nature], which in its beautiful products shows itself as art, not merely by chance, but as it were intentionally, in accordance with a lawful arrangement and as purposiveness without an end, which latter, since we never encounter it externally, we naturally seek within ourselves, and indeed in that which constitutes the ultimate end of our existence, namely the moral vocation . . .[30]

He promises at this point to return to the question of the 'purposiveness of nature' in the *Critique of the Teleological Power of Judgement*, and it is to this work that we shall now turn.

Kant's answer to the question of how far it is possible to entertain, as a certainty, the idea of an intentional end (a design), and hence a purposiveness, in nature, is short and blunt: to convert nature, in itself, into an intelligent being 'would be absurd'; to place another (intelligent) being above nature as its architect is 'presumptuous'.[31] This is not, however, in Kant's eyes at least, a rejection of theology: for he believes that 'the concept of God and the (practical) conviction of his existence' can be made to follow from the 'fundamental ideas of morality', that 'respect for the moral law represents the final end of our vocation to us quite freely, as the precept of our own reason'.[32] How much or how little can be deduced from our reverence for the moral law is a question we have already dealt with. What is important here, however, is not the grounding that Kant gives for theology, but rather the grounds that he excludes by virtue of their incompatibility with reason. For this argument from moral feeling is, he says, 'the only argument that leads to a determinate concept of the object of theology'.[33]

This 'argument', giving rise to the subjective requirement of theology, is reminiscent of his definition of vain wishing: a man in serene enjoyment of his existence needs to be grateful, a man who must make a sacrifice feels the need to believe he is carrying out some inexorable command, a man who is guilty and yet unpunished feels the need to render an account: 'In a word, he needs a moral intelligence in order to have a being for the end for which he exists, which is the cause of him and the world in a way suitable to this end.'[34] The mind, 'inclined to the enlargement' of its sentiments of gratitude, obedience, and humiliation, 'voluntarily conceives of an object that is not in the world in order, where possible, to demonstrate its duty toward such an object'.[35] The original moral bent of our nature, as a subjective principle, will not, he concludes, allow us to be satisfied with the world as an end but leads us to introduce into it an underlying supreme cause that governs that world according to moral principles.[36] We *feel* ourselves striving after some universal highest end, and without assuming such a Cause, would be in 'danger of seeing that effort as entirely futile in its effects'.[37]

According to Kant it would be 'vain' to 'dig for incentives behind these feelings' [of gratitude, obedience, and humiliation], since they are, as modes of mental disposition towards duty, 'immediately connected with the purest moral disposition'.[38] This would seem to ignore the very palpable motive of consolation to be discerned in the expansion of our feelings into the positing of an object, not in this world, that takes cognizance of those feelings, and, moreover, gives point to a striving that would otherwise appear futile. Be that as it may, these are the grounds of Kant's ethico-theology:

> [The] inner *moral* vocation of human existence has made good that which was wanting in the knowledge of nature, by directing us to conceive of the supreme cause, for the final end of the existence of all things, for which no principle other than an *ethical* principle of reason is sufficient, with properties by means of which it is capable of subjecting the whole of nature to its sole aim (for which nature is merely its instrument) (i.e. to conceive of it as a *deity*).[39]

What is important to note here are the forms of argument that Kant rejects in advancing this as 'the only argument that leads to a determinate concept of the object of theology'. Most significant among these rejected arguments, for our present purposes, is the physicotheological, that is, the argument, so popular in Kant's time, that claims the external world gives evidence of design, and that from the nature of this design we can deduce the nature of the designer.[40] According to Kant, while a consideration of the existence of the world, in particular in its teleological aspect, may inspire us to go in search of a theology it can never, in itself, produce such a theology:[41]

> [Physicotheology], no matter how far it might be pushed, can reveal to us nothing about a *final end* of creation; for it does not even reach the question about such an end. It can thus certainly justify the concept of an intelligent world-cause, as a merely subjectively appropriate concept for the constitution of our cognitive faculty of the possibility of the things that we make intelligible to ourselves in accordance with ends; but it cannot determine this concept any further in either a theoretical or a practical respect; and its attempt does not fulfil its aim of establishing a theology, but always remains merely a physical teleology, because the relation to ends in it always can and must be considered only as conditioned within nature; hence the end for which nature itself exists (the grounds for which must be sought outside of nature) . . . cannot even become a question. . . . [It] can never, even if we were capable of having an empirical overview of the whole system as long as it concerns mere nature, elevate us beyond nature to the end of its existence, and thereby to the determinate concept of [an intelligent world-cause].[42]

We can only get from the empirical data of the external world to the idea of a deity, by means of the practical employment of reason, not by its theoretical employment. For the theoretical employment of reason 'always demands that no properties be assumed in the explanation of an object of experience that are not to be found among the empirical data for its possibility', and the idea of a deity is simply unnecessary from this point of view.[43] His objection to physicotheology, then, is not that there is no God, but simply that, whether there is one or not, the very notion of physicotheology is self-contradictory, is an attempt to employ reason beyond the proper bounds of reason. Indeed, even in his exposition of ethicotheology, Kant is at pains to insist that theology is purely a 'subjective requirement': its entertainment 'is not necessary for the expansion or improvement of our knowledge of nature and, in general, for any sort of theory'.[44]

It would be no overstatement of the case, then, to assert that Kant would *not* be inclined to entertain as meaningful the notion that the contemplation of external nature could reveal its final end. That the subject may, however, have a strong motive for believing that it is possible is attested by the very fact that Kant proposes another way to arrive at the same conclusion (the existence of the object of theology), by means of a route – ethicotheology – which itself, by his own admission, will not satisfy reason in its theoretical employment. Kant, of course, says that the existence of moral feeling only warrants the 'supposition' of God, but in this feeling that such a supposition is warranted, and in the form (faith) which it takes, we can discern the operation of an interest, namely that, given that we feel ourselves, in the experience of moral feeling, striving after some universal highest end, without an adequate object for this end we would be in 'danger of seeing that effort as entirely futile in its effects'.

The idea, then, of being able to discern in nature an intention to offer us some form of satisfaction, that is, that idea which is implied by what Kant calls the 'interest of reason', is at once one that Kant could not entertain as a meaningful concept, and yet one which he had the strongest interest in entertaining. Moreover we can see how, given the supposition (or conviction) produced by the moral argument, the subject might feel justified in interpreting nature itself, if not as *evidence* of such a supposition, then at least as a phenomenon that is, in some sense, *in line with* this supposition.[45] This last point is especially relevant in connection with the particular form of satisfaction involved here, that is, the 'disinterested' satisfaction of free beauty.[46] Indeed, in the closing pages of the *Critique of the Teleological Power of Judgement*, Kant returns to the point he has made in the previous critique. In a footnote to a discussion of how our reverence for the moral law points towards a cause in harmony with moral perspective he writes that

> The admiration of the beauty as well as the emotion aroused by the so diverse ends of nature, which a reflective mind is able to feel even prior to any clear representation of a rational author of the world, have something similar to a *religious* feeling about them. Hence they seem to act on the mind, by means of a kind of judging that is analogous to the moral, primarily through the moral feeling (of gratitude and veneration toward the

cause that is unknown to us) and thus by the arousal of moral ideas, when they inspire that admiration which is connected with far more interest than mere theoretical contemplation can produce.[47]

Now the feeling that we may infer the divine from external nature is, according to Kant, an illusion. He does, however, hold that we can, in a sense, infer the divine from our experience of moral feeling, and that the feeling inspired by such beauty is analogous to moral feeling. Nevertheless this analogy will not allow him to assert that the idea of the beauty of nature being revelatory of the divine is justified, since the experience of this beauty is not an experience of moral feeling, rather it only takes on the colour of moral feeling (gratitude and veneration towards an unknown cause) by virtue of our interpreting the object as designed to be beautiful. The experience of beauty, then, whether it is 'disinterested' or not, can only serve to support the suppositions of ethicotheology if the subject grounds what gives it kinship with moral feeling in that physicotheology which Kant rejects.

In another context, in the *Critique of the Aesthetic Power of Judgement*, Kant declares that, despite the fact that the beautiful forms of nature 'speak strongly in behalf of the realism of the aesthetic purposiveness of nature', that is, in support of the plausible assumption that beneath the production of the beautiful there must lie a preconceived idea acting for the benefit of our imagination, nevertheless, since the forms of nature are all explicable in terms of their functions, and since it is the aesthetic judgement itself, rather than empirical observation of such forms, which is legislative in the matter, such an assumption is unjustifiable.[48] Thus, he concludes, nature's capacity to originate beautiful forms is not a proof that they are intended to be beautiful: it is we who receive nature with favour, and not nature that shows us a favour.[49] Yet, just how eloquently the beautiful forms of nature do plead for their own divine origin may be judged from the fact that for two thousand years in Europe beauty was taken as not merely revelatory of the divine, but only explicable in itself in terms of being such a revelation. For the ineffable (or 'disinterested') satisfaction of beauty, that is, a satisfaction, and even a sense of yearning, that neither arises from, nor points towards, any mundane satisfaction, found its adequate object in an intimation of a divinity, and the separation from that divinity implicit in the very worldly conditions of the judgement.[50]

This is, of course, philosophically, almost a separate universe from that inhabited by Kant. Indeed it is specifically in connection with how admiration for nature may, through a misapprehension, turn into a belief that it is purposely designed for us, that Kant speaks of Plato's thought (the source of this theory of beauty) giving way to visionary rapture (*Schwärmerei*).[51] Yet this is precisely the concept implicit in what Kant calls the 'interest of reason' that, he asserts, can be aroused by the beauty of nature. It would seem, then, that such an interest, whether or not it is evidence of the germ of a good moral disposition, is certainly evidence of a germ of visionary rapture or enthusiasm.

Not, that is, a peculiar, identifiable, systematic enthusiasm (fanaticism), but rather a human predisposition to the mode of thought that is common to all particular visionary raptures.

It is, of course, Kant himself who first proposed that this interest of reason was bound up with our feeling about natural beauty, in order to account for the superiority he *felt* natural beauty enjoyed over artificial beauty, to justify the then emerging (and now popular) feeling that moral goodness and a taste for natural beauty are somehow connected, and to explain why we might feel that something has been lost from the experience of a beauty when we discover we have misapprehended its provenance. He does not say that this interest is given to us as an interest *in* the experience of the beauty, or even that we are conscious of it as an interest when it is, as he claims, aroused antecedently *by* the beauty. Rather it is, according to Kant, what must be inferred from the freedom, the superior attractiveness, and the vaguely moral tenor, of that experience. It is not possible, then, to argue that the interest cannot be repressed in the experience of beauty itself, since Kant is aware that it is at work, albeit antecedently, in that experience. For, though Kant does find it a theoretical necessity to posit such an interest, he does not claim that the subject is aware of it in the experience itself. (Just as he does not posit that the subject is aware of the grounding that he proposes for the sublime, but rather is only aware, by subreption, of the 'sublimity of the object'.)

The concept implied by the 'interest of nature', then, is both not entertainable by Kant as a concept, and yet can plead eloquently enough to him to allow him to let it slip in as, if not evidence for, then, at least in line with his ethicotheology, despite the fact that it depends upon the physicotheology he explicitly rejects.[52] This concept, then, takes precisely that form which is requisite for qualifying it as the same kind of concept we saw at work in the sublime and in Frederick's poem: it gives rise to an interest strong enough to account for its repression in the form of beauty. In this way the process posited above as being at work in the instance of the bird song – with its inversion of the relationship between the 'interest of reason' and the beauty – becomes viable:

1. Kant perceives the sound, insofar as it is the song of a bird, as, potentially, expressive of joyousness.
2. He is aware that this can be interpreted as a projection of his own feelings.
3. He wishes to feel, in the 'interests of reason', that it is really nature that is expressing itself.
4. In order to entertain the idea that nature really is expressing itself he suppresses the consciousness of this wish by suppressing the consciousness that his response depends upon the idea that the sound is the expression of joyousness.
5. He cognizes the sound, in itself, as a free beauty (a beautiful *bare form* of nature).

It is important to note, as was said before, that there is no question of any kind of beauty, dependent or free, until we reach the last of these stages. Beauty is the result of the process, not an element in that process. As in the examples of dependent beauty already examined, it is the idea, given to us through the symbolic qualities of an object, of the satisfaction of a desire for transcendence, cognized as impossible to rationally entertain, yet, at the same time, too desirable to completely relinquish, that is entertained by the subject in finding the natural object beautiful. It is the very entertainment of the idea in this way that *is* the beauty of the object.

The relationship of the subject to the symbolic qualities of the sound, as bird's song, parallels, then, the relationship already proposed between the subject and what is asserted in Frederick's poem, that is, the subject must take the assertion, or, in the case of the song, the significance of the assertion, both as if it were true (significant) *and* as if it were not asserted (signified) at all. This, as we saw, accounts for the ultimate ineffability of the poem's effect for Kant. What remains to account for is the, as it were, 'immediate ineffability' of free beauty, that is, its dependence not only a repressed concept, but also on not appearing as dependent. In fact, of course, this question is answered by the exposition given above. For, as we have seen, it is not the assertion (the joyousness, or whatever the bird singing would express) in itself that arouses the 'interest of reason', it is rather the significance of its being an assertion at all. The bird song cannot satisfy this interest if we are conscious that we are interpreting the sound itself as expressive, for in doing so we would be introducing ourselves as a condition of that expressiveness, and thus disqualifying the sound from being free in the sense that the 'interest of reason' demands. It is not then merely what is expressed by the sound, but the very fact of our interpreting it as expressive that must be suppressed in order for us to find that sound beautiful. The beauty is, then, necessarily cognized as free, since it cannot exist at all if it is cognized as in any way dependent.

In what is cognized as dependent beauty, on the other hand, it is the *content* of the expression that answers the desire, and thus we may remain aware of a vague suggestiveness – the aesthetic idea – though we cannot ultimately say what is suggested. (There is a certain justice, then, in Kant's contention that free beauty is the 'purer' of the two forms.) It seems safe to conjecture, however, that we will always make beauty as 'free' as we possibly can, though outside nature, and particularly in the case of what is obviously intended as expressive, this positing of freedom is far more difficult for the subject to achieve. Insofar as the subject has the strongest possible interest in not cognizing the precise grounds of their judgement we might say that all dependent beauty aspires to the condition of free beauty.

9

Conclusion

This much can certainly be said about the empirical interest in objects of taste and in taste itself, namely, that since the latter indulges inclination, although this may be ever so refined, it also gladly allows itself to blend in with all the inclinations and passions that achieve their greatest variety and highest level in society, and the interest in the beautiful, if it is grounded on this, could afford only a very ambiguous transition from the agreeable to the good. (Kant *Critique of the Power of Judgement*, §41, pp.177–8 [298])

As was suggested in the Introduction, the principal importance of the *Critique of the Power of Judgement* for the history of aesthetics lies in its role as a catalyst. The most enduring legacy of the *Critique* is less any particular thesis that Kant advances than the nature of the reaction it inspired among Kant's immediate successors, in particular Schiller, Schelling and Hegel. That rummaging among the details of individual subjectivity for the grounds of the aesthetic, which Kant rejects, did, of course, continue for a while within writing on taste; indeed, the associationism of Alison and Jeffrey at the turn of the nineteenth century would positively have demanded such rummaging as the proper course for its development. But such development was not to take place.

Though Kant is frequently included as a precursor of Romanticism, there is, as we have seen, little in his aesthetics that justifies this status. (Not excepting his discussion, hardly touched on in the present commentary, of 'genius'.) Nevertheless, within his lifetime, 'Kantians' such as Schiller were already extending, or distorting, his work towards those twin fixed points of the cognitive and the ethical that would dominate aesthetics for the next two centuries. It is Schiller, Schelling, Hegel and Schopenhauer, rather than Kant, who can be more properly called the creators of modern aesthetics – a discourse fundamentally grounded in a reaction against that Enlightenment which Kant, at least elsewhere in his philosophy, might be said to exemplify. The precise relationship of the third *Critique* itself to certain Enlightenment principles is, of course, a moot point. Mothershill has suggested that Kant's motive in the third *Critique* may have been 'to make the whole [critical] system less austere and more congenial'.[1] If so, then the role of the aesthetic in Kant's philosophy can certainly be taken as foreshadowing the place to which aesthetics would subsequently be assigned – to the epilogue, to the relaxed moment, to where what *seems* and what *must be* are apparently reconciled. For aesthetics has become, within philosophy, the last refuge of miracles.

In the alternative grounding I have offered to the phenomenon which is Kant's object there is some evidence as to why this should be so: why Romantic aesthetics should have so conclusively triumphed, and persisted, despite the emergence of inimical and powerful trends elsewhere in philosophy. For, given the nature of the aesthetic itself, it is only necessary to let the subject's feelings have their head, providing this subject itself be idealized, to produce an aesthetics that is also anti-Enlightenment: certain where no certainty is possible. (This is not, of course, to say that there is anything irrational about aesthetic pleasure *per se*: pleasure in itself is not the kind of thing that can be rational or irrational.) It is in no one's interest to 'explain away', as Schelling put it, the 'miracles of art'. The kind of interest in which the aesthetic is grounded is a fundamental one, a matter of our implicit rather than professed or even conscious motives. Yet it is these latter kinds of motive that aesthetics has hitherto tended to appeal to in grounding the aesthetic: it is the true and good, according to aesthetics, that are mobilized by aesthetic experience. It is doubtful, however, that the motives we profess have that self-consistency that would make them strong enough to create an aesthetic experience; though doubtless, in the form of culture, they are a determining factor in the way in which the object of the more fundamental desire that creates the aesthetic is embodied. Though the aesthetic may throw up a host of appraisals based on automatic preconscious or unconscious evaluations (very probably at odds with our deliberate, conscious evaluation of what *should* be), yet still aesthetics feels it must make the aesthetic answerable to the ethical and the cognitive. Aesthetics, as a part of culture, is predisposed to favour the values we are content with entertaining; and, even where less than creditable motives apparently play a role in the experience, aesthetics is anxious to show how such mobilization is nevertheless instrumental in some greater, that is, more than privately defensible, good.[2]

Yet so long as aesthetics seeks to justify rather than explain aesthetic pleasure/value it must have recourse to metaphysics, albeit metaphysics under the guise of psychology (as, for example, in I. A. Richards or Rudolf Arnheim). It is not surprising, then, that aesthetics should have clung so long to the dream of formalism: an approach that may have originated as a natural response to the inscrutability of the aesthetic – its immediate, apparently non-conceptual character – but which became in time merely a way of avoiding asking fundamental questions about the nature of the aesthetic *per se*. It now seems extraordinary how, for so long, casual references to Kant's deduction, vague talk of 'form' or 'play', could have stood in the place of any attempt at the explanation of what must be fundamental to aesthetics: the aesthetic.

The responsibility for this state of affairs does not, of course, lie entirely with Kant. Hegel is right when he 'accuses' Kant of being too much of the eighteenth century: too much concerned with the aesthetic as pleasure, and too little willing to assert the transcendental value of aesthetic experience, to make anything truly grandiose of the aesthetic. Where Kant does, however, foreshadow the wreck of aesthetic speculation in the nineteenth and twentieth centuries is in his rejection of the possibility of a psychological explanation for aesthetic experience: a rejection that, as we have seen, follows only from the unwarranted supposition that aesthetic judgement can possess subjective universal validity. In effect, though this can hardly have been Kant's intention, this demand for universal validity undid, at a stroke, all that had been achieved in aesthetics during the course of Kant's century.

This is not to say that eighteenth-century aestheticians were unconcerned with establishing potential universal validity in matters of taste. On the contrary, the eighteenth century was much exercised with the notion of the 'standard of taste'. Even Burke, the first edition of whose *Enquiry* paid little heed to such a notion in comparison with the attention it pays to the phenomenology of taste in action, felt it necessary in the second edition to develop the often repeated argument that, since taste is a form of judgement, such judgements must be amenable, like those of reason, to impartial arbitration as to their validity.[3] Others sought to establish the existence of a standard through an analogy with the senses, arguing that, since the organs of perception can exhibit varying degrees of health, or demonstrably greater or lesser powers of discrimination, so taste (in the sense of aesthetic preference) must likewise be capable of admitting of differing degrees of correctness in relation to some ideal norm. Hume's 'Essay on Taste' (which appeals to this last argument, among others) can be taken as exemplary of the eighteenth-century approach, in its concern with such a standard, the arguments it employs, and their inconclusiveness. No matter how ardently such a standard may have been desired, the parameters within which aesthetics was pursued in the eighteenth century were not conducive to the production of such a standard. Perhaps, without the wrench of the more general reaction against the Enlightenment, aesthetics might have come to reconcile itself to whatever conclusions its commitment to reason required. For a standard of taste is, strictly speaking, one more entity than is necessary to hypothesize in order to account for the existence of judgements of taste. Kant acknowledges this insofar as not only is his notion of subjective universal validity necessarily unusable as a practical standard by virtue of its ideality, but even this form of validity is not argued for but merely presupposed.

Yet the eighteenth century's concern with the establishment of a standard does echo in Kant's text: at precisely that point where the argument is most forcibly bent to the demands of the presupposed universal validity, that is, in the rejection of the possibility of a psychological explanation for taste. This echo can be interpreted, as indeed can the presupposition of universal validity itself, as expressive of the same impulse underlying the eighteenth century's desire for a standard of taste, and the nineteenth and twentieth centuries' implicit presumption that such a standard exists. That impulse arises from *felt* universal validity that characterizes every judgement of taste.

One cannot arrive at a standard of taste without starting out with its presupposition. The (philosophically) problematic nature of the feeling underlying this presupposition is indeed Kant's starting point. He begins with the conflict between the judgements appearing to be no more than 'the reflection of the subject on his own state (of pleasure or displeasure)', while nevertheless also appearing to that same subject to possess a more than private validity: the pleasure which the subject experiences is marked by a 'consciousness of separation of everything that belongs to the agreeable and the good from the satisfaction that remains to him'.[4] The beautiful object is, then, experienced as an object of *necessary* satisfaction. This way of stating the case is perhaps a little misleading, for it is not that the subject is conscious of feeling a pleasure in connection with an object, casts about to discover *personal* reasons to account for the satisfaction, either in terms of the agreeable or the good, and then, on failing to do so, decides that their judgement was one of taste; rather it is simply that the beauty, or the aesthetic merit, appears to the subject as a quality of the object itself. It is not my intention, however, to recast Kant's original antinomies. Whether we arrive at the antinomy of an apparently groundless pleasure by the formula which Kant uses, in which both the subjectivity and the claim to universal validity of the judgement appear to arise almost by default, or whether we simply say that the experience immediately strikes us as qualitatively different, albeit in an inexplicable way, from either, on the one hand, a judgement connected with desire, or, on the other, an objective judgement, the fundamental antinomy remains the same. Indeed, Kant's way of formulating the problem has the merit of emphasizing from the outset the, for reflection, inherently problematic nature of that judgement.

Eighteenth-century writers, by and large, strove to cut the Gordian knot of this antinomy with the assertion that the necessity which the individual judgement of taste lays claim to is a real necessity: that the judgement is exemplary of a common sense. Since tastes are not uniform, however, nor indeed enduring even in a single subject, this solution necessarily entails adopting the position that the subject can make mistakes in attributing beauty to objects. The instance Kant gives of the partial young poet, for example, can be seen in this way. Kant himself talks of how time may render the poet's judgement 'more acute' and bring his evaluation of his own poems into line with that of his contemporaries.[5] But what if the next generation were unanimous in their praises for the poet's early work? And if the subsequent generation passed it over as dated? And if now it was universally considered the high point of that poet's career? A consensus on the value of a work of art or (what is more rare) on the beauty of an object is evidence of nothing about the object except that at a certain time there is a consensus on its value. Such a conclusion will not, however, satisfy the impulse for validity that arises from aesthetic experience itself. Consider for example the vantage point implied in Hume's pronounce-ment: '[The] beauties, which are naturally fitted to excite agreeable senti-ments, immediately display their energy; and *while the world endures*, they maintain their authority over the minds of men.'[6] As we saw in the last chapter, we have every interest in wishing our beauty to belong to the object in itself.

The arguments habitually brought forward for the objectivity of taste (by analogy with reason or the senses, or by appeal to the test of time) were manifestly too weak for Kant to employ, and, as we have seen, he directly rejects forms of them in the course of advancing his own thesis. He is too much the philosopher to allow the feeling that something must be so to become an argument that it is so. Nevertheless, he still wishes to leave open the possibility that it might be so. Hence the idealism of his result: some judgements do have subjective universal validity, though we cannot know which ones. However, the introduction of even this limited form of universal validity, since it is, and indeed can only be, introduced as a presupposition, must have the effect of warping the analysis of the aesthetic.

As we saw in Chapters 1 and 2, once we have set aside the stipulation that the judgement of taste may potentially lay legitimate claim to subjective uni-versal validity, what Kant actually establishes regarding this form of judgement is only that it represents the subject's *feeling* of immediate delight in the object: the object of taste is one that is *cognized by the subject* as an object of necessary satisfaction. If, however, this felt necessity should, at least potentially, be capable of corresponding to a real necessity, a further condition appears to be requisite: the ruling out of any determining factor that might admit of contingency. This is precisely the line Kant takes. That this follows from the stipulative definition of taste (with its demand for universal validity), rather than from the phenomenology of taste (with its emphasis on the subject's cognizance of the 'disinterestedness' of their own pleasure), is signalled by the fact that the thesis entails a situation in which a subject could be fulfilling all the conditions of the phenomenology (cognizing the object as an object of nec-essary satisfaction) yet not be making what Kant would call a judgement of taste, or, at least, not a 'pure' judgement of taste. Surely, however, the more plausible argument would be that, if it is possible for a subject to mistakenly believe their judgement is disinterested when it is in fact determined by con-tingent factors, or even interests, there is no reason to presume that the felt necessity of the judgement should ever correspond to a real necessity. There is, indeed, no philosophical justification for such a presumption; it is unnecessary, and, as with his predecessors' quest to establish a standard of taste, Kant's motive in making it appears to be principally lead by the desire to place beauty in the world rather than in the individual subject.[7] (The notion of '*subjective* universal validity' will, of course, only appear to be a compromise so long as we do not ask what other kind of universal validity there could possibly be.)

I must emphasize, however, that I do not wish to put in question the justness of the antinomy from which Kant begins. A judgement of taste is only identifiable as such, according to Kant, through its contrast with judgements on the agreeable and disagreeable: the object must be cognized as an object of necessary satisfaction. This much we must grant, if we are still to have such a thing as a judgement of taste; with, however, the proviso that this distinction between the different forms of judgement refers only to the subject's cognizance of their own judgement. Where Kant oversteps the limits of what he can establish is in the claim that a judgement of taste is 'pure only insofar as no merely empirical satisfaction is mixed into its determining ground'.[8] It is this supposition that leads him to assert that 'charm or emotion' *cannot* have any share in the judgement by which something is declared 'beautiful', and to the *a priori* rejection of the possibility of a psychological explanation for taste.[9] What he singularly fails to bring forward is any reason for supposing that the felt disinterest distinguishing the judgement must correspond to a real disinterest in its determining ground. Indeed, his own phenomenology and grounding allow the possibility of the subject registering what are actually interested judgements as judgements of taste.

Though the psychological explanation that has here been drawn from Kant's phenomenology (once the presupposition of possible subjective universal validity is laid aside) does posit an interest in the determining ground of all judgements of taste, it also, nevertheless, preserves the condition that such judgements be cognized by the subject as necessary, or 'disinterested'. Not all interest, of course, need entail holding that gratification is a real possibility. There may be a satisfaction merely in entertaining a desire. Kant himself describes this phenomenon in his discussion of vain wishing: those 'desires in a human being as a result of which he stands in contradiction with himself'.[10] Such self-contradictory, or consciously vain, desires manifest themselves, according to Kant, in those instances where we seek the production of an object by means of representation alone, without any hope of succeeding, and with the full knowledge that success would be impossible; as, for example, when we wish to undo the past, or to annihilate the interval that divides us from a wished-for moment, when we pray for the aversion of inevitable evils, or when we entertain, in defiance of reason, an idea as certain, for the sake of the pleasure, or avoidance of pain, this certainty affords us. Though we are conscious, writes Kant, of the inefficiency of our representations as causes of their objects, every wish or longing still involves a reference to cause, and is not deterred from straining towards its object by this consciousness.[11]

Kant is not, of course, here characterizing mere misconceptions. In the case of such 'fantastic desires' the subject must remain aware that the desire is entertained in defiance of reason, hence the 'strain' involved: the desire must be preserved from dissolution in the face of the consciousness, inspired by reason, of its futility. That it is so preserved would seem to indicate that the very entertaining of the desire entails a certain satisfaction for the subject, if only in the form of avoiding the pain that a relinquishing of the desire would bring.

Hence the paradoxical nature of longing: it is something the subject at once suffers and yet *indulges* in. The similarity between the scenario of the fantastic wish and the way in which Kant himself justifies calling the representations of the imagination involved in judgements of taste 'aesthetic ideas', on the grounds that 'they at least strive toward something lying beyond the bounds of experience, and thus seek to approximate a presentation of concepts of reason', was noted in Chapter 6 above.[12] What I have done in dealing with the sublime, and with free and dependent beauty, is to show how a form of this same psychological tendency, or dynamic, can be seen to operate in the very constitution of the judgement of taste.

The aesthetic instance starts, I have argued, with the subject being suddenly struck by a significance either in the object itself or in their relationship to that object. What the object signifies for the subject is the satisfaction of a desire for transcendence, a satisfaction that is cognized as necessarily impossible, yet, at the same time, the idea of which is too desirable to completely relinquish. (The object does not, of course, appear as an agent of this satisfaction, but rather as expressive of it.) Such are the desires that we have seen operating in the case of the sublime, where the subject entertains the certainty of the supremacy of the will, in the case of the identification of the dying *philosophe* with the setting sun, where the subject entertains the certainty of the soul's immortality, and in the case of the bird's song, which is allowed to imply, through its 'evidence' of the adaption of nature to our pleasure, that the universal highest end implicit in our striving has a real existence beyond that striving. In each of these cases the idea that is entertained is one that Kant has elsewhere explicitly denied can be entertained as a certainty they are, indeed, ideas, concerning which a claim to certainty would qualify, in Kant's eyes, as enthusiasm or visionary rapture. For Kant, to acknowledge them even as desires, then, would be to compromise any notion he might entertain of their fulfilment, by the introduction of what he would necessarily recognize as a contingent, and interested, element.

The way in which interest might be seen at work in taste was first dealt with in connection with sublimity, which Kant himself describes as 'combined' with emotion.[13] Yet, even though Kant's grounding is driven by the *a priori* requirement that the grounding of the experience accommodate the possibility of subjective universal validity, in practice he must acknowledge that no instance of what appears to the subject to be sublimity can ever be proved to be grounded otherwise than in the domination of one interest of sensibility by another. For if we allow that the pleasure involved does arise from the *feeling* of reason's superiority over sensibility, then this pleasure presupposes that sensibility has (in its own interests) set aside the requirement (of reason) that the instance in question be distinguishable from instances of one interest of sensibility dominating another, and has done so for the sake of entertaining the pleasurable feeling of reason's superiority. The pleasure, then, is grounded in the entertaining of the illusion of the superiority of reason to sensibility. For the *feeling* that reason is dominating sensibility could only be the result of a state of mind in which sensibility was dominating reason.

Likewise the pleasure of beauty was shown to depend upon the way in which the subject, by a certain subreption, entertains that pleasure as 'disinterested', and hence ascribes the cause of the feeling to the merely sensible qualities of the external world. The difference in the way this may happen constitutes the difference between what Kant calls free and dependent beauty, that is, between beauty and other aesthetic merits.[14] In the case of dependent beauty (for example, Frederick's poetry) the subject is conscious of entertaining some, albeit ultimately ineffable, idea in connection with the object, though they still feel that their pleasure is, paradoxically, attributable to the object itself. We feel that the idea somehow justifies our pleasure, and may indeed assert (as in criticism) a necessary connection between pleasure and the idea insofar as we can formulate it. Nevertheless we can neither point to an objective principle, nor the satisfaction of a universally intersubjective desire, that would establish such a connection as necessary.

With (free) beauty, by contrast, there is no cognizance of a concept. The reason for this, I have suggested, is that the very fact of significance in this instance is also part of what is signified, so that it would be impossible for the object to function as a symbol were it to be perceived as at all symbolic. This we saw with the case of the bird's song in which it was not the significance (the joyousness, or whatever the bird singing would express) of the object in itself that would have promised the fulfilment of the transcendental desire (that the universal highest end implicit in our striving have a real existence beyond that striving), but rather the significance of its appearing significant at all. To be conscious of in any way interpreting the sound itself as expressive would be to introduce ourselves as a condition of that expressiveness, thus precluding the sound from intimating a satisfaction of the desire that nature should 'answer' us of, as it were, its own accord. It was not then merely what was expressed by the sound, but the very fact of our interpreting it as expressive which had to be repressed in order for us to find that sound beautiful. Beauty, we might say, depends upon not appearing dependent.

Merely to entertain a vain desire is not, of course, to have an aesthetic experience. Rather, it is the peculiar way in which the desire is entertained that constitutes the particular character of beauty and other aesthetic merits. This involves both the entertainment of the idea of what would constitute the fulfilment of the desire, and recognition that this fulfilment is impossible, that it exists *only as* an object of desire. In order for the former to take place the consciousness of the latter must be suppressed. The impossibility of doing this entails the more comprehensive suppression of the very fact that it is a desire that is being entertained. The two contradictory orientations must be held in some form of balance. It is not, however, that the aesthetic and this form of entertaining the desire are separate matters, rather the aesthetic *is* this form of entertaining the desire: the repression takes the form of what we call 'beauty', 'sublimity', 'profundity', 'grace', and so on. The very entertainment of the idea in the way described is, for the subject, the aesthetic 'quality' of the object.

It is for this reason that, even in the case of aesthetic merits other than beauty, that is, those instances in which we are conscious of entertaining something like a concept (the aesthetic idea) in connection with the object, the ultimate grounds of our pleasure remain indeterminable. For it is one of the essential characteristics of taste that it is not only the entertaining of a certain idea, but also a way of not entertaining that idea as a rational concept. This is what distinguishes aesthetic experience from other manifestations of vain wishing such as faith, prejudice, or mental derangement.[15] The concepts involved in these last are always, as it were, beleaguered by reason to a greater or lesser extent, and the holding of them takes on a certain colour from this fact. (Many identifiable prejudices, for example, are of the grim sort. Only the tenacity with which they are held in the face of contrary evidence betrays the satisfaction they afford the subject.) The aesthetic, by contrast, is a concept that has been transmuted entirely into feeling, and the pleasure of entertaining the idea, the intimation of transcendence, albeit mixed, as it so often is, with some wistfulness, is our only cognizance of what is taking place.[16]

Taste, then, could be described as 'arrested desire'. Moreover it seems likely that the kind of interest involved, that is, a desire for transcendence of the conditional, will be the same irrespective of what form the taste takes, that is, that differences in taste arise from differences in the terms in which the subject conceives of transcendence, which differences must ultimately depend upon the subject's experience of the conditional, rather than from fundamental differences in the kind of desire entertained. For this reason, though these terms will be an individual matter, to the extent that the individual's psychology reflects their milieu (period, class, age, sex, experience of objects intended for aesthetic consumption, and so on) so will their taste reflect that milieu. We have seen an example of such a phenomenon in Kant's admiration of Frederick's poetry: poetry which today appears almost a dead letter.

Having demonstrated the possibility of an alternative grounding for the phenomenon that is Kant's object, and suggested the profound, if indirect, effect of his *a priori* rejection of the possibility of a psychological explanation for taste on the subsequent history of aesthetics, my task, with regard to the aesthetic in Kant, is at an end. However, given that the alternative grounding of the aesthetic proposed is hardly orthodox, I wish to conclude by clarifying certain points concerning that grounding; not in the hope of forestalling any possible objections, but in order to ensure that the formulation of such objections may be pertinent. In particular there are three potential misunderstandings, which I shall deal with in descending order of plausibility.[17]

First, it must be emphasized that the object that expresses the satisfaction of the 'fantastic desire' is not itself the object of that desire. It is the state of affairs that the object symbolizes that arouses the interest, not the object to which the subject ascribes their aesthetic experience.[18] Hence the justice of saying that the subject's pleasure in the object is 'disinterested': the interest involved is not one that the object, simply as an object, could satisfy. This is not, of course, to set any limits to the kind of object that can be involved in the aesthetic instance. This object may be itself the object of another interest to the subject: Romantic love provides a good example of the potential coexistence of these two kinds of interest centred on what is ostensibly a single object. In order for the pleasure in an object to be aesthetic it is not necessary that the object or its real existence be a matter of indifference to the subject, but only that, as Kant says, the pleasure in the object that is designated a judgement of taste be felt *apart from any interest* in this real existence. It is not, however, a matter of the straight choice between disinterest and interest that Kant makes it: though the judgement may arise independently of any interest in the existence of the object, it depends upon an interest in the state of affairs that object symbolizes for the subject.

A second possible misunderstanding, though one so profound that its possibility would not have occurred to me had I not actually encountered it, would be to take the preceding description of the aesthetic for the description of a *reaction to* the aesthetic.[19] There is, as far as I can discover, no way in which the alternative grounding of the aesthetic advanced in the later chapters of this book could be made consistent either with the notion that beauty itself signifies the potential satisfaction of a 'fantastic desire', or, conversely, that the expression of such a satisfaction is itself beautiful. The subject's ascription of beauty, or any other aesthetic merit, to an object is posited not as the cause but rather the result of the mental process outlined, and nothing that could properly be termed an aesthetic quality, property, or experience is either necessary, or indeed possible, as a constituent element in that process. Aesthetic experience and the particular way that the 'fantastic desire' is entertained are not separate matters; rather aesthetic experience is this way of entertaining the desire. The theory ceases to be a theory of the aesthetic on any other terms.

One final, and perhaps trivial, misunderstanding that a previous formulation of this thesis has met with concerns not so much its content as the consequences to be drawn from it. Specifically the perception that such a thesis is 'puritanical', insofar as it makes the aesthetic a self-generated pleasure based upon a mental state akin to, if not identifiable with, delusion.[20] Insofar as the thesis is intended to be analytical, rather than evaluative, this objection is beside the point. Nevertheless, insofar as that thesis does leave little space for the attribution of any obvious instrumental value, in terms of the ethical or cognitive, to the aesthetic, I take it that it could be employed as a premise in a further argument intended to establish the worthlessness, or even perniciousness, of aesthetic experience *per se*. However, I have no wish to develop such an argument. Indeed it is the perception that the thesis is puritanical that contains the puritanical element, for it seems to rely on the premise that any experience that does not possess instrumental value in terms of the ethical or cognitive is worthless – even if that experience is, by definition, a pleasure.

I see no incongruity between the grounding of aesthetic experience I have provided and unashamed indulgence in such experience. (Its implications for the pretensions of the humanities may, however, be more substantial.) However, as with the potential misunderstanding previously dealt with, this present one does imply a mindset that faithfully reflects certain basic tendencies in aesthetics since Kant.

In conclusion I wish to address the question of the extent to which the aesthetic theory advanced here is a matter of 'reducing' the aesthetic to some other category. Certainly reductionism, in the sense of the analysis of a complex phenomenon into its simpler components, and the pursuit of an understanding of that phenomenon through the relationships between those components, has been the intention of the preceding analysis of the aesthetic. However, I do not wish to leave the reader with the impression that this work has been arguing that the aesthetic is, in any sense, 'really something else'.

Where I have most radically parted company with Kant is over his demand, following on from the presupposition of possible subjective universal validity, that no interest be part of the determining ground of the pure judgement of taste, so that no 'charm or emotion', as the expressions of such interest, can have any part in such a judgement. Though I have made emotion essential to the aesthetic, nevertheless, as was noted earlier, I do not believe that the aesthetic itself can justly be classified as an emotion. (In the nineteenth century aesthetic experience was quite commonly so classified, though on the basis of its phenomenology rather than because it was thought to be grounded in interest.) Those experiences that are usually referred to as 'emotions' have this much in common with aesthetic experience, that the interest they signify is only implicit in the form they take. (Moreover, as with the aesthetic, it is possible to experience a particular emotion, believe one can identify the event that precipitated it, yet still be unable to discover a causal connection between the two.) Nevertheless, prototypic emotions (such as anger or love) express a *tendency to act*, or at least imply a stimulus towards a definite form of behaviour, in line with the subject's interpretation of their relationship with the environment. The emotion, which signals that some value or goal of the subject has been engaged (whether to be advanced or thwarted), is, then, itself interpretable as a drive, in the sense that it motivates the subject to do something about their environment. This is also true, though in perhaps a weaker sense, of those emotional states that are complex (grief), ambiguous (awe, determination, satisfaction), or even apparently contentless (excitement, arousal, distress, agitation). With the aesthetic, by contrast, there is, even in my hypothesis, a sense in which the apparent, or felt, 'disinterest' does correspond to a real abnegation of interest. For if emotion can be characterized as a response to adaptional meaning, then the aesthetic is a response to a meaning that informs us we cannot adapt, that no further action is possible. There is neither the advancement nor thwarting of a goal or value, though we could say there is the germ of both: the initial advancement (the transcendental desire) is self-thwarted, though the form this self-thwarting takes is such that pleasure (in the entertainment of the idea of the satisfaction of that desire) is the outcome. (In this respect the nearest parallel phenomenon to the aesthetic, to be found in psychological literature, is probably the neurotic symptom as described by Freud.) Hence, all courses of action that might arise in association with the aesthetic cannot be related, even symbolically, to the kind of interest that is involved, but are rather *necessarily* displacements: possession of the 'aesthetic object', imitation, creativity, the humanities, romance, the greater part of what is called 'human sexuality'.

Aesthetic experience is equally distinct, for a different reason, from mood (happiness, apprehensiveness, melancholy), though perhaps a case could be made for including certain moods under the category of the aesthetic. ('Mood', too, seemed at one time an appropriate characterization of the mental state involved in the aesthetic.) While it is difficult to draw a sharp distinction between emotions and moods, the latter tend to have a longer duration, a more diffuse character, and to often lack contextual provocation. Like emotions, they may be characterized as reactions to the subject's appraisal of their relationship to the environment, though the appraisal appears to be on a more general level than is the case with emotion. However, though this more general existential reference brings the mood closer to aesthetic experience, nevertheless, the very lack of a specific object or event as a stimulus to the feeling necessarily sets it off from such experience.

Thus, while the aesthetic is grounded in precisely those interests that are ultimately responsible for emotion, it would be misleading to try to reduce it to an emotion. Indeed, that the aesthetic exhibits such marked differences from those phenomena (emotions and moods) which can be seen as closest to it in type, is a good indication that it should most properly be regarded as *sui generis*; providing, of course, that we do not take this 'autonomy' as an exemption from the general economy of human interests.

Notes

INTRODUCTION

1 Schelling *The Philosophy of Art*, pp.11–12.
2 Burke *A Philosophical Enquiry into the Origin of our Ideas of the Sublime and Beautiful*, p.1. Johnson, though he may have been no more impressed with Burke's theory (as distinct from his style) than anyone else, nevertheless considered Burke's work to be 'an example of true criticism' insofar as it was fundamentally concerned with 'the workings of the human heart'; Boswell *Life of Johnson*, p.415 [October 16, 1769].
3 Usher *Clio*, p.107.
4 Townsend's recent *Hume's Aesthetic Theory* is an object lesson in this regard.
5 Hegel *Aesthetics*, I, p.33.
6 *ibid.*, p.32.
7 *ibid.*, p.33.
8 Many of my arguments with the secondary literature will turn around those points at which Kant's commentators have been unable to shake this prejudice.
9 See Kirwan *Literature, Rhetoric, Metaphysics*, pp.76–8; *Beauty*, pp.58–60; *Sublimity*, Chapters 6–7 *passim*. A full discussion of the philosophical background to the theory may be found in Copleston *A History of Philosophy: Volume VII: Fichte to Nietzsche*, especially Part I *passim*, and a treatment of the same background that links it directly to the aesthetics of the period in Chapters 2–3 of Schaeffer's *Art of the Modern Age*.
10 Hegel *Aesthetics*, I, pp.56–7; 60.
11 Schelling *The Philosophy of Art*, pp.11–12.
12 Reid *Essays on the Intellectual Powers of Man*, p.490. Reid, in his treatment of grandeur in 1785, deprecates his predecessors for their tendency to 'resolve everything [beauty, harmony, grandeur, right and wrong] into feelings and sensations', insisting rather that 'the object has its excellence from its own constitution and not from ours' (p.495). Such a massive shift from the psychological to the metaphysical did not, of course, go completely unchallenged, even if only indirectly. In 1834 Fechner was complaining that Kant, Hegel and Schelling had pursued aesthetics only 'from above', from the viewpoint of ideal concepts of beauty or art in relation to the true and the good. Without wishing to denigrate such a viewpoint he felt that it must be better balanced by an aesthetics pursued 'from below', that is, from the viewpoint of the empirical, so that aesthetic laws might be balanced with aesthetic facts; *Vorschule der Aesthetik*, I, pp.1–6.
13 It is, therefore, surprising to discover, on turning to the now decidedly obscure world of nineteenth-century academic aesthetics in English (Knight, Haven, Wayland, Day, Bascom), that aestheticians of this period (for whom Kant was the arch 'subjectivist') considered their primary task to be to challenge the apparent popular triumph of the associationism of Alison and Jeffrey. Alison's seminal associationist text, *Essays on the Nature and Principles of Taste*, had appeared in the same year as the *Critique of the Power of Judgement*.

14   Croce, for example, makes short work of Herbert Spencer.

15   Justification for linking such heterogeneous figures as Gadamer and Lyotard can be found in Kirwan *Literature, Rhetoric, Metaphysics*, pp.176–7.

16   There are, of course, several twentieth-century figures (Richards, Langer, Goodman, Arnheim) who would not, at first, appear to fit this description. There is space here only to aver that I am not overlooking such figures in my generalization.

17   See Hegel *Aesthetics*, I, pp.34–5. To consider only a single, though telling, example, there is Danto's assertion that in his *Transfiguration of the Commonplace* he had put all question of the nature of the aesthetic itself 'on ice'; 'A Future for Aesthetics', p.275. See also Danto *After the End of Art*, pp.193–8. Hegel believed, of course, that his own aesthetic theory had put an end to the need for fundamental speculation on the nature of the aesthetic itself, as opposed to the examination of its manifestations. The point here is that modern aesthetics pursues these manifestations without having a clear notion of what the aesthetic is. This is not intended as disparagement. Many interesting things can be said about art and even aesthetic experience, even in the absence of an aesthetic theory, or, as in the case of Hegel himself, and Adorno, despite the presence of a nonsensical one.

18   Details of Guyer and Allison's works can be found in the references at the end of this work. My engagement with specific details of their interpretations will be found throughout the footnotes. The student should note that Allison's work, though of a later date, in no sense supersedes Guyer's.

19   Kant himself sets a precedent for such uses of the aesthetic in his treatment of the sublime, though only after first exempting it from the realm of taste. I have presented a version of this thesis on the aesthetic in my *Beauty*. However, given some of the radical misunderstandings that work has encountered, I have no qualms about repeating myself here. The responsibility for much of this misunderstanding perhaps largely lies in my attempt there to combine instruction with entertainment. The reader of the present work will soon discover that I have abjured any attempt at providing the latter on this outing. While the former work strove for colour, the present is resolutely monochrome. Unfortunately perhaps, Kant himself, with his 'fantastic desires', 'striving', and 'longing', has obliged some of that colour to return.

20   My apparent prescience in this matter is due to an anonymous reader for Continuum who actually did raise these objections in a form I paraphrase below. I here express both my gratitude, and the sincere hope that I have not misrepresented their views.

21   This reading certainly receives extensive justification in the text; not least perhaps by the fact that it adequately explains why, at various crucial points throughout the *Critique*, this normally most relentless of philosophers should appear to simply stop making sense. The reading has been most forcefully advocated by Allison (*Kant's Theory of Taste*, pp.7–8; 61; 78; 98–143; 146–9; 176–81; 374 n.28), though it is by no means peculiar to him. Smith, for example, also interprets Kant as being primarily concerned with justifying the claim of judgements of taste to universal validity, but asserts that Kant ultimately 'recognizes the tautologous nature of [his] entire demonstration', and that he has come up 'axiologically empty-handed'; *Contingencies of Value*, pp.64–71. Budd, too, describes Kant's intention being 'a justification of the claim to universal validity intrinsic to a judgement of taste, a proof that the claim to intersubjective validity can be well founded'; *Values of Art*, p.27. See also note 10 to Chapter 3 below.

22   Anyone skimming this book to find out 'what Kant says' is very likely to come a cropper, as indeed they would deserve to.

23   The very genesis of the present work might illustrate this. It began as a projected paragraph in my *Beauty*, grew rapidly to an appendix longer than that work itself, and then to its present size, without ever departing from the limits of its original intention: the drawing out of certain specific implications of Kant's text.

24   With regard to this secondary literature I must note here that there are several currently

influential accounts, or employments, of Kant's text which I do not consider simply because they are irrelevant to the concerns of the present work; for example those of Clement Greenberg, Paul de Man, Jacques Derrida, and Thierry de Duve. Conversely, references to a great deal of eighteenth-century material that is germane to situating Kant's discussion, particularly with respect to the sublime, have been shorn from this final version since it will appear in my forthcoming *Sublimity*. The reader is referred to that work where appropriate.

25   Guyer says that his interest is confined to the 'intersubjective validity of the judgement of taste', and that he limits his discussion of the 'larger systematic pretensions of the third Critique to their bearing on this issue'; *Kant and the Claims of Taste*, p.393. Given the detail in which he considers the text, however, this still amounts to a thorough examination of those 'pretensions'. I have resisted the temptation to offer an account of such questions for the very good reason that they are already thoroughly analysed from a variety of standpoints in the great majority of more recent commentaries to be found in the references; Guyer's work, together with Ginsborg's *The Role of Taste in Kant's Theory of Cognition*, and the first part of Allison's *Kant's Theory of Taste*, are particularly to be recommended.

1 THE DESCRIPTION OF TASTE I

1   Hume *A Treatise of Human Nature*, p.471. This aspect of the fundamental orientation of eighteenth-century aesthetics might be usefully recovered as an antidote to the wishful thinking that still dominates this branch of philosophy.

2   Kant *Critique of the Power of Judgement*, §15, pp.111–13 [226–9].

3   *ibid.*, §1, p.89 [203].

4   *ibid.*, Introduction, pp.75–6 [189].

5   *ibid.*, First Introduction, p.25 [223]).

6   Kant's rejection of the idea that the judgement of taste is a form of knowledge is, of course, most directly aimed against Baumgarten. (Though perhaps also against Moritz' notion of the intrinsic purposiveness of the beautiful object; see Moritz 'On the Concept of That Which is Perfect in Itself' *passim*.) However, the idea of beauty as a form of revelation may be found in a host of writers – from Plotinus to Heidegger and Sircello. It retained sufficient potency in the eighteenth century to make it worth Kant's while to dismiss it. Baumgarten, for example, had defined 'beauty' as 'the perfection of sensuous knowledge'; *Reflections on Poetry*, §§115–17, pp.77–9. (For Kant's implicit response to Baumgarten, see *Critique of the Power of Judgement*, §15, pp.111–12 [226–7]; §44, p.184 [304–5].) Diderot's entry on beauty in the *Encyclopédie* defines beauty as that which 'can reveal to my understanding the idea of relation', adding that it is only the indeterminacy of these relations, the ease with which we group them, and the pleasure which accompanies the sensation, that lead us to believe beauty is an affair of feeling rather than reason; 'The Beautiful', p.138.

7   Kant *Critique of the Power of Judgement*, §5, p.96 [211]; §2, pp.90–1 [205].

8   *ibid.*, §2, p.90 [204]. For an interesting discussion of the relationship between aesthetic pleasure and other kinds of pleasure in Kant, see Zuckert's 'A New Look at Kant's Theory of Pleasure'.

9   Kant *Critique of the Power of Judgement*, §5, pp.94–5 [209–10]. This characterization of the immediacy of beauty is, of course, by no means peculiar to Kant. Leibniz had described taste as 'something like an instinct', distinguished from understanding by the fact that it 'consists of confused perceptions for which we cannot give an adequate reason'; 'Remarks on Three Volumes Entitled *Characteristicks of Men, Manners, Opinions, Times*' (1715) in *Philosophical Papers and Letters*, II, pp.1022–32 (p.1031). 'No sooner the eye

opens upon figures, the ear to sounds', writes Shaftesbury, 'than straight the beautiful results'; *Characteristicks*, II, pp.414–15. Likewise Addison in *The Spectator* No.411, June 21, 1712; Hutcheson *An Inquiry into the Original of our Ideas of Beauty and Virtue*, p.10; the article 'Taste' in Chambers' *Cyclopaedia*; Montesquieu 'An Essay on Taste', p.265; Burke *A Philosophical Enquiry into the Origin of our Ideas of the Sublime and Beautiful*, p.92; Hume *A Treatise of Human Nature*, pp.546–7; Reynolds *Discourses on Art*, p.20 (I, 1769); Rousseau *Emile*, p.340; Diderot *Isolated Thoughts on Painting* (1798) in *Selected Writings*, pp.327–41 (p.329).

10   Kant *Critique of the Power of Judgement*, §4, p.93 [208].

11   *ibid.*, §§4–5, pp.94–5 [208–9]. Zangwill takes issue with Kant's claim that there is always an interest at work in the agreeable; 'Kant on Pleasure in the Agreeable', pp.167–76. His strongest counter-example to Kant's claim is, however, humour, which, while it is obviously not a matter of beauty, is certainly a matter of taste, and, therefore, ultimately, perhaps comprehended by the category Kant calls 'dependent beauty'.

12   Kant *Critique of the Power of Judgement*, §5, pp.94–5 [209–10].

13   *ibid.*, Introduction, p.76 [190].

14   Crawford, for example, mistakenly finds there to be a conflict between Kant's quite compatible assertions that there may be an interest in the existence of a beautiful object and that the pleasure of beauty is disinterested; *Kant's Aesthetic Theory*, pp.25; 44–50. Kant himself, however, though he makes the present distinction in §41, seems to briefly lose sight of this distinction in his remark about the interest in art taken by the connoisseur; *Critique of the Power of Judgement*, §42, p.179 [300].

15   Hutcheson *An Inquiry into the Original of our Ideas of Beauty and Virtue*, p.11.

16   This last point is worth bearing in mind since Kant's insistence on the disinterested nature of the pleasure has often mistakenly been interpreted as the advancement of the theory that a particular form of 'disinterested' contemplation is necessary to the instance of beauty. (As, for example, by Taminaux in *Poetics, Speculation, and Judgement* (pp.55–61), Scruton in *Kant* (p.84), Townsend in 'From Shaftesbury to Kant: The Development of the Concept of Aesthetic Experience' (pp.219–21), and Berleant in 'Beyond Disinterestedness' (pp.242–3). Lyotard also attributes a form of aesthetic attitude to Kant, going so far as to (erroneously) cite Kant's use of the examples of the evanescent patterns created by fire and running water, as instances of typically Kantian beauty; *The Inhuman*, p.32. In fact these examples are given by Kant (*Critique of the Power of Judgement*, §22, pp.126–7 [243–4]), as illustrations of objects which charm the imagination, but which are not beautiful.) In connection with this distinction see Zangwill's 'UnKantian Notions of Disinterest'. Another way of misinterpreting the kind of 'disinterest' involved is demonstrated by Nancy, when he asserts that Kant, in finding the solution to the antinomy of taste, in the harmony of the faculties, the 'self-enjoyment of reason', thereby 'finishes off' the aesthetic; 'The Sublime Offering', pp.31–3.

17   Kant *Critique of the Power of Judgement*, §9, p.104 [219].

18   For such appeals to consensus, most often conceived of as the outcome of the 'test of time' see Pope *Essay on Criticism*, ll. 181–94; Addison *Spectator* No.409, June 12, 1712; Hutcheson *An Inquiry into the Original of our Ideas of Beauty and Virtue*, pp.68–9 (though Hutcheson is, for his time, remarkably coy about a standard of taste); Burke *A Philosophical Enquiry into the Origin of our Ideas of the Sublime and Beautiful*, pp.17–24; Reynolds *Discourses on Art*, p.117 (VII, 1776).

19   Kant *Critique of the Power of Judgement*, §22, pp.96–7 [240].

20   *ibid.*, §6, pp.96–7 [211].

21   *ibid.*, p.97 [211].

22   *ibid.*, §§18–22, pp.121–4 [236–9].

23   *ibid.*, §8, pp.98–9 [213–14].

24   *ibid.*, p.101 [261]; p.99 [213].

25 *ibid.*, §33, p.165 [284–5].
26 *ibid.*, §8, p.101 [215–16].
27 *ibid.*, [216].
28 *ibid.*, §32, p.162 [281].
29 *ibid.*, [281–2].
30 *ibid.*, p.163 [282].
31 *ibid.*, §8, p.101 [216].
32 *ibid.*, §32, p.163 [282].
33 *ibid.*, §34, p.166 [285–6]. The reference to Hume is to the following passage: '[Nature] is more uniform in the sentiments of the mind than in most feelings of the body, and produces a nearer resemblance in the inward than in the outward part of human kind. There is something approaching to principles in mental taste; and critics can reason and dispute more plausibly than cooks or perfumers. We may observe, however, that this uniformity among human kind, hinders not, but that there is a considerable diversity in the sentiments of beauty and worth, and that education, custom, prejudice, caprice, and humour, frequently vary our taste of this kind'; 'The Sceptic' (1742) in *Essays Moral, Political, and Literary*, pp.159–80 (p.163).
34 Hume 'Of the Standard of Taste' (1757) in *Essays Moral, Political, and Literary*, pp.226–49 (p.241) (my emphasis).
35 Kant *Critique of the Power of Judgement*, §13, pp.107–8 [223].
36 *ibid.*, p.108 [223].
37 *ibid.*, §14, pp.109–10 [225]
38 *ibid.*, §8, pp.100–101 [215–16].
39 Mothershill *Beauty Restored*, pp.317–20; 400. Though I have singled out Mothershill and Savile in this section, the tendency dealt with here goes back at least as far as Hegel; see, for example, his *Aesthetics*, I, pp.56–61. Thirty years ago Coleman wrote that the 'first difficulty' Kant presents to contemporary aesthetics is the 'seeming irrelevance' of his concern with beauty; *The Harmony of Reason*, pp.21–2. Like Mothershill, Coleman sees aesthetic pleasure as determined at least in part by an ability to discern style, historical influences, and patterns of composition, and thus finds it a shortcoming of Kant's account that it will not account for 'erroneous aesthetic judgements' (pp.82–3). Körner similarly treats Kant's thesis as if it were principally a theory of art, and suggests that the failure of that thesis to encompass the possibility of 'aesthetic mistakes' can be rectified if we allow that the subject falls into error through 'not having seen the object properly', that is, through the subject's inability to discern that structure of the work of art which 'discloses itself to us only after much attention, labour and patience'; *Kant*, pp.187–8. Interestingly, while for most of the twentieth century Kant's work was distorted by the assumption that, since it was a work in aesthetics, whatever it asserted about beauty must apply to art, Cousin, in lectures first given in 1818, asserts that though Kant considered beauty 'in the soul and in nature', he 'did not even touch the difficult question of the reproduction of the beautiful by the genius of man'; *Lectures on the True, the Beautiful, and the Good*, p.125. In recent years a closer study of Kant has led to some rectification of the prevailing twentieth-century view (see, for example, Cohen and Guyer's introduction to their *Essays in Kant's Aesthetics*, where they acknowledge that Kant's concentration on nature must confuse the modern aesthetician, McCloskey's rebuttal of Wollheim and Goodman's objections to Kant's concentration on beauty in her *Kant's Aesthetic* (pp.6–17), and Allison's assertion, in his *Kant's Theory of Taste*, that Kant's treatment of fine art is 'parergonal to the theory of taste' (p.279)), but everything in the contemporary prosecution of the subject of aesthetics militates against Kant's being taken on his own terms. As a random instance one might here cite Korsmeyer's assertion that Kant was 'wrong' to believe that disgust is incompatible with 'aesthetic liking', since the disgusting is often portrayed in art objects which are objects of 'aesthetic liking'; 'Disgust', pp.43–5. The two

uses of the expression 'aesthetic liking' here, if they are not actually incompatible, at least serve two areas of response of quite different scope: Kant is saying that something cannot be at the same time the object of disgust and an object of pleasure; Korsmeyer is asserting that an object may employ the disgusting to produce a subsequent pleasure. On a quite different philosophical plane there is Lyotard's appeal to Kant for support when asserting that the aesthetic is being destroyed by the ability of modern technology to reproduce objects independent of their 'initial reception', so that the experiencing of them is no longer an experience of the 'here and now'; *The Inhuman*, p.50 (see also pp.34–5; 109–12; 114–18). Lyotard's confusion of immediacy with 'authenticity' is, however, self-evidently incompatible with one of the founding axioms of Kant' theory: that only judgements/feelings of pleasure that do not defer to the provenance (originality, authenticity, and so on) or even real existence of their object can properly be called 'aesthetic'.

40   This is very much connected to the changes in the focus of criticism from predominantly evaluative, with the exposition of merits mostly confined to their reproduction in the criticism, to a form of criticism which is predominantly analytical, and in which evaluation is often merely implicit in the criticism's existing at all. We will return to this subject in the next chapter.

41   Mothershill's approach can be seen as a reaction against the 'pure form' aestheticians of the likes of Pater or Bell, who insisted on using the word 'beauty' to mean aesthetic merit while defining the experience of their 'beauty' in terms which Kant restricted to the experience of free beauty (see, for example, Pater *The Renaissance*, pp.105–9, and Bell *Art*, Chapters I–II *passim*). The obvious inappropriateness of beauty as a model for the experience of art led to a rejection of the use of the word 'beauty' in favour of 'aesthetic merit'. So far so good. At the same time however another approach (as, for example, Collingwood in *The Principles of Art*, p.37) was to claim that beauty only belonged to aesthetic merit and was used inappropriately whenever it was used for things that were merely beautiful. It is in this second tradition that Mothershill and Savile stand. In arguing against the notion that the model of free beauty is inappropriate for art, however, it is against an argument advanced by the 'pure form' aestheticians, rather than Kant, that they are really arguing. Moreover the very fact that they use the same vocabulary as these aestheticians, leads them to retrospectively blame Kant for holding the views that such aestheticians mistakenly took of him. This tangled web is dealt with at some length in Kirwan *Beauty*, Chapter 8.

42   Mothershill *Beauty Restored*, pp.323–31; 372.

43   *ibid.*, pp.423; 222–4.

44   Savile *The Test of Time*, pp.166–81. For a detailed criticism of Savile's argument, particularly in relation to natural cases, see Janaway 'Beauty in Nature, Beauty in Art'.

45   Kant *Critique of the Power of Judgement*, §32, pp.163 [282].

46   Mothershill *Beauty Restored*, p.327.

47   *ibid.*, pp.150; 167; 174.

48   Savile *The Test of Time*, p.183.

49   Mothershill *Beauty Restored*, p.348.

50   Beauty, however, will have its revenge. So that even after absolutely identifying aesthetic value and 'beauty', Mothershill still finds the pull of connotation too strong for such an identification, and ultimately makes the very distinction which elsewhere she has explicitly suppressed, that is, the distinction between what is, in her own words, not '*only* beautiful' but also 'complex, difficult and profound' (pp.422–4). See Kirwan *Beauty*, p.162 n.84.

51   Mothershill *Beauty Restored*, p.163.

52   See also my discussion of Dutton's attack (in his 'Kant and the Conditions of Artistic Beauty', pp.226–31) on Kant's aesthetics as a model for the philosophy of art; Kirwan *Beauty*, pp.114–15. This (mistaken) idea, that Kant's concerns are somehow rendered out-

moded by modern aesthetics, not indeed because the problems he addressed have been solved, but rather because these problems have become irrelevant, is in danger of becoming something of an orthodoxy. According to Adorno it is changes in the actual practice of art that have caused this redundancy (*Aesthetic Theory*, pp.94; 163–6), but others see it more in terms of the increased sophistication of aesthetics itself: Diffey, speculating on the future of aesthetics, records, in passing, his conviction that Anglo-American aesthetics is 'overcommitted' to the Kantian paradigm; 'On American and British Aesthetics', p.175 n.1. Guyer, too, has recently written of the pernicious influence of Kant in encouraging the tendency for most subsequent aesthetics to 'reduce art to some single essential aspect'; 'Kant's Conception of Fine Art', p.275. (I would agree with this, but argue that Kant is only interested in a single aspect – taste – and that the fault, apropos art, lies with his successors. Though, even with regard to taste, the open-minded student is likely to find more food for thought in Hutcheson or Alison than in Kant.) See also Margolis 'A Small Prophecy' and *What, After All, Is a Work of Art?*, p.106. Dickie holds Kant's 'obscure, misguided speculations' responsible for the demise of the rational discussion of taste, and sees his major influence as lying in the rise of the theory of the 'aesthetic attitude'; *The Century of Taste*, pp.3–4. His judgement that Kant's theory 'cannot hold a candle to the highly sophisticated theory of Hume's "Of the Standard of Taste"' (p.114) is supported by an analysis of Kant's theory that, with a complete disregard of any of his modern commentators, takes everything in the most absurd possible sense (pp.85–122), set against an analysis of Hume's theory that gives the most favourable possible interpretation to everything (pp.123–48). Indeed, Dickie holds up Hume's very omissions for particular praise. It is part of the 'sophistication' of Hume's theory, according to Dickie, that he expands the list of 'taste properties' *without* attempting to find a unifying principle (pp.145–6), that he does not appeal to teleology (p.151), that he does not exclude colour from the domain of beauty (p.143), and that he does not assert that there are qualities in objects naturally fitted to produce the feeling of beauty (or at least, since, in fact, he does assert this, does so, according to Dickie, only 'casually'). If the position implied by all these omissions is a significant advance in the theory of taste one might wish that Hume could have been a little more positive about his reason for making them since, given that the essay is less than 25 pages long in a modern edition, as mere omissions they seem to constitute no great achievement.

53 See Kirwan *Beauty*, Chapter 8. An excellent discussion of the relationship between Kant's 'anthropology of aesthetic experience' and the subsequent concentration on theories of art in German philosophy is to be found in the first two chapters of Schaeffer's *Art of the Modern Age*.

54 Kant's notion of immediacy and disinterest has also been attacked from a quite different direction – on the grounds not that it is a mindless pleasure but rather that it is not sufficiently mindless to qualify as anything other than a cultural construct – by Bourdieu, in his *Distinction*. According to Bourdieu Kant's principle of pure taste is nothing other than a 'refusal', a disgust for objects which impose enjoyment and a disgust for the crude, vulgar taste which revels in this imposed enjoyment; *Distinction*, p.488. The pure aesthetic, he argues, is 'the rationalization of an ethos: pure pleasure, pleasure totally purified of all sensuous or sensible interest, perfectly free of all social or fashionable interest, as remote from concupiscence as it is from conspicuous consumption, is opposed as much to the refined altruistic enjoyment of the courtier as it is to the crude, animal enjoyment of the people' (p.493). Kant's analysis of the judgement of taste, he concludes, 'finds its real basis in a set of aesthetic principles which are the universalization of the dispositions associated with a particular social and economic condition' (p.493). (Bürger makes a similar point about class interest; not so much with regard to Kant's characterization of aesthetic judgement as with what he sees as Kant's claim to its universal validity; *Theory of the Avant-Garde*, pp.42–3. An extreme formulation of the same thesis can be found in

Eagleton's *The Ideology of the Aesthetic*, pp.93–8. A critical examination of Eagleton's, and Derrida's, use of Kant can be found in Armstrong; *The Radical Aesthetic*, pp.30–5; 47–50.) Such a judgement naturally follows from Bourdieu's own contention that aesthetic experience is the result of the sublimation of instincts, so that the closer people's judgements adhere to norms of morality or agreeableness the more 'natural' they are, but this is a contention that would need to be more firmly established before it could be used as counter-argument to Kant's account. (Kant did at one time himself see taste as arising from the sublimation of instincts; see 'Conjectures on the Beginning of Human History' *passim.*) It is true that details of Kant's account, such as his rejection of the lower senses as potential sources of aesthetic experience, tend to lend weight to Bourdieu's thesis, but since such deductions do not in fact follow from the original antinomy but rather from the fact that Kant has prejudged the outcome of his enquiry, reading such prejudices back into the very formulation of the antinomy is not justified. Kant does deduce an ethos from taste, though this ethos does not belong organically to it. (It is Bourdieu who ultimately confuses ethos with aesthetic.) A very different political implication is given to Kant's *sensus communis* by Arendt, who, while acknowledging that taste may appear to be 'an essentially aristocratic principle of organization', nevertheless argues that the manifestation of personality, and the implicit refusal to be 'overwhelmed . . . by the world of the beautiful' inseparable, in her view, from the judgement of taste, is a significant instance both of resistance to coercion, and deference to the sense of community; *Between Past and Future*, pp.220–6. (See also Arendt *Lectures on Kant's Political Philosophy*, pp.66–74.) This thesis appears to rest on a strikingly objectivist notion of the aesthetic, which the present work does not share. For a sympathetic account of Arendt's use of Kant see Curtis *Our Sense of the Real*, pp.114–23; for criticism of her thesis, from both political and philosophical points of view, see Ferguson *The Politics of Judgement*, pp.102–13, and Cascardi *Consequences of Enlightenment*, pp.132–74. Gadamer gives a brief, useful, but not entirely reliable, history of the notion of the *sensus communis*, *Truth and Method*, pp.19–29. He assigns a crucial role to Kant in that history, by virtue of his 'radical subjectivization' of the aesthetic, and his rejection of any role for a *sensus communis* in the ethical or the cognitive (pp.38–55).

55   Kant *Critique of the Power of Judgement*, §34, p.166 [285–6].
56   *ibid.*, §8, p.101 [216].
57   *ibid.*, §7, p.98 [212].
58   *ibid.* [213].
59   *ibid.*, §8, p.101 [216].
60   *ibid.*, §9, p.102 [217].
61   *ibid.* Kemal attributes to Kant the much stronger claim that 'the very structure of judgement . . . is a constant negotiation between individual and community' in that, while beauty 'depends on a feeling . . . *first* that feeling must be confirmed by other judgements', since 'lack of confirmation [by the social formation] would reduce pleasure to a merely subjective response rather than an act of judging aesthetically'; *Kant's Aesthetic Theory*, pp.71; 124 (my emphasis). (It is a striking instance of what Kant calls the 'tendency to follow a habitual train of thought' that Kemal can argue, in the face of Kant's own explicit assertion that the judgement of taste is merely subjective, that being 'merely subjective' would disqualify a response from being a Kantian judgement of taste.) Yet, though Kant will ultimately assert that there are *a priori* principles of taste, and, therefore, by implication, true and false judgements of taste, he can only do so on the premise that taste is autonomous, that is, is *not* such a deference to consensus. A 'judgement' that waited to be confirmed would disqualify itself from being an authentic judgement of taste. Moreover, since the principle that Kant discovers is *indeterminate*, there is nothing other than authentic (that is, 'merely subjective') judgements of taste that could serve as the basis for such a consensus: 'Since an aesthetic judgement is not an objective and cognitive judgement, [its] necessity cannot be derived from determinate concepts, and is therefore not

apodictic. Much less can it be inferred from the universality of experience (from a complete unanimity in judgements about the beauty of a certain object). For not only would experience hardly supply sufficient evidence of this, but it is also impossible to ground any concept of the necessity of these judgements on empirical judgements'; *Critique of the Power of Judgement*, §18, p.121 [237].

62 Kant *Critique of the Power of Judgement*, §7, p.98 [213].
63 *ibid.*, §19, p.121 [237].
64 *ibid.*, §20, p.122 [237–8].
65 *ibid.*, §22, p.123 [239]. Indeed, at this stage Kant can still ask whether the existence of this 'indeterminate norm of a common sense' is in fact necessary as a constitutive principle of the possibility of the experience or not (p.124 [239–40]).
66 *ibid.*, §22, p.124 [240].
67 *ibid.*, p.123 [239].
68 Especially if we compare such 'disagreements' with those that might arise from a difference over cognitive judgements in which both sides appeal to the same objective principle.
69 Kant *Critique of the Power of Judgement*, §22, p.85 [240].
70 Diderot 'In Praise of Richardson' (1762) in *Selected Writings*, pp.82–97 (p.94).
71 Kant *Critique of the Power of Judgement*, §7, p.97 [212].
72 *ibid.*, §34, p.165 [285].
73 Kant 'On a Newly Arisen Superior Tone in Philosophy', p.58.
74 Hume *A Treatise of Human Nature*, pp.546–7.

2 THE DESCRIPTION OF TASTE II

1 Kant *Critique of the Power of Judgement*, §10, p.105 [220].
2 *ibid.*, §§10–11, pp.105–6 [220–1]; §17, p.120 [236].
3 *ibid.*, §15, pp.111–13 [226–9].
4 *ibid.*, p.112 [227–8].
5 *ibid.*, §17, p.120n [236].
6 *ibid.*, §16 p.115 [231].
7 *ibid.*, p.114 [229].
8 *ibid.*
9 *ibid.*, pp.114–15 [230].
10 *ibid.*, §17, p.120 [236].
11 Carritt asserts that such a distinction 'simply does not exist'; *The Theory of Beauty*, p.113. He does, however, go to the trouble of a confutation (pp.113–19). Cassirer, by contrast, deliberately passes over the sections concerning this distinction in his *Commentary on Kant's Critique of Aesthetic Judgement*, Beardsley does not even mention it in his exposition of Kant's theory in *Aesthetics from Classical Greece to the Present* (pp.210–25), Osborne, in his *Aesthetics and Art Theory*, sees it as simply an error (p.118), and Dickie, despite the various interpretations recently advanced, dismisses the concept of what he calls 'accessory beauty' as inexplicable; *The Century of Taste*, p.114. Pluhar mentions the distinction under the heading 'Beauty and Fine Art', but his treatment is cursory; 'Introduction' to Kant *Critique of Judgement*, pp.lxvi–lxviii. Kemp avoids the problem by asserting that judgements of dependent beauty are not judgements of taste at all, but merely bear 'some resemblance' to them, being rather judgements based on the conformity of the object to our normative idea of such objects; *The Philosophy of Kant*, p.105. Crawford likewise asserts that in describing 'dependent beauty' as a 'judgement of taste' Kant cannot be using the latter phrase in the strict sense of 'the product of a disinterested act of judging an object noncognitively'; *Kant's Aesthetic Theory*, pp.24–5. Like Kemp, he concludes that a judgement of dependent beauty 'is to be analysed as an assessment of a

close approximation to the perfection or ideal of the kind' (p.114). Budd takes a similar line, interpreting 'dependent beauty' as a 'combination of a pure judgement of taste . . . with a judgement of qualitative perfection', while conceding that the concept 'suffers from a number of obscurities', and that Kant may possibly have meant that the delight involved arises not from the presence of a pure judgement of taste but rather from the very judgement that the object is qualitatively perfect; 'Delight in the Natural World: Kant on the Aesthetic Appreciation of Nature. Part I: Natural Beauty', pp.10–11. Guyer proposes two explanations for the contradiction that 'dependent beauty' appears to contain: firstly, that Kant is perhaps merely stating a commonly held opinion – that beauty is a form of perfection – rather than himself positing the existence of such a thing as dependent beauty, or, secondly, that he is proposing that there are judgements of taste which do involve (are 'restrained' by) concepts of purpose, but which are not fully determined by such concepts; *Kant and the Claims of Taste*, pp.244–53. This is, however, according to Guyer, 'an inadequate interpretation of Kant's claim that judgements of dependent beauty *presuppose* concepts of what objects should be' (p.247). (Guyer enlarges on the second alternative in his 'Dependent Beauty Revisited', written in reply to what he sees as Wicks' misrepresentation of his views in Wicks' 'Dependent Beauty as the Appreciation of Teleological Style'. Wicks' response to Guyer can be found in 'Can Tattooed Faces Be Beautiful?'; see also his 'Kant on Beautifying the Human Body'.) Zammito interprets Kant's distinction as a confused attempt to develop a theory of taste that could encompass more than just such 'trivial' phenomena as sea shells, flowers, and arabesques; *The Genesis of Kant's Critique of Aesthetic Judgement*, pp.124–9. Bernstein makes the distinction 'wholly-dependent on Kant's moral theory'; *The Fate of Art*, pp.32–5; 36–8. Scruton attacks the distinction on the grounds that there is only dependent beauty, that is, that it would be 'absurd' to suppose that someone could say a thing was beautiful unless they knew what it was; 'Aesthetics', p.17. (This is obviously a thesis that presumes a rather idiosyncratic definition of 'beautiful'.) Lorand takes the view that, since the beauty of an object depends upon its context, and every object must, inescapably, have a significance, all beauty must be dependent; 'On "Free and Dependent Beauty" – A Rejoinder', pp.250–3. (She is answering Stecker's and Lord's replies to her earlier 'Free and Dependent Beauty'; see also Stecker 'Lorand and Kant on Free and Dependent Beauty' and Lord 'A Note on Ruth Lorand's "Free and Dependent Beauty: A Puzzling Issue"'.) Kant was 'wrong', she writes in a later paper, for 'neglecting the fact that non-conceptual value is and must be preconditioned'; 'The Purity of Aesthetic Value', p.20. (Though I broadly agree with this conclusion, I do not believe that it is strictly relevant to Kant's distinction, as we shall see in the next section.) Likewise Dutton rejects the very existence of free beauty, and even discerns such a rejection by Kant himself in the course of the later sections of the *Critique of the Power of Judgement*; 'Kant and the Conditions of Artistic Beauty'. Allison, while acknowledging that the distinction is problematic, insofar as judgements of dependent beauty do not appear to be judgements of taste at all, suggests (following Gammon's 'Kant: *parerga* and *pulchritudo adhaerens*') that while the beauty of a dependently beautiful object is recognized by a pure judgement of taste, nevertheless the 'overall assessment' of the object is conditioned by a concept of the object's perfection: 'a judgement of adherent beauty is not *purely* a judgement of taste, though the taste component within the complex evaluation itself remains *pure*'; *Kant's Theory of Taste*, p.290 (see also pp.138–43; 290–8).

12   Chambers *Cyclopaedia*, p.94.
13   Kames *Elements of Criticism*, I, pp.244–5. Something similar is to be found in Addison's distinction between 'primary' and 'secondary' pleasures of the imagination (*Spectator* No.411, June 21, 1712; *Spectator* No.416, June 27, 1712); in Hutcheson's distinction (which appears to be Kames' most immediate model) between 'absolute' and 'comparative' beauty (*An Inquiry into the Original of our Ideas of Beauty and Virtue*, p.13); in Hume's

distinction between the naturally beautiful and the beautiful that depends upon the 'humour' of the beholder ('Of the Standard of Taste' (1757) in *Essays Moral, Political, and Literary*, pp.226–49 (pp.243–4)); in Reynolds' distinction between 'the beauty of form alone', that is, the beauty of symmetry and proportion, and that beauty which is the result of an effect on the imagination 'by means of association of ideas' (*Discourses on Art*, p.212 (XIII, 1786)); and in Alison's distinction between the 'natural beauty' of forms, that is, that beauty which results from those qualities in forms 'in themselves' that are 'expresssive to us', and 'relative beauty', that is, that beauty which is the result of our 'discovering' evidence of design, fitness, or utility in the form (*Essays on the Nature and Principles of Taste*, p.299). None of these distinctions exactly parallels Kant's, nor would I wish to imply that Kant took up a form of this distinction merely because it was the convention. Rather what I wish to emphasize by this rehearsal is the fact that Kant, like his predecessors, is addressing a real problem within the theory of taste. Indeed, since first drafting this note I have come across a recent work by Zangwill arguing that Kant's 'invaluable but misunderstood' distinction could be resurrected, though shorn of his terminology and specific views on aesthetic judgement, in order to produce a 'feasible aesthetic formalism'; *The Metaphysics of Beauty*, pp.55–81. Unfortunately, there is not here room to do justice to the way in which Zangwill develops this argument.

14 Kant *Critique of the Power of Judgement*, §16, p.114 [229]. For the historical context of Kant's assertion about the beauty of the abstract, and the influence of this assertion on the rise of formalist aesthetics, see Morgan 'The Idea of Abstraction in German Theories of Ornament from Kant to Kandinsky'.

15 Kant *Critique of the Power of Judgement*, §16, pp.114–15 [230].

16 *ibid.*, p.114 [229].

17 *ibid.*

18 Reynolds *The Idler* No.82.

19 Kant *Critique of the Power of Judgement*, §2, pp.90–1 [205].

20 *ibid.*, §16, pp.115–16 [231].

21 Budd claims that the concept of dependent beauty is rendered necessary by Kant's need to 'introduce a qualification into his account in order to accommodate judgements of artistic value'; *Values of Art*, p.30. Budd understands dependent beauty to refer to an object exemplifying 'the function of the kind of object it is a beautiful specimen of' (p.31). This makes sense in view of the example he himself chooses – a church – but it is perhaps more difficult to see how, given that the function of a work of art is to appeal to taste, it could be applied elsewhere. Indeed he seems to ignore the fact that dependent beauty is a kind of beauty, and to retract his own distinction, when he writes that 'given the satisfaction of the requirement that the work is a successful realization of the artist's intention, its artistic value is determined by whether it is beautiful' (p.31). McAdoo is closer to the mark when he advances Kant's 'dependent beauty' as an anticipation of Sibley's anti-formalism; McAdoo 'Sibley and the Art of Persuasion', pp.36–8. (He is principally referring to Sibley's 'Aesthetic Concepts'.)

22 For a further discussion of the place of music in Kant's outline of the arts see Weatherston's 'Kant's Assessment of Music in the *Critique of Judgement*', Kivy *Philosophies of Arts* (pp.12–17), and (partly in response to Kivy) Bicknell 'Can Music Convey Semantic Content?' (pp.256–60). (In light of the widespread criticism of Kant during the twentieth century for his 'reduction' of the aesthetic to the mindless, it is interesting that Gilson advances Kant's attitude to music as illustrative of his philistinism; see Gilson *The Arts of the Beautiful*, pp.152–3; *Forms and Substances in the Arts*, pp.182–3.) Schaper presents an extended argument against the idea that Kant's distinction is intended to create a hierarchy of taste in her *Studies in Kant's Aesthetics*, pp.78–98.

23 Kant *Critique of the Power of Judgement*, §22, p.126 [242–3].

24 One might, of course, claim it is the sound of the line that is beautiful (though to Kant

this would be the agreeable rather than the beautiful) but it seems impossible to claim, calligraphy aside, that the beauty is the result of neither sound nor sense.

25 Kant *Critique of the Power of Judgement*, §15, pp.112–13 [228]. How or why these two different kinds of apprehension of the same object should be possible, or why, on any particular occasion, it should be one rather than the other Kant does not, at this stage, make clear.

26 *ibid.*, p.113 [228].

27 *ibid.*, §16, pp.114–15 [230].

28 *ibid.*, p.115 [230].

29 It may be a different object insofar as it does not strike you as dependently beautiful, though this does not mean that, asked to choose the horse that most immediately struck you as beautiful from among one hundred horses, you would choose a different horse to Kant.

30 While regretting that Kant should be under the necessity of using 'beauty' to refer to what is, by his own definition, not beauty, I will nevertheless carry on, for the most part, using the expression 'dependent beauty', since to use the term 'aesthetic merit' in the context of the discussion of a work in which 'aesthetic' has quite a different meaning would only add to the confusion. Moreover, as we have seen, Kant does not exclude the possibility that 'free beauty' can be found in art, yet the expression 'aesthetic merit' is often now used to mean whatever particular merit is found in a work of art. This unfortunate combination of facts would place us in the situation of having to say, at least in order to be consistent with some uses of 'aesthetic merit', that sometimes beauty (free beauty) is an 'aesthetic merit' (dependent beauty).

31 If we consider the use of 'aesthetic' within the contemporary discipline of aesthetics this distance between Kant's 'aesthetic' and our own becomes even more marked. The notion of the intelligibility of 'aesthetic merits' (or dependent beauties) has come to dominate both the theory and the practice of art in the twentieth century; to the extent of the almost universal, if only implicit, acceptance of the institutional definition of 'art', in which an associated concept of a certain kind is the only property which an object need be perceived (by the artworld) as 'possessing' in order for that object to qualify as art, and, therefore, to be part of the subject matter of aesthetics.

32 Addison in *The Spectator*, Nos.409; 411–21, June–July 1712.

33 Kant *Critique of the Power of Judgement*, §49, p.192 [313–14]. The germ of this apparently paradoxical notion of an idea that is aesthetic (in Kant's sense) can be found in Baumgarten's discussion of poetry as the perfection of *sensate representations*; *Reflections on Poetry*, §§3–8, pp.38–9. Such representations, according to Baumgarten, are not distinct, as are the representations of the intellect, but rather possess what he calls *extensive clarity*: the more that is gathered together in a confused complex concept, which also conveys what is represented as good or bad, the more powerful the effect, and the more *poetic* the representation (§§14–18, pp.23–6; 42–3; 47–8). Kant's own treatment of such ideas, however, seems to owe its working out more to the discussion of poetry in Part Five of Burke's *Philosophical Enquiry into the Origin of our Ideas of the Sublime and the Beautiful*, the hint for which may be traced back to Addison's *The Spectator* No.416, June 27, 1712, and No.418, June 30, 1712. A similar notion of poetry, explored quite speculatively, can be found in Diderot's *Lettre sur les sourds et muets* (1761).

34 Kant *Critique of the Power of Judgement*, §49, p.192 [314].

35 *ibid.*, pp.193; 194 [315; 316].

36 It is not surprising that Kant should claim that it is in poetry that 'the faculty of aesthetic ideas can reveal itself in its full measure'; *Critique of the Power of Judgement*, §49, p.193 [314]. Literature is the most obviously conceptual of the arts, its very material (language) being inescapably symbolic, and for this reason it stood at the pinnacle of the hierarchy of arts in the eighteenth century. Reynolds, for example, writes that painting is only entitled

to be called a Liberal Art, only able to rank itself as 'a sister of poetry', insofar as the painter endeavours to captivate the 'imagination' of the spectator not by means of the power of imitation, but by the 'grandeur' of the 'ideas' expressed; *Discourses on Art*, pp.51; 43 (III, 1770).

37 Kant *Critique of the Power of Judgement*, §51, p.197 [320].

38 *ibid.*, pp.197–8 [320]. Dickie deals at some length with the connection between aesthetic ideas in art and nature; *The Century of Taste*, pp.112–14. However, through mistakenly interpreting Kant's subject as the aesthetic idea as it might exist in the mind of a producer (artist) rather than a beholder, he concludes that by an aesthetic idea in nature Kant means evidence of 'God's purposiveness striving to intimate to human beings something beyond the bounds of their experience' (p.113).

39 Kant *Critique of the Power of Judgement*, §45, pp.185–6 [306–7].

40 *ibid.*, §65, pp.246–7 [375].

41 *ibid.*, §44, pp.184–5 [305–6]; §45, pp.185–6 [306–7]; §58, pp.224–5 [350–1]. Unless, of course our taste is for works of art that appeal to our intellect (conceptual art), though in such cases it could be argued that an aesthetic idea is at work in the subject's representation of their own liking of the work. This is not a question, however, that Kant felt it necessary to address.

42 Kant *Critique of the Power of Judgement*, §65, pp.246–7 [374–6].

43 *ibid.*, §51, pp.197–8 [320].

44 *ibid.*, §17, p.116 [231]; §8, p.101 [215–16].

45 *ibid.*, §17, p.116 [231–2].

46 *ibid.*, §32, p.163 [282].

47 *ibid.*, §17, pp.116–17 [232].

48 *ibid.*, p.117 [232–3].

49 *ibid.*, pp.117–19 [233–5].

50 Though he elsewhere says that 'strictly speaking . . . perfection does not gain by beauty, nor does beauty gain by perfection'; the effect of the two together being a consequence of two separate, though harmonious, states of mind (§16, p.115 [231]).

51 *ibid.*, §17, p.120 [236]).

52 *ibid.*, p.116 [231]. Likewise Reynolds, for all his emphasis on the principles of art, asserts that 'Could we teach taste or genius by rules, they would be no longer taste and genius'; *Discourses on Art*, p.45 (III, 1770).

53 Kant *Critique of the Power of Judgement*, §49, pp.193–4 [314–16].

54 That a work of art is, by definition, an appeal to taste, is perhaps a contentious point, but, as I have suggested elsewhere (Kirwan *Literature, Rhetoric, Metaphysics*), if it is not such an appeal it would appear to be no more than a very crude and inefficient form of something else.

55 Many years ago now Osborne suggested that a sharper distinction should be drawn between taste and aesthetic judgement; the former being the domain of those objects that we like, and the latter that of those objects we 'seek contact' with 'for the expansion of awareness and deepening of experience or insight that appreciative commerce with them brings'; 'Introduction' to *Aesthetics*, pp.1–24 (p.16). The remarks above should have made it clear that I do not believe either that these domains are separable, or that taste should be identified, as Osborne identifies it, simply with 'affection'. Nevertheless, a distinction between 'taste' meaning individual preference, and 'taste', meaning the standard enshrined in the (current) outcome of the test of time, or in the preferences of the most cultivated, was commonplace in the eighteenth century. Indeed, so commonplace was it that while examples of its use are abundant it is rarely spelt out explicitly; an exception is Kames in his *Elements of Criticism* (III, pp.351–74). It is a distinction very clearly brought out by Madame de Staël in Chapter XIV of her *Germany*.

56 Indeed it would be more accurate to say that twentieth-century academia was hostile rather than indifferent to the notion of taste.

57 Hence Budd's claim that it is a strong argument against Kant's 'ill-conceived and ill-motivated notion of an "aesthetic idea"', that it implies 'that it is impossible for anyone to have a good reason to believe that a work of art she experiences as the expression of a certain set of aesthetic ideas is experienced by another person as the expression of the same set of ideas', and, even worse, that 'nobody would be able to identify *for herself* the aesthetic ideas expressed in a work of art'; *Values of Art*, pp.33; 182. On the contrary, these seem strong arguments in favour of the notion.

58 Kant *Critique of the Power of Judgement*, §49, p.193 [315].

59 *ibid.*, §16, p.115 [230].

60 *ibid.*, §34, p.166 [285–6].

61 *ibid.*, §22, p.126 [243].

62 *ibid.*, §42, pp.181–2 [301–2].

63 *ibid.*, §22, p.126 [243].

64 *ibid.*, pp.126–7 [243–4].

65 I have had just this experience myself on a country platform where all the birds of Kitaku turned out to be coming from a loudspeaker. Though, if wistfulness can be an aesthetic merit (dependent beauty), then such mechanical reproduction is not necessarily without aesthetic merit – whether such a merit was intended or not. A similar case has been reported to me of the effect of discovering that the greenness of a pair of green eyes was attributable to art rather than nature; though here no aesthetic merit was subsequently discerned.

66 Kant *Critique of the Power of Judgement*, §49, p.194 [316]

67 *ibid.*, §42, pp.180–1 [300–2].

68 And vice versa. As one who knows the biological function of the shape, colour and scent of flowers (so that teleologically they stand for me on the same footing as mould), I aver that this knowledge appears irrelevant to the aesthetic potential of flowers. Consider the hypothetical case of Kant discovering the flowers were artificial.

69 Kant *Critique of the Power of Judgement*, §42, p.181 [301–2].

70 *ibid.*, §51, p.197 [320].

71 *ibid.*, pp.197–8 [320].

72 See Kirwan *Beauty*, pp.59–62.

73 Kant's touching so indirectly on this question has, indeed, led many commentators on the *Critique* to simply ignore the phenomenon of 'free beauty' (modern 'beauty') altogether, and concentrate instead on that 'dependent beauty' which can be squared with the modern concept of aesthetic value.

74 Hume *A Treatise of Human Nature*, pp.546–7.

75 The subject may, of course, be unaware of the true grounds of their feeling. It is, for example, a psychological commonplace that disapproval is often 'really' envy, that anger is often, or perhaps always, 'really' fear, and so on. But such assertions, if they mean anything, can only mean that the real anger, that is, the anger that is felt, is grounded in fear. It would be nonsense otherwise to talk of fear giving rise to anger.

76 Sometimes, indeed, the more a critic 'demonstrates' the value by appealing to the meaning, the more tenuous the connection between that meaning and any value may come to seem.

77 In fact Kant offers his 'key' to the critique of taste at an early stage: in the 'second moment' of the analytic of the beautiful, at a point which the present exposition left behind some time ago. In the first edition of the *Critique of Pure Reason* (1781) Kant claimed in a footnote that a critique of judgement was impossible since there can be no *a priori* laws by which our judgements of taste are directed. In the second edition (1787) he adds the qualification 'determinate' to '*a priori*', thereby implying that there can be indeterminate *a priori* laws of taste. This change has often been pointed out. What is less often noted is that the rest of the footnote, concerning the futility of trying to bring the critical treatment of the beautiful under rational principles, is left unaltered.

3 THE GROUNDS OF TASTE

1 Kant *Critique of the Power of Judgement*, §36, pp.168–9 [288].
2 *ibid.*, §6, p.97 [211].
3 *ibid.*, §57, p.220 [346].
4 *ibid.*, [345–6].
5 *ibid.*
6 According to Kant Burke's approach consists of 'observations' rather than 'explanations': *Critique of the Power of Judgement*, First Introduction, p.38 [238]. Physiology and psychology are, of course, by no means distinct entities in this period. (See, for example, the discussion of eighteenth-century theories of insanity in Porter's *Mind Forg'd Manacles*, pp.169–228.) Appropriately for the age of taste it is the action of changes in temperature on a specimen of sheep's tongue that Montesquieu brings forward as experimental evidence in support of his thesis that 'imagination, taste, sensibility, and vivacity' are all dependent on climate; *The Spirit of Laws*, XIV, §2, p.103.
7 Kant *Critique of the Power of Judgement*, First Introduction, p.38 [238].
8 *ibid.*, p.39 [238]. Guyer holds that Kant does, indeed, offer 'a speculatively psychological explanation of our pleasure in the beautiful', and that it is only by considering that he does offer such an explanation that the *Critique of the Power of Judgement* can be squared with the conclusions of the *Critique of Pure Reason: Kant and the Claims of Taste*, pp.10; 96–9.
9 Hume 'Of the Standard of Taste' (1757) in *Essays Moral, Political, and Literary*, pp.226–49 (p.230).
10 Kant's first statement of the deduction comes in §9, entitled 'Investigation of the question: whether in the judgement of taste the feeling of pleasure precedes the judging of the object or the latter precedes the former'. Some commentators have interpreted 'judging of the object' as synonymous with 'judgement of taste', despite the fact that this produces a nonsensical question, and, given that Kant does conclude that such a judgement (of the object) must precede that pleasure (which he nevertheless asserts is the only way in which the judgement of taste is cognized), an even more nonsensical answer. The kind of 'judgement' Kant has in mind here will be dealt with in the present chapter, but it is worth considering one of the effects of Kant's approaching the deduction from the viewpoint of this question of priority. Since, as Kant says in §9, the 'subjective unity of the relation [judged present by the subject] can make itself known only through sensation', there is no reason to suppose that this relation (between imagination and understanding) will be brought into play by the same objects in all subjects; *Critique of the Power of Judgement*, §9, p.104 [219]. It is only by making the presupposition (commonplace in eighteenth-century discussions of taste) that, since whatever is at the basis of judgements of taste is apparently disinterested, it must be called into play in a uniform manner, that Kant can make the deduction itself a proof that it does. This circularity has been much discussed in the secondary literature on the *Critique*. See, for example, Kemp who argues that Kant makes the judgement precede the pleasure since if it did not this pleasure would be merely subjective and private; *The Philosophy of Kant*, p.102. Crawford likewise takes the line that Kant gives priority to the judgement over the pleasure in order to assert the existence of a universal validity; *Kant's Aesthetic Theory*, pp.69–74. Guyer rejects the idea that Kant claims, in the *Critique of the Power of Judgement*, that a recognition of intersubjective validity is a condition of any judgement of taste, though he does attribute such a belief to Kant in the period preceding the writing of that work, and interprets some of the more unsustainable claims of the *Critique* as the result of Kant's own lack of clarity with regard to his mature theory; *Kant and the Claims of Taste*, pp.15; 29. (He offers further reasons for Kant's inclusion of such a claim in the *Critique* on pp.154–60.) Guyer addresses, at some length, the question of whether Kant claims we can actually be directly conscious of the harmony of the faculties (the 'judgement' of the title to §9) independently of the

pleasure it gives us, and concludes that Kant is ultimately asserting that, though such a judgement must precede the pleasure, it must be in some way unconscious, since it is 'the feeling of pleasure itself which is the ground for thinking that the object produces the harmony of the faculties, rather than the reverse' (pp.99–105). (Caygill, by a very different route, comes to the same conclusion; *The Art of Judgement*, pp.324–38.) Allison specifically attacks Guyer's interpretation on the grounds that to deny the intentionality of feeling for Kant would imply that the pleasure 'must be regarded as an inference-ticket, from which the free harmony is then inferred', and this would render the judgement of taste an 'empirical causal claim, and a rather problematic one at that'; *Kant's Theory of Taste*, pp.51–4. Zammito interprets this 'judgement' of §9 as the 'act' of reconfiguring, or playing with the form, and sees in Kant's distinction between the 'judgement' and the pleasure the intention to differentiate the active pleasure of taste from the passive pleasure of the agreeable; *The Genesis of Kant's Critique of Aesthetic Judgement*, pp.106–115. Similarly, Ginsborg rejects the idea that the 'judgement' and the pleasure are to be sharply distinguished, arguing that to feel disinterested pleasure is to judge an object beautiful; *The Role of Taste in Kant's Theory of Cognition*, pp.70; 72. She interprets Kant's apparently paradoxical claim (in §9) that the feeling of pleasure is *consequent* on its universal communicability to mean only that my state of mind in judging the object beautiful is one that assumes the judgement that 'everyone who perceives the object should share' this feeling of pleasure: it is Kant's 'way of conveying that the feeling of pleasure makes manifest the act of claiming the universal communicability of one's state of mind' (pp.71; 73). (This is similar to the thesis I have advanced in Chapter 1.) This interpretation makes Kant's description of the harmonious interplay of imagination and understanding (the 'judgement' of §9) not an explanation of the separate, psychological, grounds of taste but rather 'a derivative and metaphorical characterization of a state that is fundamentally to be understood . . . in purely logical or conceptual terms' (p.74). (Ginsborg pursues this argument in depth in the first chapter of her book; pp.3–41.) In contrast with these approaches, Schaper uses the distinction, between the pleasure and the 'aesthetic experience' (Kant's 'judgement'), made in §9, to assert that the relationship between the two is not a necessary one, thereby leaving room for the idea of a standard of taste; 'The Pleasures of Taste', pp.53–5. Kemal, moving even further in the same direction, gives 'communicability' a very strong sense, interpreting Kant to mean that we cannot know we have made a judgement of taste (as opposed to a judgement on the merely agreeable) until it is confirmed by other subjects; so that 'more than anything else, our particular claims that objects are beautiful denotes a relation between subjects'; *Kant's Aesthetic Theory*, pp.88–99. It is possible that none of these commentators has sufficiently distinguished the two general uses of 'taste' in the eighteenth century mentioned in note 55 to the last chapter: one to refer to the private act of judging, the other to participation in a public institution of 'good taste' (consider, for example, Johnson's assessment of Milton, or the scrabble to establish *legitimacy* for such new forms as the novel); rather as today some distinguish, hierarchically, art and entertainment, without actually consulting their own taste in the matter at all. That these two senses are somewhat confused in Kant's text accounts perhaps for the fact that support can be drawn from it for such widely differing interpretations as Ginsborg's and Kemal's.

11   Kant *Critique of the Power of Judgement*, §35, pp.167–8 [287].

12   *ibid.*, §9, p.102 [217].

13   *ibid.*

14   *ibid.*, Introduction, p.77 [191].

15   *ibid.*, §21, p.123 [238].

16   *ibid.* [238–9]

17   *ibid.*, §61, p.233 [359]. Kant's theory will not provide specific *a priori* properties for beautiful forms any more than Hutcheson's. This is generally recognized among modern com-

mentators. Guyer, for example, asserts that Kant's theory of taste and his formalism are 'not so intimately connected as has traditionally been supposed'; *Kant and the Claims of Taste*, pp.209–10. Likewise Caygill *Art of Judgement*, pp.285–99. (Indeed, Caygill makes this *aporia* the actual subject of the third critique. Bernstein makes a similar claim, describing the *Critique of the Power of Judgement* as an 'act of mourning on the coming into being of autonomous aesthetics'; *The Fate of Art*, pp.7; 60–5. Mortensen similarly gives Kant a key role in the rise of the concept of 'disinterest', and its, in his view, concomitant tendency to elitism in aesthetics; *Art in the Social Order*, pp.157–62.) Likewise Crowther, who argues that Kant confuses the logical conditions of cognition (necessarily singular) with the psychological process (possibly varied) whereby subjects discriminate and respond to form; *The Kantian Sublime*, pp.64–77. Allison, rightly, holds that there is no contradiction between Kant's formalism and his emphasis on aesthetic ideas, since the expression of such ideas requires a form; *Kant's Theory of Taste*, pp.288–9. Some, however, find it more convenient to deny that Kant is a formalist at all. Kemal, for example, interpreting the *Critique of the Power of Judgement* as a book on aesthetics in the modern sense, emphasizes the fact that Kant talks both of the 'free play' of the faculties and, in discussing poetry, the 'play with ideas'. However, he glides over the fact that it is the play, not the ideas, that are, according to Kant, the source of the effect; *Kant's Aesthetic Theory*, pp.145–51.

18   Though Zammito characterizes Kant's purpose in the *Critique of the Power of Judgement* to effect a 'Copernican revolution' in aesthetics – to shift the basis of the judgement of taste from the object to the subject, and, ultimately, to the subject's reason – such an ambition would have been a strange one in 1790, given that no such revolution was then necessary; *The Genesis of Kant's Critique of Aesthetic Judgement*, pp.89–94. Such a view ignores both the parallels between Hutcheson's 'final cause' and the grounding Kant provides, and Kant's own formalism, as evinced in the quotation above. Kant, seemingly with Hutcheson's own assertion of the superior beauty of one simple geometrical figure to another in mind, emphatically rejects the idea of such figures being a type of beauty, on the grounds that they are too determinate (*Critique of the Power of Judgement*, 'General remark on the first section of the Analytic', pp.124–7 [240–4]) but something like Kant's conception of a fugitive uniformity amid a more complex variety would serve Hutcheson's own theory better.

19   Hutcheson *An Inquiry into the Original of our Ideas of Beauty and Virtue*, pp.95–7. In Hutcheson's scheme, of course, the universe becomes evidence of the *ultimate* intelligibility of our own existence in a way that does not occur in Kant. We shall return to this point in Chapter 8.

20   Kant *Critique of the Power of Judgement*, §21, p.123 [238–9]. This uniformity emerges, however, only by default: an *unconditioned* command as to 'how we ought to judge' is presupposed by judgements of taste inasmuch as 'they would have the satisfaction known to be *immediately* connected with a representation' ('General remark on the exposition of aesthetic reflective judgements', p.159 [278]).

21   *ibid.*, §32, pp.163–4 [283]; §33, pp.164–5 [284–5].

22   *ibid.*, §22, pp.123–4 [239–40].

23   *ibid.*, §9, p.104 [219].

24   *ibid.*, §57, p.219 [344].

25   *ibid.*, §35, p.168 [287]; §31, p.162 [281].

26   Guyer, borrowing the vocabulary of the *Critique of Pure Reason*, characterizes Kant's appeal to a supersensible substratum as a foundation for the universal validity of taste as 'pseudo-rational', and the product of a 'transcendental illusion'; *Kant and the Claims of Taste*, p.7. He rightly points out that the noumenal neither follows from nor is necessary to the concept of the harmony of the faculties (pp.338–46). Its main function, avers Guyer, appears to be to dispose of any scepticism about the universal validity of particular

subjects. Schaeffer attributes Kant's deduction to 'specific requirements of Kantian philosophy – which seeks a direct experience of the supersensuous that it elsewhere declares to be impossible (whence the paradoxical character, which is purely formal, of aesthetic teleology); it is not called for by specific aesthetic considerations'; *Art of the Modern Age*, pp.26–7. Schaper, too, rejects Kant's 'last step to a seemingly triumphant disclosure of the supersensible'; *Studies in Kant's Aesthetics*, pp.131–2. Mothershill describes the concept of the supersensible substratum as 'a refuge for ignorance', and its introduction into the *Critique of the Power of Judgement* as 'mechanical and high-handed'; 'Hume and the Paradox of Taste', p.281. Budd declares that the deduction 'depends upon a rather murky conception of the mental mechanisms at work in perception of the world'; 'Delight in the Natural World: Kant on the Aesthetic Appreciation of Nature. Part I: Natural Beauty', p.6. Savile notes that the reader is 'taken aback' by the sudden appearance of the supersensible in Kant's account, which has hitherto placed such emphasis on the subjective; *Kantian Aesthetics Pursued*, p.41. Savile rejects the notion that Kant is offering a further positive explanation of the necessity of judgements when he brings forward the supersensible, and instead sees the most likely, or, at least, excusable, reason for its introduction lying in its serving a purely negative role: as another way of saying that 'the necessity to [judge something beautiful] cannot be provided with any fuller explanation than that when all is taken into account there remains nothing else to think, and that there remains nothing else to think for the reason that the response of delight that the beautiful object calls forth is one that is entirely proper to it, given that it has the material and intellectual constitution which it does and that it is presented to us in the social and cultural setting in which it is' (pp.61–2). This seems to take us right back to the initial observations that though critics can argue more plausibly than cooks, beauty, in itself, is still the *je ne sais quoi*. Other commentators, however, have been more sympathetic to its introduction. Zammito, for example, interprets Kant as saying that the subject inevitably must think of the supersensible, and that the only way to do so is through symbolism; *The Genesis of Kant's Critique of Aesthetic Judgement*, pp.91–4. Hence the inclusion of the supersensible in Kant's discussion. (Scherer, interpreting the concept in perhaps the same way, but putting quite a different value on such an interpretation, rhapsodically asserts that it is Kant's justifiable intention to show how aesthetic judgement reconciles the phenomenal and the noumenal; *The Crisis of Judgement in Kant's Three* Critiques, pp.189–95.) This does not, however, constitute a justification of its appearance. Pluhar takes Kant's own line when he claims that the concept of the supersensible is implicit in the deduction itself; 'Introduction', pp.lxi–lxvi. Allison sees the appeal to the supersensible as 'neither a desperate attempt to bolster the original deduction of taste now a mere exercise in architectonics', but rather 'an attempt to lay the foundation for the account of beauty as the symbol of morality'; *Kant's Theory of Taste*, p.254 (see also pp.208–11). These differences would seem to arise more from differences in the interpretation of the notion of the supersensible itself.

27 Kant *Critique of the Power of Judgement*, §31, p.162 [281].

28 Croce *Aesthetic as Science of Expression and General Linguistic*, pp.280–2. Ferry, though without mentioning Neoplatonism by name, also makes Kant's solution at least contain an echo of the Neoplatonic theory of beauty as an intimation of the divine when he writes that, for Kant, 'The Beautiful is, precisely, one of [those objects which can symbolically evoke the Idea of God required by reason]; as a *partial* reconciliation of nature and spirit, of sensibility and concepts, it functions as a contingent trace – dependent on the real itself – of this necessary idea of reason'; *Homo Aestheticus*, p.88. This does not, of course, make Kant's theory dependent on the supernatural, but only on the idea of the supernatural. Moreover, Ferry is here writing of Kant's description of an effect of the beautiful, not its cause. More recently Dickie has confused this distinction, arguing that the 'central task' of the *Critique of the Power of Judgement* is to 'justify believing in an unexperienced teleo-

logical world', and that, according to Kant, in experiences of beauty 'the tracings of God's purposiveness' are revealed; *The Century of Taste*, pp.91; 106. Deleuze argues just the opposite: that the *Critique of the Power of Judgement* is intended to demonstrate the redundancy of the divine from an explanatory point of view; *Kant's Critical Philosophy*, p.96. We shall see why such widely divergent interpretations are possible in Chapter 8 below.

29 Kant *Critique of Pure Reason*, pp.268, 272.

30 Kant *Critique of the Power of Judgement*, §§56–7, pp.214–15 [338–9].

31 *ibid.*, §57, p.218 [342]. It should be noted here how Kant returns to the supposition, only hinted at previously, that the 'aesthetic idea' is fundamental to beauty.

32 It is worth noting that the existence of a standard of taste, which is a highly speculative matter, is treated as such by Kant; is treated, indeed, with more circumspection than many a more avowedly prosaic theorist has treated it. As was noted before, despite the parallels with Hutcheson's theory, Kant quite definitely, as we shall see in Chapter 8, rejects what is metaphysical in Hutcheson's account.

33 That a universal validity of specific judgements does not follow from the harmony of the faculties as Kant appears to want to make it do is generally agreed upon among Kant's commentators. Coleman observes that Kant's concept of beautiful form is not sufficiently developed to rebut the objection of the relativist who might argue that there is no reason why the *sensus communis* should respond similarly in all societies or at all times; *The Harmony of Reason*, pp.152–6. Kant's affirmation of the standard of taste is also rejected by Guyer (*Kant and the Claims of Taste*, p.132), Schaper (*Studies in Kant's Aesthetics*, p.64), and McCloskey (*Kant's Aesthetic*, pp.82–9). Guyer deals with what he identifies as three different attempts by Kant to establish the rationality of aesthetic judgements; *Kant and the Claim of Taste*, pp.279–307; 308–30; 331–50. The first two fail, according to Guyer, for internal reasons, and the third 'transgresses Kant's own . . . limits on metaphysics' (p.278). Guyer does, however, see Kant's explanation, based on the harmony of the faculties, as successful, in the sense that it can explain 'how we may take a pleasure in objects which is truly independent of individual interests and concerns, and which is rooted in an objective . . . which may surely be attributed to everyone' (p.328). 'Whatever its flaws', he concludes, 'Kant's aesthetic theory certainly comes closer to explaining both the uniqueness and the rationality of aesthetic judgements than previous attempts' (p.329). Crowther takes a similar line in *The Kantian Sublime*, pp.140–2; see also his 'The Significance of Kant's Pure Aesthetic Judgement'.

34 Kant *Critique of the Power of Judgement*, §57, p.217 [341].

35 *ibid.*, Preface, p.58 [170]. After three decades of intense interest in the third critique in the English-speaking world, it seems that commentators are at last turning away from the attempt to find in that critique either a fully developed, comprehensive aesthetics or a solution to the standing problem of the nature of the aesthetic itself. Indeed it would have been strange if such a theory had lain so long hidden in so conspicuous a text. Instead aesthetics is beginning to incline more towards Schopenhauer's verdict that Kant's achievement was to distinguish precisely what the problem of the aesthetic was, by locating it in the hitherto (and, arguably, subsequently) neglected realm of the subject, but that, having marked out the correct path, Kant himself 'missed the mark'; *The World as Will and Representation*, I, p.530. Henrich, for example, after praising Kant in terms similar to those used by Schopenhauer, and before setting out his own interpretation of what he calls Kant's 'unacceptably metaphorical' notion of 'harmonious play', asserts that the *Critique of the Power of Judgement* accomplishes 'almost nothing' with respect to the elucidation of this key concept; *Aesthetic Judgement and the Moral Image of the World*, pp.33–40.

36 Many of these commentators, as we have seen in Chapter 1, being primarily interested in the nature of art, take Kant to task for neglecting the role of concepts in beauty. As we have also seen, however, the *Critique of the Power of Judgement* does contain the description of a kind of beauty that is more appropriate to the modern conception of aesthetic

merit than beauty that might be grounded in a harmonious activity of the faculties in apprehending an object that appropriately combines unity and heterogeneity. This other form of 'beauty' is, of course, dependent beauty; so called, however, because it, too, is an object of taste, that is, because the 'aesthetic idea' is, ultimately, no more amenable to an analysis that would 'prove' its value than is the 'combination of unity and heterogeneity' possessed by what Kant calls a *beautiful form*.

4 THE SUBLIME

1 Kant *Critique of the Power of Judgement*, 'General remark upon the exposition of aesthetic reflective judgements', p.149 [226].

2 Schaeffer holds that in the *Critique of the Power of Judgement* 'the theory of the sublime is a mere side issue that is not easy to integrate into aesthetic judgement as a whole'; *Art of the Modern Age*, p.3. Guyer, in *Kant and the Claims of Taste*, deliberately does not deal with the sublime. One reason is that Kant's 'analysis of this particular aesthetic merit will not be of much interest to modern sensibilities' (a statement he naturally retracted 14 years later in light of the upsurge of interest in what at least purported to be 'Kantian sublimity'; *Kant and the Experience of Freedom*, pp.187–8); *Kant and the Claims of Taste*, p.400 n.1. Moreover, Kant's treatment of sublimity strikes Guyer as an afterthought, 'a concession to the standard topics of eighteenth-century aesthetics (or taste!)', and one that 'adds nothing' to Kant's inquiry into the relation between subjective aesthetic response and intersubjective aesthetic validity (*ibid*). (Allison, too, holds that the account of the sublime, together with that of fine art and genius, 'serves to frame Kant's theory of taste, rather than constituting an essential part of it'; *Kant's Theory of Taste*, p.272. He avers that Kant's attitude towards the sublime is 'deeply ambivalent', and that he only decided to include it at the last moment (pp.303–7).) I think that Schaeffer and Guyer (in *Kant and the Claims of Taste*) are right in their judgement on the relation of the sublime to Kant's analysis of taste, insofar as Kant asserts that the sublime is not a matter of taste. However, I deal with the sublime here on the premise that Kant is wrong, and that the sublime is a matter of taste. Even starting from this premise, however, I would still agree with Guyer's judgement that Kant's analysis is a concession to standard topics in eighteenth-century aesthetics, insofar as the sublime is only one of a host of aesthetic affects, and its apparent fundamentality in 1790 was an historical accident. I have gone into the rather mundane reasons why the sublime achieved such prominence in the eighteenth century (and why it regained that prominence at the end of the twentieth) in my *Sublimity*.

3 It can be said, without exaggeration, that there is nothing original in Kant's account of the sublime, not even his proposed grounding. The currently widespread belief to the contrary arises from a general ignorance of writing on the sublime in the eighteenth century, outside of the idiosyncratic example of Burke. See the first three chapters of Kirwan *Sublimity*.

4 Kant *Critique of the Power of Judgement*, §23, p.128 [244].

5 *ibid.*

6 *ibid.*

7 *ibid.*, §24, p.131 [247].

8 *ibid.*, §23, p.129 [245].

9 *ibid.* [245–6].

10 *ibid.*, p.130 [246].

11 *ibid.*, pp.128–9 [245].

12 *ibid.*, p.130 [246]; §24, p.131 [247]. In his earlier *Observations on the Feeling of the Beautiful and Sublime* he had divided the sublime into three: the terrifying, the noble, and the splendid (p.48).

13 Kant *Critique of the Power of Judgement*, §25, pp.133–4 [250].
14 *ibid.*, §26, p.135 [251].
15 *ibid.*, p.138 [255].
16 *ibid.*, p.139 [255].
17 Kant *Critique of the Power of Judgement*, §26, p.140 [256]. Kames uses the same instance of mental progression as an example of a grand conception; *Elements of Criticism*, I, pp.272–3.
18 Kant *Critique of the Power of Judgement*, §26, pp.135–6 [251–2]. The misapprehension that Kant restricts the sublime to nature (in contrast to art) appears to be rather widespread in the 'tertiary' literature.
19 Kant *Critique of the Power of Judgement*, §28, p.144 [260–1]. For war and God, see *ibid.*, pp.146–7 [262–4].
20 *ibid.*, p.144 [260].
21 The phrase 'delightful horror' is to be found in Burke; *A Philosophical Enquiry into the Origin of our Ideas of the Sublime and Beautiful*, p.73. Kant does not use the phrase, though such a characterization is implied by his description. Moreover he refers to Burke as 'the foremost author' on the empirical exposition of the sublime; *Critique of the Power of Judgement*, 'General remark on the exposition of aesthetic reflective judgements', p.158 [277].
22 See Chapter 1 of Kirwan *Sublimity*.
23 Kant *Critique of the Power of Judgement*, §26, p.138 [255].
24 *ibid.*, §27, p.141 [258].
25 *ibid.*, p. 142 [258].
26 *ibid.*, §28, pp.144–5 [261–2].
27 *ibid.*, §26, p.140 [256–7].
28 *ibid.*, §25, p.134 [250].
29 *ibid.*, §27, pp.142–3 [259]; §28, p.145 [261].
30 *ibid.*, §27, p.142 [259].
31 *ibid.*, pp.141–2 [258].
32 *ibid.*, pp.140–1 [257–8].
33 *ibid.*, §28, p.144 [260].
34 *ibid.* [261].
35 *ibid.*, pp.144–5 [261].
36 *ibid.* [261–2].
37 *ibid.*, p.145 [261–2].
38 *ibid.*, §26, pp.137–40 [254–6].
39 *ibid.*, §25, p.134 [250].
40 *ibid.*, 'General remark upon the exposition of aesthetic reflective judgements', pp.151–2 [269].
41 *ibid.*, p.152 [269].
42 *ibid.*, p.156 [274].
43 *ibid.*, p.152 [269].
44 *ibid.*, pp.149–50 [266].
45 *ibid.*, §23, p.128 [244].
46 *ibid.*, §25, p.133 [249]; §28, p.147 [264]; §26, p.139 [256].
47 *ibid.*, §23, p.130 [246].
48 *ibid.*, p.129 [245–6].
49 *ibid.*, p.130 [246].
50 *ibid.*, §24, p.131 [247].
51 *ibid.*, §23, pp.128–9 [244–5].
52 *ibid.*, 'General remark upon the exposition of aesthetic reflective judgements', p.151 [269].

53   *ibid.*, §30, p.160 [279].
54   *ibid.* [279–80].
55   *ibid.*, pp.160–1 [280].
56   *ibid.*, p.161 [280].
57   *ibid.*, 'General remark upon the exposition of aesthetic reflective judgements', p.149 [266].
58   In fact it is far more common for eighteenth-century commentators to enumerate sublime things than beautiful things. Their lists demonstrate that there is not only a clear consensus on what is sublime but also a definite spectrum of objects, running in a natural sequence from the most abstract or formless – the thought of the size of the universe, or a noble action – to the most concrete – tigers and serpents. See Kirwan *Sublimity*, Chapter 1.
59   Kant *Critique of the Power of Judgement*, §28, p.147 [264]; §23, p.130 [246].
60   *ibid.*, 'General remark upon the exposition of aesthetic reflective judgements', pp.152–3 [270–1].
61   *ibid.*, §28, p.146 [262].
62   *ibid.*, pp.144–5 [261].
63   *ibid.*, §27, p.141 [257]; 'General remark upon the exposition of aesthetic reflective judgements', p.152 [269].
64   Jeffrey 'Review of *Essays on the Nature and Principles of Taste*', pp.23–4. This is Jeffrey's elaboration on an example given by Alison in his *Essays on the Nature and Principles of Taste* (pp.146–8). Alison's other main example – the mistaking of a distant rumbling for the onset of an earthquake – is not well chosen, as the standpoint of relative safety which sublimity requires is singularly lacking in the direct experience of this particular natural phenomenon.
65   Blair includes sublimity, alongside beauty, under the heading of pleasures of taste, or of the imagination, though he distinguishes it on the grounds of its 'more precise and distinctly marked' character; *Lectures on Rhetoric and Belles Lettres*, p.29. Later he writes that while the emotion of sublimity is 'very distinguishable' from that of beauty, the latter cannot, indeed, be considered so homogeneous as the former (p.51). Beauty, he writes, extends 'to a much greater variety of objects than sublimity; to a variety indeed so great, that the feeling which beautiful objects produce, differ considerably, not in degree only but also in kind, from one another' (pp.51–2).
66   Kant *Critique of the Power of Judgement*, §27, p.143 [260]. Indeed, it is the comic rather than the sublime, which really stands out as distinctive, in point of effect, among dependent beauties. Some theories of the comic make all comedy depend on the same teleology as Kant has given to the sublime! While such theories certainly do not give an adequate account of comedy as a whole, there are obviously some kinds – 'black comedy', and slapstick, for example – to which they, and Kant's teleology of the sublime, would seem to apply.
67   Guyer, in his *Kant and the Experience of Freedom*, has given an extensive justification of Kant's distinction between the sublime and the beautiful, in terms of significant psychological and phenomenological details (pp.192–228). It should be clear from the foregoing that I am not at all arguing that the sublime is not distinct from the beautiful, but only that there is nothing in the distinction that Kant makes – unless, that is, we unconditionally subscribe to the grounds he provides for each – which would justify his making sublimity the object of some other kind of judgement than a judgement of taste.

5 REASON AND MORALITY IN THE SUBLIME

1   Kant *Critique of the Power of Judgement*, §30, pp.160–1 [279–80].
2   *ibid.*, §27, p.141 [257–8].

3   *ibid.*, pp.140–1 [257–8].

4   *ibid.*, 'General remark on the exposition of aesthetic reflective judgements', p.156 [274].

5   *ibid.*, §24, p.131 [247].

6   *ibid.*, §27, p.141 [257].

7   *ibid.*, §29, p.148 [264]. It is far from clear what evidence might be advanced to support this claim, but whether or not it is true is irrelevant here.

8   *ibid.*, §25, pp.131–4 [248–50].

9   *ibid.*, §39, p.172 [292].

10 *ibid.*, §23, p.129 [245–6].

11 *ibid.*, §29, p.148 [264–5]. As, for example, Johnson in the Highlands; *A Journey to the Western Islands of Scotland*, pp.60–1.

12 Kant *Critique of the Power of Judgement*, 'General remark on the exposition of aesthetic reflective judgements', p.151 [268].

13 See Kirwan *Sublimity*, Chapter 3 *passim*. The vague feeling that certain tastes (though no longer the sublime) are inextricably bound up not merely with a certain 'degree' of culture, but also with a certain 'degree' of moral sensitivity is, of course, still with us.

14 Kant *Critique of the Power of Judgement*, 'General remark on the exposition of aesthetic reflective judgements', p.151 [268].

15 *ibid.*, §29, p.149 [265].

16 *ibid.*, [265–6].

17 Kant *Groundwork to the Metaphysic of Morals*, p.67.

18 *ibid.*, pp.62–5.

19 Kant *Critique of Practical Reason*, pp.83–4.

20 *ibid.*, p.64.

21 *ibid.*

22 Kant *Perpetual Peace: A Philosophical Sketch*, p.116. In *Groundwork to the Metaphysic of Morals* Kant writes that 'all men have already of themselves the strongest and deepest inclination towards happiness, because precisely in this Idea of happiness all inclinations are combined into a sum total' (p.64).

23 Kant *Perpetual Peace: A Philosophical Sketch*, p.116.

24 Kant *Groundwork to the Metaphysic of Morals*, p.76.

25 *ibid.*, pp.75–6.

26 Kant *Critique of Practical Reason*, p.83.

27 Kant 'On the Common Saying: "This May be True in Theory, but it does not Apply in Practice"', p.69.

28 *ibid.*

29 *ibid.*

30 Kant *Groundwork to the Metaphysic of Morals*, p.71. 'For the matter of that, not even does a man's inner experience with regard to himself enable him so to fathom the depths of his own heart as to obtain, through self observation, quite certain knowledge of the basis of the maxims which he professes, or of their purity and stability'; Kant *Religion Within the Limits of Reason Alone*, p.57.

31 Kant *Critique of the Power of Judgement*, §40, p.174n [294].

32 Kant *Groundwork to the Metaphysic of Morals*, p.120.

33 *ibid.*

34 Kant *Critique of Practical Reason*, pp.78–9. Indeed not only is this respect not counter to our status as sensuous beings, but, according to Kant, that respect, in being 'an effect on feeling and thus on the sensibility of a rational being . . . presupposes the sensuousness and hence the finitude of such beings' (p.79).

35 I will use 'respect' and 'reverence' promiscuously throughout this discussion, in line with the fact that the translations referred to translate the same German word *Achtung* as both. Paton says that he translates the word *Achtung* as 'reverence' rather than the more common

'respect', since it appears to him that the feeling Kant describes is 'almost akin to religious emotion'; *The Categorical Imperative*, p.63.

36 Kant *Groundwork to the Metaphysic of Morals*, p.120.
37 *ibid.*, p.66.
38 *ibid.*, p.120.
39 *ibid.*, p.66n.
40 Kant *Critique of Practical Reason*, p.80.
41 *ibid.*, pp.81–2.
42 *ibid.*, p.80.
43 Kant *Critique of Practical Reason*, p.132n.
44 *ibid.*, p.89. An advantage, indeed, which it arguably enjoys over Kant's own approach to the subject also.
45 Kant *Groundwork to the Metaphysic of Morals*, p.103.
46 *ibid.*, pp.103–4.
47 Kant, it seems, had at one time subscribed to the moral feeling thesis. In Beck's discussion of this question he refers to Duisburg Fragment 6, where Kant, according to Beck, asserts that morality is a necessary condition of happiness, that only virtue can bring about happiness (though it does not always necessarily do so), and that this happiness is not the source of the worth of morality. Nevertheless, in this fragment, according to Beck, Kant's position is that 'to feel that we are the authors of a state of being worthy of happiness . . . is itself a positive self-contentment, and this constitutes the human worth of morality'; *Commentary on Kant's Critique of Practical Reason*, p.215. It is only later, Beck continues, that Kant replaced the idea of the happiness resulting from morality as the motive of morality, and replaced it with the doctrine that moral happiness is not a motive but merely a corollary effect of moral purpose (p.216).
48 Kant *Groundwork to the Metaphysic of Morals*, p.96.
49 Kant *Critique of the Power of Judgement*, 'General remark on the exposition of aesthetic reflective judgements', p.156 [274].
50 *ibid.*
51 *ibid.* [275].
52 Kant *Groundwork to the Metaphysic of Morals*, p.89.
53 *ibid.*, p.89n. Damisch makes a brief and rather unusual case for Kant's positing of sexual appetite as the root of all judgements on women's beauty; *The Judgement of Paris*, pp.55–7. Shell discusses the role, or rather the significance of the absence of a role, for female beauty in the *Critique of the Power of Judgement* in her *The Embodiment of Reason*, pp.219–24.
54 Kant 'On the Common Saying: "This May be True in Theory, but it does not Apply in Practice"', p.71 (my emphasis). 'The majesty of the moral law (as of the law on Sinai) instils awe (not dread, which repels, nor yet charm, which invites familiarity); and in this instance, since the ruler resides within us, this *respect*, as of a subject toward his ruler, awakens a *sense of the sublimity* of our own destiny which enraptures us more than any beauty'; Kant *Religion Within the Limits of Reason Alone*, p.19n.
55 Kant 'On a Newly Arisen Superior Tone in Philosophy', p.68.
56 Kant *Critique of Practical Reason*, p.89 (my emphasis).
57 *ibid.*, p.87.
58 Kant *Anthropology from a Pragmatic Point of View*, p.65; 'On a Newly Arisen Superior Tone in Philosophy', p.72n.
59 Kant 'On a Newly Arisen Superior Tone in Philosophy', p.71.
60 *ibid.*, p.87.
61 Kant *Critique of the Power of Judgement*, 'General Remark on the Exposition of Aesthetic Reflective Judgements', pp.153–4 [271].
62 Kant *Critique of Practical Reason*, pp.120–1.
63 *ibid.*, p.121.

64 *ibid.*
65 *ibid.*
66 *ibid.*, p.122.
67 *ibid.*, pp.122–3.
68 Kant *Groundwork to the Metaphysic of Morals*, pp.96–7.
69 *ibid.*, p.120.
70 Kant *Critique of the Power of Judgement*, 'General remark on the exposition of aesthetic reflective judgements', pp.156–7 [275].
71 Paine, for example, after remarking that 'the sublime and the ridiculous are often so nearly related that it is difficult to class them separately', instances both the story of Joshua commanding the sun and moon to stand still, and the phrase 'Let there be light' (exemplary of the sublime even for Longinus, let alone most eighteenth-century writers) as illustrating the 'puerile', 'pitiful', and 'ridiculous' effects of unsuitable assays on sublimity; *The Age of Reason*, pp.751n; 828n.
72 Kant *Critique of the Power of Judgement*, 'General remark on the exposition of aesthetic reflective judgements', pp.157–8 [276].
73 The sublime was, almost by definition, transporting and irresistible. See Kirwan *Sublimity*, Chapter 1.
74 Kant *Critique of the Power of Judgement*, 'General remark on the exposition of aesthetic reflective judgements', p.157 [275].

6 THE ANATOMY OF AN AESTHETIC IDEA

1 Kant *Critique of the Power of Judgement*, §59, p.227 [353]. The rather tentative tone of Kant's suggestion that beauty at least 'prepares us to love something . . . without interest' ('General remark on the exposition of aesthetic reflective judgements', p.151 [267]) is to be found elsewhere in the eighteenth century. Reynolds, for example, describes the arts as 'an inferior school of morality', in that they cultivate 'the pleasures of the mind, as distinct from those of the sense'; *Discourses on Art*, p.149 (IX, 1780). 'Whatever abstracts the thoughts from sensual gratifications,' he continues, 'whatever teaches us to look for happiness within ourselves, must advance in some measure the dignity of our nature', since, even if 'refinement of taste . . . does not lead directly to purity of manners, [it] obviates at least their greatest depravation, by disentangling the mind from appetite' (pp.150–1). A more modern statement of the same kind of idea can be found in Crowther's 'The Significance of Kant's Pure Aesthetic Judgement', in which Crowther implies, on the basis of pure aesthetic judgement's disclosure of our 'free-belonging to the world', a more direct link than I have drawn here between Kant's thesis and morality. Allison holds that a potential connection between taste and morality 'lies at the very heart of Kant's project, though it presupposes, and therefore cannot help to ground, the normativity of the pure judgement of taste'; *Kant's Theory of Taste*, pp.195; 212–8. For a detailed discussion of the immediate German context of the attempted conflation of the aesthetic and the moral in the concept of the *schöne Seele*, see Norton *The Beautiful Soul*, Chapters 4–6 *passim*.
2 Kant *Critique of the Power of Judgement*, §59, pp.227–8 [354].
3 *ibid.*, 'General remark on the exposition of aesthetic reflective judgements', p.154 [271].
4 *ibid.*, p.154n [272].
5 *ibid.*, pp.154–5 [272–3]. (In light of the definition Kant gives, Meredith's 'sentimentality' appears preferable to Guyer and Matthews' 'oversensitivity'.) Kant's strictures here on what is evidently the contemporary cult of 'Sensibility' are comparable to Mackenzie's similarly based attack on the 'sentimental novel', comparing the dangers of the 'enthusiasm of sentiment' with those of religious enthusiasm, in an untitled article in *The Lounger* (No.20, June 18, 1785). What is noteworthy is how both Mackenzie, in his own

novels, and Kant, in that choice of argumentative illustration that reflects his admiration of Rousseau, both today appear guilty of precisely the sentimentality they indict.

6   Kant *Critique of the Power of Judgement*, 'General remark on the exposition of aesthetic reflective judgements', pp.157–8 [275–6]. It is in this positive sense that 'melancholy' is used in Thomas Gray's *Elegy Written in a Country Churchyard* (1751).

7   Kant *Critique of the Power of Judgement*, 'General remark on the exposition of aesthetic reflective judgements', p.154 [272].

8   *ibid.* [272].

9   *ibid.* The relationship between the sublime and enthusiasm was, indeed, a close and problematic one during the eighteenth century. See Kirwan *Sublimity*, Chapter 2 *passim.*

10   As we have seen above, every strenuous feeling, which excites the consciousness of overcoming a resistance and leaves behind an impression of the mind's strength and resoluteness (even in the case of anger, desperation, or impetuous action) is aesthetically sublime, while the 'yielding', though it may be beautiful, leads to enervation of the heart and insensibility to duty. In Kant the emphasis is definitely on the superiority ('manliness') of the sublime – Kant cites, as examples of manly sublimity of soul, the waging of war (providing civilians are respected), and decries the 'weakness' that comes from prolonged peace; *Critique of the Power of Judgement*, §28, p.146 [263]. (Meredith translates Kant's *Weichlichkeit* here as 'effeminacy' (p.113). In this regard see Kant *Observations on the Feeling of the Beautiful and Sublime*, pp.76–96. For a discussion of the role of gender in Kant's account of the sublime see Gould 'Intensity and Its Audiences', and Battersby 'Stages on Kant's Way'.) Later Schelling will speak of the sublime (which he restricts to art) as a source of 'heroic resolve', and a means of 'cleansing' oneself of pettiness, cowardice, weakness, and intellectual flaccidity; *The Philosophy of Art*, pp.87–90. It is not surprising that Adorno should claim that Kant, by 'situating the sublime . . . in overwhelming grandeur . . . directly affirmed his unquestioning complicity with domination'; *Aesthetic Theory*, p.199. More recently Huhn has described the sublime as 'the justification of domination and violence', and the making of 'domination pleasurable and violence beautiful'; 'The Kantian Sublime and the Nostalgia for Violence', p.269. (Rosiek accuses Kant of blindly celebrating the powers of reason, and indulging in a superfluous 'vocabulary of violence and displeasure . . . with a satisfaction that is perhaps less than reasonable and disinterested'; *Maintaining the Sublime*, p.35.) This thesis, while a useful response to the recent positing of the sublime (in, for example, Crowther's *The Kantian Sublime*, Lyotard's *Lessons on the Analytic of the Sublime*, Budd's 'Delight in the Natural World: Kant on the Aesthetic Appreciation of Nature. Part III: The Sublime in Nature', pp.245–7, or Budick's *The Western Theory of Tradition*) as somehow aesthetically and morally superior to the beautiful, nevertheless, as I hope my account will show, overstates the case.

11   Kant *Critique of the Power of Judgement*, 'General remark on the exposition of aesthetic reflective judgements', pp.154 [272].

12   *ibid.*, p.155 [273].

13   *ibid.*, pp.155–6 [274].

14   The relationship between the sublime and the moral, as was indicated in the last chapter, had been seen as problematic. See Kirwan *Sublimity*, Chapter 3 *passim.*

15   Kant *Critique of the Power of Judgement*, §49, p.194 [316]. Allison objects to the idea of connecting the sublime with aesthetic ideas on the grounds of the great difference in the operation of the imagination in the two cases: in 'the beautiful and its expression of aesthetic ideas, the imagination points to the supersensible in virtue of its being . . . *too* rich for the understanding', while, by contrast, in the sublime it is the imagination's '*inability* to realize the demands of reason, that accounts for the manner in which it points to the supersensible'; *Kant's Theory of Taste*, pp.340–1. The point is well taken, but the notion of an aesthetic idea in the sublime is pursued here precisely because Kant fails to establish

that aspect of the grounding of the sublime (that is, its 'essentially negative manner of presentation') upon which this distinction rests.

16 Kant *Critique of the Power of Judgement*, §49, p.192 [314].

17 I am using 'symbolic' here in the sense that Kant gives the word in §59.

18 Addison *The Spectator* No.411, June 12, 1712.

19 Historically, of course, the 'false sublime' was a well-established category in aesthetic discourse. It is to be found in Longinus himself, and in most eighteenth-century discussions of the sublime, including Kant's own earlier *Observations on the Feeling of the Beautiful and Sublime*.

20 Kant 'On the Common Saying: "This May be True in Theory, but it does not Apply in Practice"', p.69.

21 Kant *Groundwork to the Metaphysic of Morals*, pp.71–2.

22 *ibid.*

23 Kant, as we have seen, himself defines 'sentimentality' ('oversensitivity' in Guyer and Matthews' translation) in such a way as to cover many actual instances of the sublime in the eighteenth century: 'A sympathetic pain that will not let itself be consoled, or with which, when it concerns invented evils, we consciously become involved, to the point of being taken in by the fantasy, as if it were real'; *Critique of the Power of Judgement*, 'General remark on the exposition of aesthetic reflective judgements', p.155 [273].

24 Dennis, in writing of how, in the sublime, 'the soul is amazed by the unexpected view of its own surpassing power', revealingly reflects that 'greatness of mind is nothing but pride well regulated'; *Remarks on a Book Entituled, Prince Arthur, An Heroick Poem. With Some General Critical Observations, and Several New Remarks upon Virgil* (1696) in *The Critical Works of John Dennis*, I, pp.46–144 (p.47).

25 Kant *Critique of the Power of Judgement*, 'General remark on the exposition of aesthetic reflective judgements', p.155 [273]. There are times when we have found something sublime and then almost immediately, once out of its presence, begin to doubt, often, curiously, on moral grounds, the basis of its sublimity. But the sublimity has already existed by then – we have *done* it. We can, of course say, as no doubt Kant would in the case of war, anger, or desperation, that it is the abstract principle (of the domination of sensibility) expressed that is sublime, but, in fact, we cannot even be sure of the principle.

26 Kant *Critique of the Power of Judgement*, 'General remark on the exposition of aesthetic reflective judgements', pp.152–3 [270–1]. This is another consideration that negates the usefulness of the test for sublimity mentioned at the end of Chapter 4.

27 *ibid.*, §27, p.141 [257].

28 This conclusion, which I believe is a correct assessment of the phenomenon of sublimity, also squares with the quite reasonable supposition that only the satisfaction of an interest of sensibility is capable of producing a pleasure. (How the pleasure that is attendant on mere cognition, which Kant describes in the introduction to the *Critique of the Power of Judgement*, can be reduced to an interest of sensibility is adequately demonstrated in Hutcheson's aesthetics.) Although this view of the sublime would have been unremarkable in the eighteenth century, among modern commentators on Kant's sublime only Mothershill, to the best of my knowledge, admits it: 'The sense of spiritual elevation is not an indication of actual spiritual elevation'; 'Sublime', p.411.

29 Other eighteenth-century theories of the sublime are dealt with in my *Sublimity*. With regard to the grounding of the sublime, if not the implications of that grounding, Kant's theory may be taken as a synthesis of those theories. Of subsequent theories, once one has filtered out the Kantian, those that are either overtly or covertly theological, and those which confuse the sublime with the merely overwhelming, the uncanny, the horrifying, or the disgusting, the only real contender left is probably Collingwood's account in *Outlines of a Philosophy of Art*, pp.34–44.

30 Freudian interpretations of the sublime, such as Weiskel's 'deidealization' of Kant (*The

Romantic Sublime, pp.21–8; 99–106), Kristeva's notion of the sublime as the edge of the abject (*Powers of Horror*, pp.1–31), or Herz' application of both the preceding (*The End of the Line*, pp.4–60; 217–39) suffer from two drawbacks. Firstly, they are Freudian and therefore (though not necessarily in Kristeva's case) depend on a belief in the Oedipal; secondly, and more importantly, since these three instances of interpretation are worked out, to a greater or lesser extent, in the context of examinations of the literary 'embodiment' of sublimity, the theoretician is invariably working back towards some form of positive evaluation in terms of the cognitive or therapeutic. (Criticism of Weiskel's approach in terms of his misuse of Kant can be found in Crowther's *Critical Aesthetics and Postmodernism*, pp.140–5.) Crockett (who identifies the source of the Kantian sublime in Freud's 'uncanny') goes as far as saying that 'in his notion of the sublime, Kant "discovers" what later becomes known as the Freudian unconscious'; *A Theology of the Sublime*, pp.109–12. The 'Freudian' interpretation of the sublime closest to the theory I will advance in the present work is made by Freud himself in the opening section of *Civilization and its Discontents* where he discusses the 'oceanic feeling' – a feeling which signals the persistence of that identification of ego and world which predated the formation of the reality principle; *Civilization and its Discontents*, pp.251–60.

31 Indeed from its very inception, the concept of the sublime was inseparable from the notion of the dignity of the soul. Longinus characterized the sublime as 'the echo of a noble mind' and declared the grandeur of the world to be evidence of the 'noble ends' for which we were created; *On the Sublime*, pp.109; 146.

32 Kant *Critique of the Power of Judgement*, §49, pp.192; 193; 194 [314; 315; 316].

33 It is even possible, as was noted in Chapter 4, to discern what appears to be merely an intention or potential to produce sublimity. Every instance of free beauty, too, must, of course, be exemplary (of beauty), but it is exemplary of a pleasure that is precisely *not* cognized as involving any kind of thought over and above this exemplariness.

34 Deleuze's contention, based on §49 of the *Critique of the Power of Judgement*, that the *aesthetic idea* 'expresses what is inexpressible' in the rational idea, does not, then, seem justified, though his description of how, while reason turns the simple phenomena of nature into spiritual events (love, death, and so on), it is only the aesthetic idea which gives us the intuition of a 'nature whose phenomena would be true spiritual events' is an apt one; *Kant's Critical Philosophy*, pp.56–7. Allison makes a similar point concerning how aesthetic ideas render 'thinkable' that which reason determines through its practical legislation but the understanding, in its theoretical legislation, leaves indeterminate; *Kant's Theory of Taste*, pp.208–11. Allison particularly links this with the thought of the purposiveness of nature, and its connection to the moral vocation of humanity.

35 Kant *Critique of the Power of Judgement*, §40, p.174 [294].

36 *ibid.*, p.174n [294].

37 *ibid.*, Introduction, p.65n [177–8].

38 *ibid.*, p.66n [178].

39 *ibid.*, §49, pp.192–3 [314].

40 Both Zammito and Guyer link the notion of the aesthetic idea specifically to artistic merit; Zammito *The Genesis of Kant's Critique of Aesthetic Judgement*, pp.284–91; Guyer 'Kant's Concept of Fine Art' *passim*. Guyer has the grace to confess that, in concentrating on art, he is 'mercifully spared the task of explaining in what sense natural beauty expresses aesthetic ideas' – this being a claim that Kant explicitly makes (p.281). (For comments on Guyer's paper see Wicks' 'Kant on Fine Art: Artistic Sublimity Shaped by Beauty', and Cantrick's 'Kant's Confusion of Expression with Communication', and Guyer's reply 'Beauty, Sublimity, and Expression: A Reply to Wicks and Cantrick'.) Neither they, nor indeed almost any other commentator, is, however, quite brave enough to employ, or often even mention, Kant's own example of the expression of an aesthetic idea: the lamentable lines by Frederick the Great quoted in §49. (Allison, by contrast, does mention that poetry

(though he rather arbitrarily supposes that Kant himself saw it as mediocre), and, perhaps not coincidentally, gives a more purely descriptive, rather than normative, account of aesthetic ideas; *Kant's Theory of Taste*, pp.282–4; 287. He defines such an idea as 'an indeterminately, that is aesthetically, ordered set of aesthetic attributes . . . something like a principle for the selection and organization of aesthetic attributes such that they constitute a meaningful and aesthetically pleasing whole' (pp.257–8). (I would, of course, take issue with the notion that the elements that are indeterminately ordered in the idea are themselves independently 'aesthetic attributes': rather what attributes of the idea/object count for the spectator as aesthetic is a result of the ordering.) There is a tendency, informed more by the spirit of nineteenth-century discussions of the value of art than by anything to be found in Kant or his century, to interpret Kant's notion of the aesthetic idea as the description of an intrinsically valuable experience. Thus McCloskey: 'A perceptual form which extends our perceptual powers, in being expressive of aesthetic ideas, also extends our powers of thought. [The] contemplation of such work is of value because it extends our cognitive powers, extends thought, by extending our perceptual powers'; *Kant's Aesthetic*, p.159. Likewise Makkreel: 'These ideas are used to discern order and meaning in aspects of experience left contingent by the laws of the understanding. . . . Aesthetic ideas allow us to integrate our experience in ways left contingent by the abstract system of nature based on the understanding and elaborated by reason. They draw out, in Kant's words, "a concept's implications (*Folgen*) and its kinship with other concepts" . . . Thereby aesthetic ideas can be said to contribute to the process of reflective interpretation that suggests significant affinities even where direct conceptual connections cannot be demonstrated'; *Imagination and Interpretation in Kant*, pp.112; 121. (See also Makkreel 'Sublimity, Genius, and the Explication of Aesthetic Ideas', pp.626–9). I would, of course, largely agree with the letter of this, though not the spirit. For McCloskey's and Makkreel's descriptions could apply equally to the significance-giving of the delusions of superstition or enthusiasm. It is a Romantic fallacy, and a remarkably tenacious one, that the imagination is, in itself, in Shelley's words, the 'great instrument of moral good'; *The Defense of Poetry*, p.12.

41 Kant *Critique of the Power of Judgement*, §14, p.111 [226].
42 *ibid.* Kant's definition of *Rührung* at this point would not seem to apply to such negative emotions as anger, shame, contempt, or jealousy, which could hardly be called agreeable. However, since he is specifically dealing with the pleasures of beauty and sublimity the restriction is not problematic. Kant's grounding of emotion in interest is, of course, in no way idiosyncratic: 'There would be no emotion if people did not arrive on the scene of an encounter with a desire, want, wish, need, or goal commitment that could be advanced or thwarted'; Lazarus *Emotion and Adaptation*, p.94.

7 FANTASTIC DESIRES I

1 Kant *Critique of the Power of Judgement*, §49, p.193 [314].
2 Kant, as we have seen, does both at different places in the *Critique of the Power of Judgement*.
3 Cassirer *The Philosophy of the Enlightenment*, p.278.
4 I would not, of course, argue that this should be standard critical practice. In criticism philosophy may be left, as Hume would have it, in the study – providing its existence is not entirely forgotten. (I am fully aware of what this implies for the study of literature, particularly as it has been prosecuted since the middle of the last century.) In contrast to other branches of philosophy, aesthetics has hitherto confined itself, for a variety of reasons, to constructing only such theories as can decently be seen in public.
5 Kant does not give the original French text, but rather a German prose translation

[315–16]. The original French text is given, without translation, by Meredith (p.178), while what is probably Kant's own German rendition is translated by Pluhar (p.184), and Guyer and Wood (p.193). Working on the presumption that the German translation is Kant's, I have preferred to work principally with the original text, that is, the one that actually struck Kant as exemplary of genius, for reasons that will become clear in what follows.

6   This translation (closer to the French original than any of the English translations of Kant's German) is given by Adams in his excerpts from Bernard's translation of the *Critique of Judgement* in Adams' *Critical Theory Since Plato*, p.392.

7   Kant *Critique of the Power of Judgement*, §49, pp.193–4 [316].

8   *ibid.*, §49, p.194 [316–17]. The use of the term 'aesthetic' is not a tautology here, it does not, after all, bear its modern meaning in Kant's text: for Kant an 'aesthetic attribute' is a form which does not constitute the presentation of a given concept itself, but rather is a secondary, or supplementary, representation of the imagination which expresses the implications of the object, and its kinship with other objects. We might say they are symbolic forms; §49, p.193 [315].

9   The essential role of analogy in metaphor in discussed in Chapter 2 of Kirwan *Literature, Rhetoric, Metaphysics*.

10 Henry Vaughn 'They are all gone into the world of light! / And I alone sit lingering here; / Their very memory is fair and bright, / And my sad thoughts doth clear.' (1655), ll. 1–4.

11 I am, of course, fully aware that there must be an aesthetic idea involved in my response to Vaughn's poems. However, given the nature of that response, I should be the last person to discern what that idea was, and, if I believed that I could, then, given how much pleasure I derive from entertaining that idea, I would be a complete fool to attempt to do so. (To the objection that self-knowledge *per se* is a good thing, I would answer first, that the case in question is the unexamined origin of a pleasure, not a pain, so that there is no foreseeable benefit; second, given that one cannot remove every contingent determinant of the self and still have a self, this question of 'benefit' is not so facile as it appears.)

12 Kivy appears to invert the true order here when he writes that Kant is 'driven' into the position of having to say that the poem contains an ineffable sub-text, constituted by the aesthetic ideas it contains, by his demand that the aesthetic idea should be, by definition, unamenable to formulation; *Philosophies of Arts*, pp.93–4. It is, on the contrary, *because* there is, for Kant, this ineffable suggestiveness about the poem, that he makes it exemplary of the aesthetic idea. That neither Kivy nor I feel the same way as Kant did about the poem is not the point here. However, from the point of view of the thesis that any and all readers, if their taste was 'good', should come to judge it as Kant does, Kivy's criticism is justified, and I would readily concur with his suggestion that Kant sets a precedent for the subsequent tendency, within aesthetics, to combine the formal and the ineffable into an impregnable definition of 'art', with the proviso that, since the aesthetic is, as I have endeavoured to show in both *Literature, Rhetoric, Metaphysics* and *Beauty*, that which we wish to remain ineffable, there would be strong motives for this tendency even without the precedent of Kant.

13 Metaphor and simile are not, of course, identifiable with euphemism: they only become euphemistic insofar as they are a mollification or evasion of the unpleasant. Often, indeed, the effect of metaphor can be quite the opposite.

14 Joseph Addison 'Ode' ('The spacious firmament on high') (1712), ll. 17–24.

15 Kant *Critique of Practical Reason*, p.166.

16 Della Volpe, who lumps Kant together with the Romantics and, ultimately, Neoplatonism, for his belief that the value of poetry lies in its ineffability, identifies the notion of the 'aesthetic idea' with metaphor and simile; *Critique of Taste*, pp.140–2; 178. According to Della Volpe 'the discursive or (concrete) intellectual nature of metaphor and simile remain hidden from Kant' (p.141). Indeed, he even suggests that Kant's commitment to the ultimate ineffability of what underlies the aesthetic idea is equivalent to a

belief, on Kant's part, that the subsidiary subject of any particular metaphor is merely contingent with respect to the effect of that metaphor (pp.141–2). With regard to this second claim, it would seem rather that Kant, in locating the 'genius' of the poetry in the way the image supplements the basic thought, is saying precisely the opposite. With regard to the former claim – that Kant does not take into account the discursive nature of metaphor – Kant's comments on rhetoric, which I shall discuss in the next section, and, in particular, his description of how rhetoric plays fast and loose with the understanding, would appear to contradict this. That Kant is unaware of the 'discursive' nature of the metaphor in the lines by Frederick is true, but that, as we shall see, is because he *cannot* be aware of it – any more than Della Volpe can be aware of the rhetoric that underlies the lines from Gongora which he himself presents as exemplary of 'genius' (p.141). Della Volpe here appears to confuse the ability to analyse the immediate source, or the components of an aesthetic idea, with the ability to ultimately account for its being an aesthetic idea, and for its having the effect it does. Kant's point is that an aesthetic idea is, *by definition*, unamenable to precise determination: what is amenable to such determination is not an aesthetic idea. Hence my ability to use Frederick's lines as exemplary of an aesthetic idea precisely because they do not inspire me with such an idea.

17   Kant's description of the 'interestingly', as opposed to 'insipidly', sad recluse is part of his exposition of the sublime; *Critique of the Power of Judgement*, 'General remark on the exposition of aesthetic reflective judgements', pp.157–8 [276]. It is a sigh that expresses what Johnson would have unhesitatingly dubbed the 'cant' of the age.

18   Kant *Critique of the Power of Judgement*, §45, p.186 [306–7]. See Chapter 2 above.

19   On stoicism, see *Critique of Practical Reason*, pp.115; 132n. See also Bernstein's discussion in his *Shaftesbury, Rousseau, Kant*, pp.126–8.

20   It is interesting how the expression of these desires takes on the local colour of Kant's milieu: the repressed yet fundamental piety, the admiration of stoicism (insofar as it promotes the notion – trivial from a Christian viewpoint – that happiness is the result of virtue), and, preeminently, the notion of the universe as revelatory of the divine. Not, of course, that this last is a peculiar belief of the eighteenth century, but with the rejection of the authority of revelation, it perforce took on a far greater importance than it had previously. With regard to how attractive to Kant was the idea that the order of the natural world, and in particular the beauty of that order, is a manifestation of the divine, one might consider the preface and section eight of his early *Universal Natural History and Theory of the Heavens*.

21   Kant *Critique of the Power of Judgement*, §57, p.219 [343].

22   *ibid.*, §49, p.194n [316].

23   Almost 30 years earlier Kant had described the thought of God's self-sufficiency – imagined as God addressing himself '*I am from eternity to eternity: apart from me there is nothing, except it be through me*' – as 'of all thoughts the most sublime'; *The only possible argument in support of a demonstration of the existence of God*, p.191.

24   Kant 'On a Newly Arisen Superior Tone in Philosophy', p.61.

25   *ibid.*, p.64.

26   *ibid.*, p.71.

27   *ibid.*

28   Kant *Critique of the Power of Judgement*, §49, p.194n [316].

29   'Plain old physics' may seem something of a misnomer, given the recent popularity of certain books on science, but the kind of subjects Segner discusses are genuinely old and plain now.

30   Kant *Critique of the Power of Judgement*, §51, p.198 [321].

31   *ibid.*, §53, p.204 [327].

32   *ibid.*

33   *ibid.*, p.205n [327].

34   The image of Ixion and the invocation of sublime and mighty Duty are, of course, embedded in what is very definitely an appeal to the understanding, yet, unless we wish to see them as poetry, there is nothing they can be in themselves other than examples of the very rhetoric that Kant is here decrying.

35   Burke *A Philosophical Enquiry into the Origin of our Ideas of the Sublime and Beautiful*, p.53.

36   Kant *Critique of the Power of Judgement*, §51, p.198 [321].

37   *ibid.*, §53, p.204 [327].

38   *ibid.*

39   *ibid.*, §51, p.199 [321].

40   Sidney *An Apologie for Poetrie*, p.29; Kant *Critique of the Power of Judgement*, 53, p.205 [327].

41   Kant *Critique of the Power of Judgement*, §51, p.198 [321] (my emphasis). I have discussed the relationship between literature and rhetoric at length in *Literature, Rhetoric, Metaphysics*; see particularly pp.125–51.

42   Kant *Critique of the Power of Judgement*, §51, p.199 [321].

43   Though it is illuminating to think here of those apparently figurative uses of 'poetical' to describe things which were not intended as poetry.

44   Apropos having no taste for something, there may indeed be another category: being unable to entertain the desire to which the work appeals. This might cover cases such as children's books, which will satisfy momentarily but not for long. Whether this is a separate category from the first is, however, a moot point.

8 FANTASTIC DESIRES II

1   Kant *Critique of the Power of Judgement*, §16, p.114 [229].

2   *ibid.*, §16, p.115 [231]. Or, we might add, believes they are making abstraction from it in their judgement.

3   So that, in fact, almost any object would have served the same purpose. An abandoned dog collar, for example, may do as well as a rose to embody pathos. The common associations of objects do, nevertheless, set some limits on such embodiment. While an abandoned dog collar may produce pathos in a certain context, a dog turd in the same context, and given the same significance, almost certainly will not.

4   Kant *Critique of the Power of Judgement*, 'General remark on the first section of the Analytic', p.126 [243]; §42, p.182 [302].

5   Hegel, in discussing the role of imitation in art, refers to Kant's judgement with approval, as supporting his general thesis that 'delight in imitative skill can always be but restricted, and it befits man better to take delight in what he produces out of himself'; *Aesthetics*, I, p.43. For Hegel, then, the very illusionism involved acts as a negative aesthetic criterion. (Hegel here perhaps exemplifies that tendency to promote one's aesthetic preferences to principles of aesthetics that was mentioned at the beginning of Chapter 7.) See also Smith's extended discussion of the relationship of judgement to imitation in 'Of the Nature of that Imitation which takes place in what are called The Imitative Arts'. The instance he presents of artificial fruits and flowers is of particular relevance (pp.181–2).

6   Alison *Essays on the Nature and Principles of Taste*, pp.152–5.

7   *ibid.*, pp.161–2. A modern acknowledgement of this role of association in the aesthetic appreciation of nature is to be found in Hepburn's distinction between the *sensuous component* and the *thought component* of such appreciation; 'Trivial and serious in aesthetic appreciation of nature' *passim*.

8   Kant *Critique of the Power of Judgement*, §22, p.126 [243]; §42, p.182 [302]. One reason

for such a division is, of course, the difficulty of conceiving of an object that is at once artificial and devoid of the concept of an end.

9   See, for example, the discussion of evaluative criteria in Kirwan *Literature, Rhetoric, Metaphysics*, pp.69–70; 80–3; 105–6; 121; 156–65.

10 It would not be necessary to make this point, of course, if we were using the nearest modern equivalents of Kant's free and dependent beauty – 'beauty' and 'aesthetic merit'.

11 See note 1 to Chapter 6 above, and Kirwan *Sublimity* Chapter 3.

12 Kant *Critique of the Power of Judgement*, §42, p.178 [298–9]. Allison pursues this moral significance of natural beauty in Kant at length; *Kant's Theory of Taste*, pp.227–35. According to Allison Kant's point only extends to the claim that 'natural beauty is an indicator (of undetermined reliability) of a predisposition to morality, or even of a good moral character' (p.229). See also Mothershill's verdict on this notion, and its place in Kant's work, quoted in note 52 below.

13 Kant *Critique of the Power of Judgement*, §42, p.179 [299–300].

14 *ibid.*, pp.178–9 [299].

15 *ibid.*, p.180 [300].

16 *ibid.* [301].

17 *ibid.*, p.179 [299].

18 *ibid.*, p.181 [301].

19 *ibid.*, §57, p.219 [344].

20 He does not use the terms free and dependent beauty at all in this section.

21 Kant *Critique of the Power of Judgement*, §42, p.181 [302].

22 *ibid.*

23 *ibid.*

24 *ibid.*

25 *ibid.*, p.182 [302].

26 *ibid.*, p.178 [298–9].

27 *ibid.*, p.181 [301–2].

28 *ibid.*, p.180 [300].

29 *ibid.*, [301].

30 *ibid.*, pp.180–1 [301].

31 *ibid.*, §68, p.254 [383]. He goes on to explain what he means by 'presumptuous' (*vermessen*) in a footnote to the statement: 'A judgement in which we forget to take the proper measure of our powers (of understanding) can sound very modest and yet make great claims and be very presumptuous. Most of the judgements by means of which we purport to exalt the divine wisdom are like this, since in them we ascribe intentions to the works of creation and preservation that are really intended to do honor to our own wisdom as subtle thinkers.' This description would seem to cover the whole spectrum of deism.

32 Kant *Critique of the Power of Judgement*, 'General Remark on the Teleology', pp.343–4 [481–2].

33 *ibid.*, p.344 [482].

34 *ibid.*, §86, pp.311–2 [445–6].

35 *ibid.*, p.312 [446].

36 *ibid.*

37 *ibid.*

38 *ibid.*

39 *ibid.*, pp.312–3 [447].

40 Kant presents the premises of this argument in §84 (pp.301–2 [434–5]), though there he uses them to reach the more philosophically defensible position that it is in the subject that this final end, to which nature is teleologically subordinated, is to be found.

41 *ibid.*, §85, p.307 [440].

42 *ibid.*, pp.304; 305 [437; 438].

43   *ibid.*, p.305 [438–9]. Deleuze argues that it is indeed the very function of the *Critique of the Power of Judgement* as a whole to establish that the relationship between nature and man is harmonious *not* by virtue of the divine but as 'the result of a *human* practical activity'; *Kant's Critical Philosophy*, p.69. This view is expanded in Deleuze 'The Idea of Genesis in Kant's Aesthetics'.

44   Kant *Critique of the Power of Judgement*, 'General Remark on the Teleology', p.344 [482]. To be able to argue that in ethicotheology speculation 'by no means proves its strength or extends the scope of its domain', and yet that it can be grounds for a belief in God, seems a remarkable feat to be able to pull off, but presumably this is the way Kant felt about it.

45   That this supposition does take the form of faith is quite clear in Kant's account; see his definition of faith in *Critique of the Power of Judgement*, §91. The difference between faith and conviction is a fine one.

46   Apropos the idea that nature might be designed for our general happiness, Kant says, in *Critique of the Power of Judgement*, that 'external nature is far from having made a particular favourite of man' (§83, p.298 [430]). He points to plague, famine, flood, cold, and the existence of dangerous animals to support this point, but also observes that, even with the utmost goodwill on the part of external nature, such is the 'conflict' among our 'natural predispositions', that we would still be incapable of finding happiness in external nature.

47   Kant *Critique of the Power of Judgement*, 'General Remark on the Teleology', p.344n [482]. Leibniz, for example, attacking the idea (which he attributes to Spinoza) that the beauty and goodness of the universe are 'chimeras of men who think of [God] in terms of themselves', asserts that the beauty of the universe is real, in the sense of independent of the will of God, and, therefore, that it was created to be beautiful, since if it had been created otherwise it would not be beautiful; *Discourse on Metaphysics* (1686) in *Philosophical Papers and Letters*, I, pp.464–506 (§2, pp.465–6). For Kant's earlier treatment of the inference of God from the 'order, beauty and perfection' of the world see *The only possible argument in support of a demonstration of the existence of God*, pp.132; 144; 149–50; 158.

48   Kant *Critique of the Power of Judgement*, §58, pp.221–4 [347–50].

49   *ibid.*, p.224 [350].

50   See Kirwan *Beauty*, pp.19–39.

51   Kant *Critique of the Power of Judgement*, §62, pp.235–6 [363–4].

52   With regard to this analysis the following 'tentative suggestion' by Mothershill is worth quoting at length. 'Kant was committed to rejecting all arguments for the existence of God, since they pretend to say something about ultimate reality, but he seems to have been haunted by the . . . "argument from design", according to which God is not only all-powerful but intelligent and just. If that argument were valid, then life would have coherent meaning, morality would comport with science, virtue would be rewarded. A telling observation of Kant's is that when we find some natural object, such as a wild flower, beautiful, we see it as having a purpose although we know that it does not; and that when we find a work of art beautiful, we imagine it as having grown, like a wild flower, rather than having been made, as we know it to have been, with a purpose. Therefore, if we find beauty in the universe as a whole, we see it *as if* it were the creation of an artist. There is no reason to think that the world *has* been planned, but it is cheering and invigorating to think that it *might* have been. [. . .] If the foregoing speculations are correct, then Kant's motive in the third *Critique* . . . [is] to make the whole [critical] system less austere and more congenial. That, one might argue, is a retrograde step: it is not the philosopher's job, any more than it is the scientist's, to come up with results that are attractive and inspiring'; 'Sublime', p.411.

9 CONCLUSION

1 Mothershill 'Sublime', p.411.
2 Schiller is perhaps the key progenitor in this regard; see Kirwan *Sublimity* Chapter 5.
3 Burke *A Philosophical Enquiry into the Origin of our Ideas of the Sublime and Beautiful,* pp.11–27.
4 Kant *Critique of the Power of Judgement,* §34, p.166 [285–6]; §8, p.101 [216].
5 Kant *Critique of the Power of Judgement,* §32, p.163 [282].
6 Hume 'Of the Standard of Taste' (1757) in *Essays Moral, Political, and Literary,* pp.226–49 (p.233) (my emphasis).
7 As was noted in Chapter 1, this last comes out most clearly in his rejection, in §§13–14, of the possibility of any determining role for emotion, as an expression of the subject's interests, in true judgements of taste. Any interest, he asserts, 'spoils the judgement of taste and deprives it of its impartiality', since the determining ground of such a judgement can only be 'the purposiveness of the form'; Kant *Critique of the Power of Judgement,* §13, pp.107–8 [223]. He makes some concession to those cases where the potential emotional element is impossible to overlook (the beauty of one's childhood home, or the artwork in which a strong emotional effect is at play 'alongside' the approbation), when he avers that charm and emotion 'may be combined with the satisfaction in the beautiful', though they do not determine it, and the judgement involved 'can make no claim at all to universal satisfaction' (*ibid.,* p.108). Taste that requires the addition of charms and emotions, he writes, 'is always still barbaric', and the error of believing that the true beauty of form can be heightened by charm 'is very detrimental to genuine, uncorrupted, well-grounded taste' (*ibid.*). The beauty of a painting resides in composition alone, and while such charms as colour may serve to attract those whose taste is 'crude and unpracticed', that taste is likely to be 'damaged' if such charms 'attract attention to themselves as grounds for the judging of beauty' (§14, pp.109–10 [225]). In these passages, though it could be argued that Kant is doing no more than setting limits, in line with the identity of taste as established by his phenomenology, to the use of the word 'taste', there is a much stronger normative tendency, and invocation of a usable standard, than the arguments of the rest of the *Critique* would seem to support.
8 Kant *Critique of the Power of Judgement,* §13, p.108 [223–4].
9 *ibid.*
10 *ibid.,* Introduction, p.65n [177].
11 *ibid.,* p.66n [178].
12 *ibid.,* §49, p.192 [314].
13 *ibid.,* §14, p.111 [226].
14 Although I have largely kept to Kant's terminology of 'free' and 'dependent' beauty in this work there is, as we saw in Chapter 2, a strong case to be made for renaming these two as 'beauty' and 'aesthetic merit' respectively. For, despite the fundamental traits they share, the two are sufficiently distinct to warrant separate designations. At present we are in the strange situation of finding the word 'beauty' used in aesthetics with considerably *less* precision than is to be found in common usage.
15 I do not wish to conflate these categories: I believe that the distinction between the non-rational and the irrational is a valid one. However, from the point of view of Kant's characterization of vain wishing, such a distinction is negligible.
16 The fact that with aesthetic merit we often cannot escape the consciousness of entertaining something like a concept perhaps accounts for why a certain earnestness with regard to art so often appears to shade off into something like religion.
17 My account of these potential misunderstandings is based on reactions to this same thesis concerning the aesthetic, as it has appeared in my *Literature, Rhetoric, Metaphysics* and *Beauty.*

18 It is perhaps my own failure to make this distinction sufficiently clear in my *Beauty*, that leads Lyas to propose such instances as being 'simply moved by the beauty of the river at Flatford', or having 'one's yearning for the love of one's life fulfilled', as counter-examples to the notion of an element of incorrigible yearning in the aesthetic; Lyas 'Review of *Beauty*', p.95.

19 Thus, for example, McMahon has taken my analysis of beauty for a description of what it feels like, and complained that the explanation in terms of 'transcendental metaphysics' that I seem to propose is never clarified; McMahon 'Review of *Beauty*'. (Again, I am not entirely blameless here. There is, given its most likely audience, too great a discrepancy between the style and the content of that work.) Barely a week has elapsed since the last time somebody explained to me that we find things beautiful 'because they are'.

20 This objection was made to my *Literature, Rhetoric, Metaphysics*. Unfortunately I can neither remember nor locate the review in which it was made.

References

Adams, Hazard (ed.) *Critical Theory Since Plato*, rev. ed. (Fort Worth, 1992).

Addison [Joseph] and Steele [Richard] and Others *The Spectator*, ed. Gregory Smith (1907), rev. ed., four vols (London, 1945).

Adorno, Theodor *Aesthetic Theory* (1970), trans. and ed. Robert Hullot-Kentor (Minneapolis, 1997).

Alison, Archibald *Essays on the Nature and Principles of Taste* (Edinburgh, 1790; repr., Hildesheim, 1968).

Allison, Henry E. *Kant's Theory of Taste: A Reading of the Critique of Judgement* (Cambridge, 2001).

Arendt, Hannah *Between Past and Future: Eight Exercises in Political Thought* (1961), enlarged ed. (Harmondsworth, 1977).

—— *Lectures on Kant's Political Philosophy*, ed. Ronald Beiner (Chicago, 1982).

Armstrong, Isobel *The Radical Aesthetic* (Oxford, 2000).

Battersby, Christine 'Stages on Kant's Way: Aesthetics, Morality and the Gendered Sublime' in Peggy Zeglin Brand and Carolyn Korsmeyer (eds) *Feminism and Tradition in Aesthetics* (Pennsylvania, 1995), pp.88–114.

Baumgarten, Alexander Gottlieb *Reflections on Poetry* (1735), trans. Karl Aschenbrenner and William B. Holther (Berkeley, 1954).

Beardsley, Monroe C. *Aesthetics from Classical Greece to the Present Age: A Short History* (London, 1966).

Beck, Lewis White *A Commentary on Kant's Critique of Practical Reason* (Chicago, 1960).

Bell, Clive *Art* (London, 1914).

Berleant, Arnold 'Beyond Disinterestedness' *British Journal of Aesthetics* 34 (1994), pp.242–54.

Bernstein, John Andrew *Shaftesbury, Rousseau, and Kant: An Introduction to the Conflict between Aesthetic and Moral Values in Modern Thought* (London, 1980).

Bernstein, J. M. *The Fate of Art: Aesthetic Alienation from Kant to Derrida and Adorno* (Cambridge, 1992).

Bicknell, Jeanette 'Can Music Convey Semantic Content? A Kantian Approach' *The Journal of Aesthetics and Art Criticism* 60 (2002), pp. 253–61.

Blair, Hugh *Lectures on Rhetoric and Belles Lettres* (1783), 'a new edition complete in one volume' (London, 1825).

Boswell, James *Life of Johnson* (1791) (Oxford, 1953).

Bourdieu, Pierre *Distinction: A Social Critique of the Judgement of Taste* (1979), trans. Richard Nice (Cambridge, MA., 1984).

Budd, Malcolm *Values of Art: Pictures, Poetry and Music* (Harmondsworth, 1995).

—— 'Delight in the Natural World: Kant on the Aesthetic Appreciation of Nature. Part I: Natural Beauty' *British Journal of Aesthetics* 38 (1998), pp.1–18.

—— 'Delight in the Natural World: Kant on the Aesthetic Appreciation of Nature. Part II: Natural Beauty and Morality' *British Journal of Aesthetics* 38 (1998), pp.117–26.

—— 'Delight in the Natural World: Kant on the Aesthetic Appreciation of Nature. Part III: The Sublime in Nature' *British Journal of Aesthetics* 38 (1998), pp.233–50.

Budick, Sanford *The Western Theory of Tradition: Terms and Paradigms of the Cultural Sublime* (New Haven, 2000).

Bürger, Peter *Theory of the Avant-Garde* (1974/1980), trans. Michael Shaw (Minneapolis, 1984).

Burke, Edmund *A Philosophical Enquiry into the Origin of our Ideas of the Sublime and Beautiful* (1757), 2nd ed. (1759), ed. James T. Boulton (London, 1958).

Cantrick, Robert B. 'Kant's Confusion of Expression with Communication' *Journal of Aesthetics and Art Criticism* 53 (1995), pp.193–4.

Carritt, E. F. *The Theory of Beauty* (1914), 5th ed. (London, 1949).

Cascardi, Anthony J. *Consequences of Enlightenment* (Cambridge, 1999).

Cassirer, Ernst *The Philosophy of the Enlightenment* (1932), trans. Fritz C. A. Koelln and James P. Pettegrove (Princeton, 1953).

Cassirer, H. W. *A Commentary on Kant's Critique of Aesthetic Judgement* (New York, 1938).

Caygill, Howard *Art of Judgement* (Oxford, 1989).

Chambers, E[phraim] *Cyclopaedia: or, an Universal Dictionary of Arts and Sciences*, 2 vols (London, 1728).

Cohen, Ted and Guyer, Paul (eds) *Essays on Kant's Aesthetics* (Chicago, 1982).

Collingwood, R. G. *Outlines of a Philosophy of Art* (London, 1925).

—— *The Principles of Art* (Oxford, 1938).

Coleman, Francis X. J. *The Harmony of Reason: A Study in Kant's Aesthetics* (Pittsburgh, 1974).

Copleston, Frederick *A History of Philosophy: Volume VII: Fichte to Nietzsche* (Westminster, 1963).

Courtine, Jean-François *et al. Of the Sublime: Presence in Question* (1988), trans. Jeffrey S. Librett (Albany, 1993).

Cousin, Victor *Lectures on the True, the Beautiful, and the Good* (1836), trans. O. W. Wight (Edinburgh, 1853).

Crawford, Donald W. *Kant's Aesthetic Theory* (Madison, 1974).

Croce, Benedetto *Aesthetic as Science of Expression and General Linguistic* (1901), 4th ed. (1911), trans. Douglas Ainslee, rev. ed. (London, 1922).

Crockett, Clayton *A Theology of the Sublime* (London, 2001).

Crowther, Paul *The Kantian Sublime: From Morality to Art* (Oxford, 1989).

—— *Critical Aesthetics and Postmodernism* (Oxford, 1993).

—— 'The Significance of Kant's Pure Aesthetic Judgement' *British Journal of Aesthetics* 36 (1996), pp.109–21.

Curtis, Kimberley *Our Sense of the Real: Aesthetic Experience and Arendtian Politics* (Ithaca, 1999).

Damisch, Hubert *The Judgement of Paris* (1992), trans. John Goodman (Chicago, 1996).

Danto, Arthur C. *The Transfiguration of the Commonplace* (Harvard, 1981).

—— 'A Future for Aesthetics' *Journal of Aesthetics and Art Criticism* 51 (1993) pp.271–7.

—— *After the End of Art: Contemporary Theory and the Pale of History* (Princeton, 1997).

Deleuze, Gilles *Kant's Critical Philosophy: The Doctrine of the Faculties* (1963), trans. Hugh Tomlinson and Barbara Habberjam (London, 1995).

—— 'The Idea of Genesis in Kant's Aesthetics' (1963) trans. Daniel W. Smith in *Angelaki* 5/3 (2000), pp.57–70.

Della Volpe, Galvano *Critique of Taste* (1960), trans. Michael Caesar (London, 1978).

Dennis, John *The Critical Works of John Dennis*, edited by Edward Niles Hooker, 2 vols (Baltimore, 1939–43).

Dickie, George *The Century of Taste: The Philosophical Odyssey of Taste in the Eighteenth Century* (Oxford, 1996).

Diderot, Denis 'The Beautiful' (1752), trans. Karl Aschenbrenner in Karl Aschenbrenner and

Arnold Isenberg (eds) *Aesthetic Theories: Studies in the Philosophy of Art* (Englewood Cliffs, NJ, 1965), pp.129–47.

—— *Selected Writings on Art and Literature*, trans. Geoffrey Bremner (Harmondsworth, 1994).

Diffey, T. J. 'On American and British Aesthetics' *Journal of Aesthetics and Art Criticism* 51 (1993), pp.169–75.

Dutton, Denis 'Kant and the Conditions of Artistic Beauty' *British Journal of Aesthetics* 34 (1994), pp. 226–41.

Eagleton, Terry *The Ideology of the Aesthetic* (Oxford, 1990).

Fechner, Gustav Theodor *Vorschule der Aesthetik* (1876), 2 vols (Leipzig, 1925).

Ferguson, Kennan *The Politics of Judgement: Aesthetics, Identity, and Political Theory* (Lanham, 1999).

Ferry, Luc *Homo Aestheticus: The Invention of Taste in the Democratic Age* (1990), trans. Robert de Loaiza (Chicago, 1993).

Freud, Sigmund *Civilization and its Discontents* (1930) in *Civilization, Society and Religion: Group Psychology, Civilization and its Discontents, and Other Works*, ed. Albert Dickson, *The Pelican Freud Library Volume 12* (Harmondsworth, 1985), pp.251–340.

Gadamer, Hans-Georg *Truth and Method* (1960), trans. from the 2nd ed. (1965) by Garrett Barden and John Cumming (London, 1975).

Gammon, Martin 'Kant: *parerga* and *pulchritudo adhaerens*' *Kant-Studien* 90 (1999), pp.148–67.

Gilson, Etienne *The Arts of the Beautiful* (1963) (New York, 1965).

—— *Forms and Substances in the Arts* (1964), trans. Salvator Attanasio (New York, 1966).

Ginsborg, Hannah *The Role of Taste in Kant's Theory of Cognition* (New York, 1990).

Gould, Timothy 'Intensity and Its Audiences: Towards a Feminist Perspective on the Kantian Sublime' in Peggy Zeglin Brand and Carolyn Korsmeyer (eds) *Feminism and Tradition in Aesthetics* (Pennsylvania, 1995), pp.66–87.

Guyer, Paul *Kant and the Claims of Taste* (Cambridge, MA, 1979).

—— *Kant and the Experience of Freedom: Essays on Aesthetics and Morality* (Cambridge, 1993).

—— 'Kant's Conception of Fine Art' *Journal of Aesthetics and Art Criticism* 52 (1994), pp.275–85.

—— 'Beauty, Sublimity, and Expression: Reply to Wicks and Cantrick' *Journal of Aesthetics and Art Criticism* 53 (1995), pp.194–5.

—— 'Dependent Beauty Revisited: A Reply to Wicks' *Journal of Aesthetics and Art Criticism* 57 (1999), pp.357–61.

Hegel, G. W. F. *Aesthetics: Lectures on Fine Art* (1835), trans. T. M. Knox, 2 vols (Oxford, 1975).

Henrich, Dieter *Aesthetic Judgement and the Moral Image of the World: Studies in Kant* (Stanford, 1992).

Hepburn, Ronald *The Reach of the Aesthetic: Collected Essays on Art and Nature* (Aldershot, 2001).

Herz, Neil *The End of Line: Essays on Psychoanalysis and the Sublime* (New York, 1985).

Huhn, Thomas 'The Kantian Sublime and the Nostalgia for Violence' *Journal of Aesthetics and Art Criticism* 53 (1995), pp.269–75.

Hume, David *A Treatise of Human Nature* (1739), ed. L. A. Selby-Bigge (Oxford, 1967).

—— *Essays Moral, Political, and Literary* (1777), ed. Eugene F. Miller, rev. ed. (Indianapolis, 1987).

Hutcheson, Francis *An Inquiry into the Original of our Ideas of Beauty and Virtue* (London, 1725).

Janaway, Christopher 'Beauty in Nature, Beauty in Art' *British Journal of Aesthetics* 33 (1993), pp.321–32.

Jeffrey, Francis review of *Essays on the Nature and Principles of Taste* (by Archibald Alison), *The Edinburgh Review* (1811) [Enlarged version for the *Encyclopaedia Brittanica* article 'Beauty' (1824)] in *Contributions to the Edinburgh Review* (1853) (New York, 1860), pp.13–39.

Johnson, Samuel *A Journey to the Western Islands of Scotland* (1775) in Samuel Johnson and James Boswell *A Journey to the Western Islands of Scotland and The Journal of the Tour of the Hebrides*, ed. Peter Levi (Harmondsworth, 1984), pp.33–152.

Kames, Lord [Henry Home] *Elements of Criticism*, 3 vols (Edinburgh, 1762; repr., Hildesheim, 1970).

Kant, Immanuel *Universal Natural History and Theory of the Heavens* (1755), trans. Stanley Jaki (Edinburgh, 1981).

—— *The only possible argument in support of a demonstration of the existence of God* (1763) in *Theoretical Philosophy, 1755–1770*, ed. David Walford and Ralf Meerbote (Cambridge, 1992), pp.107–210.

—— *Observations on the Feeling of the Beautiful and the Sublime* (1764), trans. J. T. Goldthwaite (Berkeley, 1965).

—— *Dreams of a spirit-seer elucidated by dreams of metaphysics* (1766) in *Theoretical Philosophy, 1755–1770*, ed. David Walford and Ralf Meerbote (Cambridge, 1992), pp.301–59.

—— *Critique of Pure Reason* (1781–7), trans. Norman Kemp Smith, 2nd ed. (London, 1933).

—— *Groundwork to the Metaphysic of Morals* (1785), trans. and analysed by N. J. Paton (London, 1958).

—— 'Conjectures on the Beginning of Human History' (1786) in *Political Writings*, trans. H. B. Nisbet, ed. Hans Reiss (Cambridge, 1991), pp.221–34.

—— 'What is Orientation in Thinking?' (1786) in *Political Writings*, trans. H. B. Nisbet, ed. Hans Reiss (Cambridge, 1991), pp.237–49.

—— *Critique of Practical Reason* (1788), trans. Lewis White Beck (Indianapolis, 1956).

—— *Critique of Judgement* (1790), trans. J. H. Bernard (1892), rev. ed. (London, 1914).

—— *The Critique of Judgement* (1790), trans. James Creed Meredith (1911) (Oxford, 1952).

—— *Critique of Judgement* (1790), trans. Werner S. Pluhar (Indianapolis, 1987).

—— *Critique of the Power of Judgement* (1790), ed. Paul Guyer, trans. Paul Guyer and Eric Matthews (Cambridge, 2000).

—— 'On the Common Saying: "This May be True in Theory, but it does not Apply in Practice"' (1793) in *Political Writings*, trans. H. B. Nisbet, ed. Hans Reiss (Cambridge, 1991), pp.61–92.

—— *Religion Within the Limits of Reason Alone* (1793), trans. Theodore M. Greene and Hoyt H. Hudson (1934), rev. ed. Theodore M. Greene and John R. Silber (New York, 1960).

—— *Perpetual Peace: A Philosophical Sketch* (1795/1796) in *Political Writings*, trans. H. B. Nisbet, ed. Hans Reiss (Cambridge, 1991), pp.93–130.

—— 'On a Newly Arisen Superior Tone in Philosophy' (1796), trans. Peter Fenves in Peter Fenves (ed.) *Raising the Tone of Philosophy: Late Essays by Immanuel Kant, Transformative Critique by Jacques Derrida* (Baltimore, 1993), pp.51–81.

—— *Anthropology from a Pragmatic Point of View* (1798), trans. Mary J. Gregor (The Hague, 1974).

Kemal, Salim *Kant's Aesthetic Theory: An Introduction* (London, 1992).

Kemp, John *The Philosophy of Kant* (Oxford, 1968).

Kirwan, James *Literature, Rhetoric, Metaphysics: Literary Theory and Literary Aesthetics* (London, 1990).

—— *Beauty* (Manchester, 1999).

—— *Sublimity: The Non-Rational and the Irrational in the History of Aesthetics* (forthcoming).

Kivy, Peter *Philosophies of Arts: An Essay in Differences* (Cambridge, 1997).

Körner, Stephan *Kant* (Harmondsworth, 1955).

Korsmeyer, Carolyn 'Disgust' in *Filozofski vestnik* 2 (1999), pp.43–62.

Kristeva, Julia *Powers of Horror: An Essay on Abjection* (1980), trans. Leon S. Roudiez (New York, 1982).

Lazarus, Richard S. *Emotion and Adaption* (New York, 1991).

Leibniz, Gottfried Wilhelm *Philosophical Papers and Letters*, trans. and ed. Leroy E. Loemaker, 2 vols (Chicago, 1956).

Longinus *On the Sublime*, trans. T. S. Dorsch in T. S. Dorsch (ed.) *Classical Literary Criticism* (Harmondsworth, 1965), pp.99–158.

Lorand, Ruth 'On "Free and Dependent Beauty" – A Rejoinder' *British Journal of Aesthetics* 32 (1992), pp.250–3.

—— 'The Purity of Aesthetic Value' *Journal of Aesthetics and Art Criticism* 50 (1992), pp.13–21.

Lyas, Colin Review of *Beauty* (by James Kirwan), *British Journal of Aesthetics* 41 (2001), pp.94–5.

Lyotard, Jean-François *The Inhuman: Reflections on Time* (1988), trans. Geoffrey Bennington and Rachel Bowlby (Cambridge, 1991).

—— *Lessons on the Analytic of the Sublime* (1991), trans. Elizabeth Rottenberg (Stanford, 1994).

Makkreel, Rudolf A. *Imagination and Interpretation in Kant: The Hermeneutical Import of the Critique of Judgement* (Chicago, 1990).

—— 'On Sublimity, Genius and the Explication of Aesthetic Ideas' in Herman Parret (ed.) *Kants Ästhetik/Kant's Aesthetics/L'Esthétique de Kant* (Berlin, 1998), pp.615–29.

Margolis, Joseph 'A Small Prophecy' *International Association for Aesthetics Newsletter* 9 (1995), pp.3–5.

—— *What, After All, Is a Work of Art?: Lectures in the Philosophy of Art* (University Park, PA, 1999).

McAdoo, Nick 'Sibley and the Art of Persuasion' in Emily Brady and Jerrold Levinson (eds) *Aesthetic Concepts: Essays After Sibley* (Oxford, 2001), pp.35–46.

McCloskey, Mary *Kant's Aesthetic* (Albany, 1987).

McMahon, Jennifer A. Review of *Beauty* (by James Kirwan), *Journal of Aesthetics and Art Criticism* 59 (2001), pp.334–6.

Montesquieu, Charles Louis de Secondat Baron de *The Spirit of Laws* (1748), trans. T. Nugent (1750), rev. J. V. Prichard (Chicago, 1950).

—— 'An Essay on Taste' (nd) in Alexander Gerard *An Essay on Taste, With Three Dissertations on the Same Subject by Mr. De Voltaire, Mr. D'Alembert, Mr. De Montesquieu* (London, 1759), pp.251–314.

Morgan, David 'The Idea of Abstraction in German Theories of Ornament from Kant to Kandinsky' *Journal of Aesthetics and Art Criticism* 50 (1992), pp.231–42.

Moritz, Karl Philipp 'On the Concept of That Which is Perfect in Itself' (1785) in *Eighteenth Century German Criticism*, trans. and ed. Timothy L. Chamberlain (New York, 1992), pp.245–251.

Mortensen, Preben *Art in the Social Order: The Making of the Modern Conception of Art* (New York, 1997).

Mothershill, Mary *Beauty Restored* (Oxford, 1984).

—— 'Hume and the Paradox of Taste' in George Dickie, Richard Scalafini and Ronald Roblin (eds) *Aesthetics: A Critical Anthology* (New York, 1989), pp.269–86.

—— 'Sublime' in David Cooper (ed.) *A Companion to Aesthetics* (Oxford, 1992), pp.407–12.

Nancy, Jean-Luc 'The Sublime Offering' in Courtine *et al.* (1988), pp.25–53.

Norton, Robert E. *The Beautiful Soul: Aesthetic Morality in the Eighteenth Century* (Ithaca, 1995).

Osborne, Harold *Aesthetics and Art Theory: An Historical Introduction* (Oxford, 1972).

—— (ed.) *Aesthetics* (Oxford, 1972).

Paine, Thomas *The Age of Reason: Being an Investigation of True and of Fabulous Theology* (1794/1795) in *Collected Writings*, ed. Eric Foner (New York, 1995) pp.664–830.

Parret, Herman (ed.) *Kants Ästhetik – Kant's Aesthetics – L'Esthétique de Kant* (Berlin, 1998).

Pater, Walter *The Renaissance: Studies in Art and Poetry* (1873), 1893 edn ed. Donald G. Hill (London, 1980).

Paton, H. J. *The Categorical Imperative: A Study in Kant's Moral Philosophy* (London, 1947).

Pluhar, Werner S. 'Introduction' to Immanuel Kant *Critique of Judgement* (1790), trans. Werner S. Pluhar (Indianapolis, 1987).

Pope, Alexander *An Essay in Criticism* (1711) in *The Poems of Alexander Pope: A one-volume edition of the Twickenham text with selected annotations* (1963), ed. John Butt, 2nd ed. (London, 1968), pp.144–68.

Porter, Roy *Mind Forg'd Manacles: A History of Madness in England from the Restoration to the Regency* (1987) (Harmondsworth, 1990).

Reid, Thomas *Essays on the Intellectual Powers of Man* (1785) in *The Works of Thomas Reid*, ed. William Hamilton, 7th ed., 2 vols (Edinburgh, 1872), I, pp.213–508.

Reynolds, Joshua *The Idler* No.82, Saturday, 10 November 1759.

—— *Discourses on Art* (1797), ed. Robert R. Wark (London, 1966).

Rosiek, Jan *Maintaining the Sublime: Heidegger and Adorno* (Berne, 2000).

Savile, Anthony *The Test of Time: An Essay in Philosophical Aesthetics* (Oxford, 1982).

—— *Kantian Aesthetics Pursued* (Edinburgh, 1993).

Schaeffer, Jean-Marie *Art of the Modern Age: Philosophy of Art from Kant to Heidegger* (1992), trans. Steven Rendall (Princeton, 2000).

Schaper, Eva *Studies in Kant's Aesthetics* (Edinburgh, 1979).

—— 'The Pleasure of Taste' in Eva Schaper (ed.) *Pleasure, Preference and Value: Studies in Philosophical Aesthetics* (Cambridge, 1983), pp.39–56.

Schelling, F. W. J. *The Philosophy of Art* (1859), trans. D. W. Stott (Minneapolis, 1989).

Scherer, Irmgard *The Crisis of Judgement in Kant's Three* Critiques*: In Search of a Science of Aesthetics* (New York, 1995).

Schopenhauer, Arthur *The World as Will and Representation* (1819/1844), trans. E. F. J. Payne, 2 vols (New York, 1969).

Scruton, Roger *Kant* (Oxford, 1982).

Shaftesbury, Earl [Anthony Ashley Cooper] *Characteristicks of Men, Manners, Opinions, Times*, 3 vols (London, 1711; repr., Hildesheim, 1978).

Shell, Susan Meld *The Embodiment of Reason: Kant on Spirit, Generation, and Community* (Chicago, 1996).

Shelley, Percy Bysshe *A Defense of Poetry* (1821) in *The Prose Works of Percy Bysshe Shelley*, ed. Richard Herne Shepherd, 2 vols (London, 1906), II, pp.1–38.

Sibley, Frank 'Aesthetic Concepts' (1959) in Joseph Margolis (ed.) *Philosophy Looks at the Arts* (Philadelphia, 1978), pp.64–87.

Sidney, Sir Philip *An Apologie for Poetrie* (1595), ed. Albert Feuillerat (Cambridge, 1923), pp.1–46 [vol.III of *The Complete Works of Sir Philip Sidney*, ed. Albert Feuillerat (Cambridge, 1922–6)].

Smith, Adam 'Of the Nature of that Imitation which takes place in what are called The Imitative Arts' (n.d.) in *Essays on Philosophical Subjects*, ed. W. P. D. Wightman and J. C. Bryce (Indianapolis, 1982), pp.176–213.

Smith, Barbara Herrnstein *Contingencies of Value: Alternative Perspectives for Critical Theory* (Cambridge, MA, 1988).

Staël, Mme. de [Anne-Louise Germaine, Baroness] *Germany* (1810), trans. and ed. O. W. Wight (Boston, 1887).

Taminaux, Jacques *Poetics, Speculation, and Judgement: The Shadow of the Work of Art from Kant to Phenomenology*, trans. and ed. Michael Gendre (Albany, 1993).

Townsend, Dabney 'From Shaftesbury to Kant: The Development of the Concept of Aesthetic Experience' (1987) in Peter Kivy (ed.) *Essays on the History of Aesthetics* (New York, 1992), pp.205–23.

—— *Hume's Aesthetic Theory: Taste and Sentiment* (London, 2001).

Usher, James *Clio: or, a Discourse on Taste*, 2nd ed. (London, 1769; repr., New York, 1970).

Weatherston, Martin 'Kant's Assessment of Music in the *Critique of Judgement*' *British Journal of Aesthetics* 36 (1996), pp.56–65.

Weiskel, Thomas *The Romantic Sublime: Studies in the Structure and Psychology of Transcendence* (Baltimore, 1976).

Wicks, Robert 'Kant on Fine Art: Artistic Sublimity Shaped by Beauty' *Journal of Aesthetics and Art Criticism* 53 (1995), pp.189–93.

—— 'Dependent Beauty as the Appreciation of Teleological Style' *Journal of Aesthetics and Art Criticism* 55 (1997), pp.387–400.

—— 'Kant on Beautifying the Human Body' *The British Journal of Aesthetics* 39 (1999), pp.163–78.

—— 'Can Tattooed Faces Be Beautiful?: Limits on the Restriction of Forms in Dependent Beauty' *Journal of Aesthetics and Art Criticism* 57 (1999), pp.361–3.

Zammito, John H. *The Genesis of Kant's Critique of Aesthetic Judgement* (Chicago, 1992).

Zangwill, Nick 'UnKantian Notions of Disinterest' *British Journal of Aesthetics* 32 (1992), pp.149–52.

—— 'Kant on Pleasure in the Agreeable' *Journal of Aesthetics and Art Criticism* 53 (1995), pp.167–76.

—— *The Metaphysics of Beauty* (Ithaca, 2001).

Zuckert, Rachel 'A New Look at Kant's Theory of Pleasure' *The Journal of Aesthetics and Art Criticism* 60 (2002), pp.239–52.

Index

References to authors are only indexed where the work of that author is either quoted or characterized.